MICHAEL BABBAGE

On The Way

An Australian Doctor In Yemen & Pakistan

First published by Dr. Michael Francis Babbage 2020

Copyright © 2020 by Michael Babbage

All rights reserved. No part of this publication may be reproduced, stored or transmitted in any form or by any means, electronic, mechanical, photocopying, recording, scanning, or otherwise without written permission from the publisher. It is illegal to copy this book, post it to a website, or distribute it by any other means without permission.

Michael Babbage asserts the moral right to be identified as the author of this work.

The photographs belong to Michael F. Babbage. Most Bible quotations are taken from the NIV. Scripture taken from the HOLY BIBLE, NEW INTERNATIONAL VERSION. Copyright © 1973, 1978, 1984 International Bible Society. Used by permission of Zondervan Bible Publishers. Occasional quotations are taken from THE KING JAMES (AUTHORISED) VERSION and from THE LIVING BIBLE. Copyright© 1971 by Tyndale House Publishers, USA. All rights reserved. Also, some Scripture quotations are taken from AMPLIFIED BIBLE, Copyright© 1954, 1958, 1962, 1964, 1965, 1987 by The Lockman Foundation. All rights reserved. Used by permission. (www.Lockman.org)

Front cover photograph: Michael on a highland road in Yemen (1973).

'The LORD your God has blessed you in all the work of your hands. He has watched over your journey through this vast desert. These forty years the LORD your God has been with you, and you have not lacked anything.' Deuteronomy 2:7

First edition

ISBN: 978-0-646-81698-2

This book was professionally typeset on Reedsy.
Find out more at reedsy.com

Contents

Introduction	iv
Preface	v
1 Birth to Newcastle, and a Special Gift	1
2 'You don't speak Arabic by any chance?'	11
3 Training in Pakistan	24
4 Journey to Yemen and Language Study	34
5 Wedding and Honeymoon	44
6 Yareem, Lyndall's Visit and Andrew's Birth	53
7 Early Days In Muharraq	71
8 Encouragements, Dangers and Provision	89
9 Furlough, Sharon's Birth and Tropical Medicine	108
10 'How shall they hear?' and a Miracle!	115
11 The Eight Mountain Treks	140
12 The Four Lowland Treks	180
13 Hepatitis	190
14 Five Years in Pakistan, and back to Yemen	196
15 The Safest Place of All	216
Epilogue	249
Acknowledgements	251
Maps and Reference Books	252
Notes	256

Introduction

'Consider what great things he has done for you.'

My main aim in writing this book has been to give an account of things I've seen the Lord doing—leading, protecting and providing for me and my family—especially in Yemen.

In concern that certain people, especially those connected with our missionary work, could possibly be endangered by my writing this account, I've changed the names of many villages and omitted most surnames. However, this in no way interferes with our being able to see the Lord's workings.

I'd like to take this opportunity to ask the reader to kindly forgive any unintentional errors which may come to light; and although it may be felt that I've occasionally included matters which seem trivial or irrelevant, I believe that they all contribute to the painting of a more complete picture, especially while overseas. Please note that there is a map of Pakistan on page 254 and one of Yemen on page 255.

I pray that many people will find the book helpful and encouraging.

Sydney, NSW

May 2020

Preface

'Don't go through Maharbisha. They're watching the city gates for you!' he said in Arabic.

I looked up from my desk in the small stick hut which was serving as my clinic. The speaker was one of six or seven Yemeni men who sat crowded together on two local-style beds, simple wooden frames tightly strung with a mesh of thin, coarse rope. I didn't recognise the man who'd spoken.

'Thank you for letting me know,' I said. The news was disturbing. I'd been planning to set out the next day on the final trek in a series of solo hikes over the nearby ranges of the Yemeni mountains. On these trips, I had been able to carry the gospel message personally to various key tribal leaders, despite some interference from authorities.

But this man's words were a warning: armed soldiers were guarding the entrance to the town which spilled over both sides of the mountain ridge, high up behind our village. To reach the plateau which I'd hoped to cover on this final trek, I would need to pass through that town.

What was I to do? I had a tremendous urge to complete my campaign to provide the word of life to those the Lord had selected, and within whose hearts he'd been working. I didn't know who they were, but, as on my previous journeys, I knew that he would lead me to them. But now my way seemed to be blocked. It's still rather sobering to know that 'day and night they kept close watch on the city gates in order to' prevent my passing that way.

I've often wondered about this message, and the way it was delivered by that visitor, a stranger. As far as possible, I'd been trying to keep my comings and goings a secret, although *he* apparently knew about them. Perhaps it would have been in keeping with my current thinking regarding who he was if he'd gone on to say, 'Don't be anxious. Is anything too hard for the Lord?'

Later that afternoon I was to discover that *this* situation certainly wasn't too hard for the Lord; and he proved it by showing me, in a most extraordinary manner, how to thwart those who were seeking to prevent the spread of the gospel to that plateau, near the north-west corner of Yemen.

Someone has said, 'One man and God is always a majority,' and I believe this to be true, even though in fact I could never have been considered as only 'one man'; family members and friends were frequently praying for me.

The Christian life can be a real adventure. My wife Adele and I have certainly had plenty of fascinating and exciting experiences, though sometimes this has meant that we faced serious dangers and trials. But the main point of my writing these memoirs is to demonstrate how the Lord was caring for us and leading us every step of the way. Isaiah 63:9 could apply to us: *The angel of his presence saved them. In his love and mercy, he redeemed them; he lifted them up and carried them all the days of old.*

As Adele and I have continued our journey 'on the way' through life, we've sought to depend on the One who said, 'I am the way'. He has never disappointed us.

1

Birth to Newcastle, and a Special Gift

1943-1970: Age 0-27

Being tall has been an important aspect of my life. I've had to get used to people meeting me for the first time and saying, 'My word! You're tall!' In some ways it's a nuisance. I stand out in a crowd when I'd prefer to go unnoticed. As a teenager, I represented my school in springboard diving, which proved quite a spectacle, as divers are generally short. Beds tend not to be long enough for me, and restricted leg room when travelling is a nightmare.

In Yemen, cheeky boys sometimes called out, 'Ya Taweel!' ('O Tall One!'). I seemed like a giant in Yemeni homes where the doorways were often quite low, and sometimes I had to bend double to get into their washrooms! But God had always intended me to serve him in Yemen, and I believe that because Arabs respect tall men, he gave me my height—all of six feet and seven inches!

I was born on July 12, 1943 in the northern Sydney suburb of Roseville. Because I was a big baby, my mother had great difficulty giving birth. When her friends saw me, they used to say, 'Shirley! What do you blow him up with?' What with Dad away in the army, her bad back, and my brother aged two and a half, it was a hard time for Mum.

When my father returned from the war and left the army, we moved for a time to the little town of Emmaville on the northern tablelands of NSW, where Dad was the only doctor. Then in 1947, when I was three and a half, he joined a general practice in another northern Sydney suburb, Epping. Our living area comprised the upstairs and the back of the surgery building, and we stayed there for the next seven years, after which my father had a new home built for us in a different part of Epping.

We began worshipping at St Philip's Church of England (later Anglican Church), Eastwood. St Philip's was an evangelical church, and so I know that the gospel message would have been taught to us at Sunday School, and the scripture teaching at school would have been Bible-based. Although I don't recall most of the lessons, I believe that as a young child I would have grasped the basics of the gospel.

I don't know a definite date on which my Christian life began, but the Lord may have counted me amongst his children from a young age. Certainly, my main interest and happiness seems to have related to things which I knew God had created, like small birds and beautiful flowers, but I began to grow as a Christian when I started going to Christian holiday camps for boys. There we were encouraged to give our lives to the Lord Jesus, which I did at each camp, until I realised that we only needed to do that once. We were also taught how to grow as Christians through daily Bible reading and prayer, regular attendance at church activities, reading missionary and other Christian biographies, and so on. One of the most lasting benefits for me from those camps came from the Bible verses set to music, as well as other Christian songs that we learned by heart. Such songs have come to mind countless times over the years, providing encouragement and direction.

My years at school, and later at university, were not happy, chiefly because I struggled academically. My father had been an outstanding scholar; he was dux of Sydney Grammar School despite being a year younger than most of his peers, and my siblings were also gifted academically. These facts, together with my sensitive personality and lack of positive affirmation at school and at home unfortunately resulted in the inferiority complex I have never been able to shake off completely. Nevertheless, I sought to point fellow students to the Lord, and helped to lead the weekly lunchtime Christian meetings.

I believe that it was the Lord's plan for me to be a doctor, despite having the odds seemingly stacked against me. First, I'd never studied Latin. However, 1961, the year I applied, was the first year that it was considered unnecessary. Second, my Leaving Certificate marks were not great; the school headmaster even kindly advised me against tackling a medical degree. Thankfully, I did scrape in and the Lord helped me to press on through the following seven years to graduation and beyond[1].

When I began at Sydney University, I joined the Evangelical Union (EU), a Christian organisation which held a large weekly lunch-time meeting for students and staff in a lecture theatre. They also ran Bible study groups within the separate faculties, including medicine. I remained a member of the EU throughout my years at university, attending weekly Bible studies and participating in other functions. Sometimes the EU organised Christian outreach to the general student body. Partly because I got up and made announcements about these and other activities from time to time in front of hundreds of my fellow medical students before a lecture began, a friendly Roman Catholic chap told me that he considered me to be a 'red-hot Anglican'!

For five consecutive years from 1962, I took part in beach missions, ten enjoyable days in camping areas at beaches, starting after Boxing Day. The Children's Special Service Mission, now Scripture Union Family Mission, organised teams of 30 or so young adults to run outreach programs for children and teenagers who were holidaying in the camping area. We presented the gospel message in ways which were appropriate for their ages while also giving them a great time of fun and entertainment. I enjoyed the fellowship with the other team members, and after each mission I felt that my spiritual batteries had been fully recharged for the year ahead.

Also, during three consecutive summer holidays towards the end of my time at university, I led the Crusader Union Intermediate Boys' Surf Camp at Gerringong, an attractive spot on the NSW South Coast where dairy country comes right down to the sea. About half a dozen of my friends helped me lead these camps which were worthwhile times, not only for the 35 or so boys who came, but also for us leaders.

As well as the beach missions and surf camps, for two or three of those years, the rector of St John's Anglican Church at Beecroft invited me to care for the primary-age and young teenage boys at their annual church family weekend house party at Chaldercot, on Port Hacking, south of Sydney. We had a lot of fun and good fellowship together.

In November 1965, after I completed fourth year medicine, my parents paid for my return air fare to Papua New Guinea for five weeks. My older brother Humphrey was working for the Australian Government as a high school teacher at Kwikila, not far from Port Moresby, but he also knew Christian people elsewhere in the country. As well as staying with him, I visited some of those places too, mostly in the highlands at Goroka and the Baptist Mission Hospital at Baiyer River. In Goroka, I stayed with an Australian couple, John Burgin and his wife Ruth. His work was primarily in coffee production. Soon after I landed, he and a young colleague of his, Jerry Chan, took me with them in their Land Rover for a routine trip of several days' through the region of Kinantu and Kundiawa, where John supervised the work of the government agriculturalist in each locality. I towered more than head and shoulders over the locals as they crowded around us.

'We want him to stay here and be our king,' they told John at one place. 'He can produce many sons who would be mighty warriors!'

This trip enabled me to experience medical missionary work first-hand. I was thinking about serving in that way in the future, though I had no country in mind.

For a few years before I completed my medical degree, I helped to lead the youth fellowship at St Philip's Anglican Church, Eastwood. The main task I was given was to organise a weekend mission to the youth of Eastwood with the Rev Geoff Bingham as the speaker. Over the weekend seven young people gave their lives to the Lord. On another Sunday evening, I led a small team to Riverstone Anglican and spoke at their youth fellowship on John 4:1-26, 'the woman at the well'. Six young people gave their lives to the Lord that evening. What a joy and an honour!

BIRTH TO NEWCASTLE, AND A SPECIAL GIFT

Upon graduating, I was appointed to the Royal Newcastle Hospital as a resident medical officer. My parents and Humphrey accompanied me as I drove up to Newcastle for the first time. I thought I didn't know anyone and was apprehensive about the prospect of beginning work as a doctor, but at just the right moment the Lord arranged one of his wonderful coincidences to encourage me. As my brother and I were approaching a small side door at the front of the main building, who should open it and come towards us but John Stace! He had graduated from the University of NSW the year before me. We had even arranged an Evangelical Union function together.

As it turned out, John was soon to leave to work somewhere else. When we met, he was hurrying to the Pathology Department across the road but was able to greet me and direct me to where I had to go. I felt a little like St Paul must have felt when he was approaching Rome as a prisoner and some Christian men who'd heard that he was coming travelled out specially to meet him. 'At the sight of these men Paul thanked God and was encouraged[2].'

As the weeks and months passed, I settled into the routines. Every three months we moved to a different department. My first term was in Obstetrics and Gynaecology, and the second was in the Emergency Department, or 'Casualty'. Soon, I made an interesting discovery. I could see that the Lord himself was teaching me! For instance, in the Casualty term, a patient who had suffered a heart attack arrived one day by ambulance. I called the rostered medical registrar and took note of how he treated the patient. Shortly after, another patient was brought in who had also suffered a heart attack. Again, I called the medical registrar and assisted him in the care of the patient. Then a third heart attack patient arrived. This time, I was able to treat the patient myself. Similarly, I noticed a cluster of patients who were in severe pain from kidney stones, and then patients with fractured bones, or with lacerations needing to be sutured, or with 'foreign bodies' in their eyes. The Lord was arranging for these patients to arrive at convenient times for me to be on hand and therefore to rapidly gain excellent experience.

As resident doctors, we worked long hours, on duty every day during the week, as well as every second night and every second weekend. We had to catch what sleep we could, so we were often tired. Once when driving home

ON THE WAY

to Sydney for the weekend, I fell asleep at the wheel and drove right across the path of a car going in the opposite direction. I only woke when the other driver gave me a blast on his horn. Providentially, a wide strip of gravel at the side of the road allowed me to quickly stop my car. I or someone else could easily have been killed!

* * *

I began attending Sunday services at the Anglican Cathedral in Newcastle when I could and joined the young adults' fellowship group known as the Canterbury Club[3]. Before long I was helping to lead this group and contributing articles for the magazine which the club produced. I hadn't been at the hospital for long before I met some other Christians on the staff, and soon we had a Bible study group going. About three years later I was particularly thankful for one of the nurses who was part of that group, Barbara Hunter, as we shall see.

Another man I invited as a speaker for the Canterbury Club was the Rev John Hutchinson, a dynamic evangelical, and a Methodist minister in Newcastle. I warmed to him, and he was to have a great impact on my life. Not long after we became friends, John left the Methodist denomination to join the Assembly of God. He invited me to stay with him one weekend, but I was rostered on duty at the hospital. However, I said that I would come the following weekend. I later discovered that he'd hoped this would happen. He wanted me to come for Pentecost, the festival celebrating the descent of the Holy Spirit, and he took this as the Lord's seal that his hand was on the arrangement.

The weekend that I went to John's church, they had organised a series of meetings at which everyone in the congregation was invited to come forward if they wished, to be baptised in the Holy Spirit through the laying on of hands and to receive the gift of tongues or other gifts of the Holy Spirit. I went to several of the meetings, and although I'd never heard anyone speaking in tongues before, I was intrigued and fascinated, though a little uncomfortable. I was deeply moved by the beauty of the language when someone spoke out the interpretation in English of a message which had been given in tongues.

I chose not to go forward and at an evening gathering in the home of one of the elders, a man challenged me with why I hadn't. I felt hurt, and drove back to the hospital that night, but the next day returned for the Sunday afternoon meeting and decided that I *would* go forward.

The main speaker that night was 'Tiny' Newbury. He had a loud voice and got excited, saying one or two things which I thought were impractical. But I went forward nevertheless, because if the Lord had something that he wanted to give me, I most definitely wanted to receive it. About half a dozen of us knelt in a row out the front, while three or four men moved from one to another, laying their hands on our heads as they prayed for us. I heard others begin to speak in tongues, but nothing happened for me.

After a little while, all three or four of those men came and laid their hands on my head together. One prayed earnestly that I might receive the gift of tongues but still I didn't receive it, though I waited there on my knees for quite some time.

'Say "Hallelujah" a few times,' suggested one of them, which I did but to no avail. At last I got up and went back to my seat, inwardly distressed.

At the tea afterwards I felt embarrassed. All I wanted to do was to get away as quickly as I could. However, soon a man called Rex, a farmer from New Zealand who planned to return there soon with his young family, came up to me.

'While you were kneeling out the front, I received a message for you from the Lord,' he told me, in a humble manner. 'Normally I would have stood up and spoken the message out as I received it, but I decided to tell you later.'

'Would you write it down for me?' I asked. What he wrote described authority the Lord was placing in me. A similar message was spoken or prayed over me several times in subsequent years by people who had never met me before, thus confirming what the Lord had given Rex to pass on to me.

After I left the meeting, it struck me how amazing it was that God should speak to me *personally*. It was not just words from the Bible (though it was based on Biblical teaching), but Rex had received a personal message for me! It specifically highlighted the authority which the Lord was placing in me, which I have taken to mainly mean authority in prayer. Awed and overjoyed, I began to praise him from my heart. As I waited for the lights to change at the Charlestown intersection, praising God out loud in the privacy of my car, I suddenly began to speak in tongues. It happened just like that. One moment I was praising God in English and then I was speaking with sounds and words I didn't understand.

I drove on for about a mile and a half, and then decided to go back to the assembly. The evening gathering had already begun, but I told the man at the door what had happened. He went in and whispered to the fellow leading the service who then asked me to come up to the front and tell the congregation. They were all thrilled and delighted. I left soon afterwards as I wanted to attend the evening service at the cathedral with my friends, and on the way, picked up a young hitchhiker, urging him to turn to the Lord. He hardly said anything, but I was absolutely bubbling over with irrepressible joy which I was unable to contain. I just had to share with him what had happened. The joy I felt then I've never experienced before or since. My tongue silently went on speaking in tongues during the prayers in the sombre old cathedral that evening; and after church, back at the hospital in the privacy of my room, I just sang and danced in the Spirit, my whole being filled to overflowing with amazing ecstasy. That most memorable evening was Sunday, June 2, 1968. I only told a few people about it over the next few years. My family took the news calmly but seemed to be quite shaken underneath. It was so remote from what we'd been accustomed to.

Now that I'd been baptised in the Spirit, John felt that I should also be baptised by immersion in water. A date was fixed for this in the Charlestown Assembly of God, and I brought some white cricket trousers up from Epping for the occasion. My family were upset about this and tried to dissuade me. Dad wrote several letters to me, pointing out that this step could well prevent my further participation in certain Christian ministries with which I was connected, such as Scripture Union and the Crusader Union, because some members of those councils were strongly opposed to Pentecostalism.

However, he said that if I was certain that it was the Lord's will, he'd come for the service. He'd felt, as a young man, that it was right for him to be baptised by immersion, and he had taken that step in a Church of Christ, but he thought that to be baptised like that in a Pentecostal church was different.

I was unhappy about the family's distress, but more was to come. A little before the due date, I heard that the head of the Assemblies of God for Australia would be coming especially. I was certain it was for me, sensing that they'd be delighted to have a doctor within their ranks, and I began at once to feel uneasy. I just wanted to remain a simple believer and did not want anything special arranged. The more I considered the matter, the more anxious I became. I found the pressure the next day so heavy that I could barely concentrate on my work. Never, before or since have I had such a sense of the hand of God weighing heavily upon me like that.

In the end, I had no alternative but to ring John and cancel my baptism. He was disappointed, but I immediately felt enormously relieved. That sense of freedom and rest was confirmation to me that the Lord had been speaking. I'd met some godly people in that assembly, but clearly it wasn't the group the Lord wanted me to link up with.

Although I've never felt the Lord's hand on me in that way since, often I have been directed or strengthened by the knowledge that he was with me, particularly before getting up to give an address, through a definite awareness of being able to feel my heart beating strongly. This may sound strange, but it has certainly been 'of the Lord' in my case.

After that period, I often spoke in tongues when I chose to, but because I'd had virtually no teaching whatever about exercising the gifts of the Holy Spirit, and because I realised that some Christians don't encourage using the gifts of the Holy Spirit, and in fact may be quite hostile towards them, I kept it largely a secret.

The following year, I was asked to be on a three-person panel during the annual combined Methodist conference in Newcastle. We were each given a few minutes to speak and then we were to answer questions from the audience. I prepared what I wanted to say, and after I'd delivered my talk and sat down, a question was directed to me. A young university student asked me to explain what it meant to be born again. I stood up quickly and went to the microphone. I opened my mouth to speak and found myself saying to the young man if, in asking the question, he meant such and such; and he replied, 'Yes'. But I hadn't chosen those words!

I then launched into an explanation in clear English and answered his question; but although it was me speaking, I hadn't chosen a single word; the Lord was speaking through me with my voice. I was perfectly conscious, but it was the Holy Spirit speaking. It was the most amazing experience and the only time anything like that has ever happened through me, even though I have spoken in hundreds of services and meetings since then. I believe that this was a 'message of wisdom', one of the gifts of the Holy Spirit.

Apart from this one time, the only spiritual gift I've used over the years has been speaking in tongues privately, in intercession and for my own prayer needs. In fact, prayer became a major part of my ministry, but except when praying with my wife, I've rarely chosen to speak in tongues with others present. Paul said, in 1 Corinthians 14:4, that 'he who speaks in a tongue edifies himself'. I've discovered that the Greek word for 'edify', apart from meaning 'to grow, build up spiritually, strengthen, encourage and comfort,' also means 'to embolden'. These words describe what the Lord did in my life so that he could send me to do his bidding; and, of course, my main purpose for writing these memoirs has been to record what I saw the Lord doing. For years I'd been considering overseas medical missionary work, and the conviction that it was the Lord's plan for me was gradually strengthening. However, considering my personality and limitations, I don't think I could possibly have done what he later led me to do in Yemen, or even to have gone there as a missionary at all, without the power of the Holy Spirit enabling me. Perhaps in a small way I was like the apostles after Pentecost. Now I could recognise and respond to my calling, but because no-one asked me what I thought about the gifts of the Holy Spirit, I continued to keep it all a secret. Then, before too long, the Lord's purposes for me began to be revealed, commencing at an engagement party.

2

'You don't speak Arabic by any chance?'

1970-1971: Age 27-28

Although I'd been feeling, with gradually increasing certainty, that the Lord would lead me into missionary service, I had no idea where it would be. I was interested in China and South America, and I'd been to Papua New Guinea; but none of these seemed his place for me.

Mrs Mary Noble, from my Eastwood church, had lent me the first volume of the biography of the missionary doctor, Hudson Taylor, who went to China in 1854. The book described how the Lord led him into fruitful ministry and provided for him. At the time, both volumes were out of print, and so some months later Mrs Noble lent me the second volume.

'Do you think I could possibly keep the books?' I asked her after I read the second one. I had gained so much from Hudson Taylor's story and wanted to re-read it. Mrs Noble was slightly taken aback, because they had belonged to her late husband, but she graciously consented. I told her on several occasions how grateful I was. Those two books have gone with me wherever we have moved. I still have them handy today. Next to the Bible, they have meant more to me than any other book. I have read and reread them, and through them have been spiritually blessed and refreshed. In fact, they featured importantly in my call to the mission field.

After I'd spent about two and a half years at the Royal Newcastle Hospital, I got the flu and had to go to bed for two days. Moved by reading Hudson Taylor's story, I once again committed my life to the Lord, still not knowing where he wanted me to serve him, and not having any inclination to stay in Australia.

The next weekend I drove to Sydney for a gathering of St Philip's Fellowship friends and others for an engagement party. It was there that Rod West talked to me.

'What do you have in mind for the future?' he asked.

'I'm planning to go to England next year to do diplomas in obstetrics and anaesthetics,' I told him, although I was secretly not looking forward to going. 'I think it will be helpful for the mission field. After that, I don't know.'

'You don't speak Arabic by any chance, do you?' he asked, jokingly. 'There's an urgent need for doctors in Yemen.'

Rod and his wife Janet had prayed for the Red Sea Mission Team (RSMT) work for years and I was immediately interested. Later that evening he and I, together with Rod's nephew, Stuart Piggin, went to visit the Australian Secretary for the RSMT, Bob Colville, who lived only about half a mile away. We chatted together about my interest in missionary work and then he gave me some RSMT literature to read.

Reading what Bob gave me, I began to think about what sort of medical work the Lord would probably lead me into. I came up with four criteria. I believed he would call me to minister in a remote location, in small clinics or mobile medical work as compared to a large hospital set up. I believed it would be in a place where there hadn't been any Christian work done before, and I thought he would call me to be part of a team which sought to live 'by faith', without making appeals for funds[4].

Next, I sought advice from the Rev Neville Anderson, the principal of the Baptist Theological College in Eastwood about medical missionary work, and possibly joining the Red Sea Mission Team.

'I suggest you go and talk to Bishop Jack Dain,' he told me.

My sister Lyndall and I had planned a five-day boat trip up the Hawkesbury

River, but on the morning that we were to begin our cruise from Bobbin Head, we went via Church House, Sydney, to see Bishop Jack Dain[5], who turned out to be one of the two official referees in NSW for the RSMT.

'Only one doctor in ten would be happy and satisfied with the type of work you would be doing in the places the Red Sea Mission Team goes to,' he told me. 'So be sure that you are being led by the Lord.'

'What sort of work is it?' I asked.

He described a medical ministry that would be remote, in a small clinic situation, in areas where there had been little Christian outreach before.

'That sounds like what I'm hoping for,' I said.

On the boat over the next five days, as I read the material that Bob Colville had given me and prayed, it became obvious that my four points were well fulfilled in the work of the Red Sea Mission Team. It felt that the Lord was leading, and as soon as I returned to Newcastle, I cancelled the six-month anaesthetics job which I'd arranged to do during the first half of the following year.

Less than two months later, on Friday, October 23, 1970, I drove down to Sydney for the weekend. An English CMS surgeon, Dr Ronnie Holland, who ran a missionary hospital in Quetta, Pakistan, would be speaking at the home of Dr and Mrs Bryson in Roseville, and I wanted to meet him. He showed slides of his work, including eye surgery; and afterwards I spent a little time speaking with him. He knew something of the Red Sea Mission Team, and I was glad that he'd only heard favourable reports.

'If you want to go to Yemen, you could stop off in Quetta on the way,' he suggested. His idea was that I should spend some months gaining experience in missionary medicine and learning to manage where there would be few diagnostic facilities or specialist doctors available, since Yemen was a developing country.

'Thank you,' I said, but I didn't think I should accept. I wanted to get to Yemen as soon as I could.

Over the next little while I filled in the detailed application forms for the RSMT and gathered the necessary references. After being processed by the Australian Home Council, the papers had to be sent off to the founder and leader of the Team, Dr Lionel Gurney, who was in Ethiopia at the time. Those papers were then sent on to several other senior Team members for their clearance, one by one—a slow procedure due to the mail services there. I had no alternative but to wait in hope that my candidature would finally be accepted.

In the meantime, I knew that the Team normally required two undertakings from candidates. One was a language-learning course run by a branch of Wycliffe Bible Translators, the Summer Institute of Linguistics. In Australia, this was a three-month intensive study course held in Brisbane over the Christmas break.

The other requirement of candidates was that they attend Bible College. I was impatient to get to the mission field, however, so I wrote to Dr Gurney outlining the Christian work with which I'd been involved, such as beach missions, boys' camps, as well as the Scripture Union ministry I was involved with in 1969 and 1970, visiting in my spare time most of the Protestant churches in Newcastle to encourage Bible reading. Was it necessary for me to go to Bible College, I asked?

While waiting to hear back, I applied for the three-month SIL course in Brisbane and was accepted. For the most part, I found the time in Brisbane hard going. I had some difficult medical cases to deal with amongst the students and the study was intensive. Even though the staff had produced what was obviously a top-quality course in linguistics, covering phonetics, phonemics and grammar, useful for those preparing to start from scratch to write down a previously unwritten language, it didn't seem relevant to me at all[6]. I was to attend a language school in Yemen where I'd be learning an already recorded language, Arabic.

I enjoyed some of the talks we had during that time, however, including one by Chuck Peck, a member of the first group who went and contacted the Auca Indians who, fifteen years before, had murdered five young American missionaries in Ecuador[7]. As well as this, two important incidents occurred in Brisbane which proved to be a source of great encouragement to me over the years.

The first incident was concerning money. Due to the Christmas and

New Year holiday season, I'd been unable to make a speedy transfer of my signature from the bank in Newcastle to one near the university in Brisbane, which left me unable to access money, apart from the cash I had brought with me, with which I had to buy my daily meals at the College cafeteria, as well as anything else I needed.

'If anyone is short of finance, there is assistance available through a temporary fund we've set up,' the SIL business manager announced one day, but I decided not to tell anyone about my situation. I'd read about similar incidents in Hudson Taylor's life when he was preparing to be a missionary, and here was an opportunity to simply trust the Lord and see if he would provide for me.

Gradually I watched the money I had with me dwindle away but I still sought to trust the Lord, and not worry. Eventually the day came when I had just enough money to buy my evening meal, but not enough for breakfast the next morning. As usual, that evening I worked away in my room on the set homework. I was about to get ready for bed when one of my fellow students knocked on the door and came in carrying half a watermelon.

'I bought too much,' he told me. 'Do you want the rest?'

I was absolutely delighted by this wonderful provision and how he 'just happened' to bring it to me.

'You're the bearer of a special blessing,' I told him.

I ate some of the watermelon before going to bed and finished off the remainder in the morning for breakfast. It was the most enjoyable breakfast of my entire life. I had now begun to live by faith! Should I continue to wait for my signature to reach the bank and still not ask for money, I wondered? But I found that being short of cash was stressful and distracting, when I was supposed to be concentrating hard on my studies, so after I'd enjoyed my watermelon breakfast, I went and accepted the business manager's offer.

About a week later my signature came through from my bank so I was able to repay what I'd borrowed, but deep down I felt slightly guilty. Hudson Taylor would have continued to trust the Lord, and not ask for money I thought, but I realise now that I shouldn't have felt guilty at all. The Lord had sent that watermelon, proving that he was easily able to provide for me; and I knew that there was money in that fund freely available for me to draw upon, which I believe the Lord had prompted the business manager to offer. I saw how vigilant I'd need to be to detect if the enemy was tempting me to shift away, even slightly, from pure motives. I might have begun to feel proud of myself for being so 'spiritual' if I'd sought to continue looking to the Lord in that way!

The second incident began to unfold a few weeks later. I'd often prayed for a wife but had felt that she'd have to be one in a million, not just to agree to marry me, but also to be willing to serve the Lord in Yemen—and with a faith mission. I also had the obstacle of Bible College to overcome. While in Brisbane, I discovered that some of my fellow students had been studying at the Sydney Missionary and Bible College at Croydon. A new, one-year course was now being offered and could be completed in less than ten months. Since I knew that the Red Sea Mission Team normally required Bible College training for all candidates, I felt duty-bound to at least enquire from SMBC whether they would accept me. I explained in my letter that because I wanted to complete the SIL course, I would be three weeks late in commencing my studies at SMBC.

The deputy principal at SMBC, the Rev Howard Green, accepted my application[8]. My loss would have been enormous if I'd ignored the Lord's promptings. If I hadn't gone to SMBC, I'd never have met my wife, and as it turned out, I was to discover just how necessary Bible College was for me. As the SMBC course progressed, I realised how poor my knowledge of Christian doctrine was, and that some of my thinking was completely wrong. For example, in my application to the RSMT, I wrote that Jesus was 'created', whereas of course, he was 'begotten, not made'. He has always lived from eternity as part of the Trinity. Dr Gurney wrote that Muslims would love me to teach that Jesus was a created being. Going to Bible College proved to be a blessing. An old saying was certainly applicable here: 'The way of duty is the way of safety.'

When the Rev Howard Green accepted my application, he also enclosed a copy of the latest college news-sheet with a photo of the previous year's student body. Scanning it, my eyes stopped on one girl in the front row,

Adele Dwight. Instantly I felt my heart beating, and somehow, I just knew that she was the one the Lord had chosen for me. Now, of course, I had her photo, and the very first day I arrived at college, on Monday, February 22, 1971, I saw her in person. Mr Green took me to the College dining hall for a late morning tea. As we entered, I saw her almost immediately, crouching down while putting some jam away in a little cupboard. At the same time, looking up, she saw me in a glance, and months later told me that she was impressed.

It would be good to get to know her, I thought, but this was more easily said than done. The male and female student accommodation facilities were separate. In lectures the girls sat in the front rows, while the fellows sat at the back. Besides that, it was not permitted for a fellow and girl to stand talking to each other at College, except briefly. At mealtimes there was opportunity to talk, but only on a strictly rostered basis. In the dining hall there were about ten large tables in two rows, with each table seating ten people. We all sat at a table for a week, and then the girls moved clockwise while the fellows moved anti-clockwise, to the next tables. This meant that Adele and I were only seated at the same table for a week every five weeks or so.

It wasn't until nine days after I arrived at College that I first spoke to Adele, on Wednesday, March 3. I was enrolled in the one-year Diploma course, while she was doing the second year of the normal two-year course, with the extra task of being student librarian. On this day I approached the library desk, and asked her to explain the catalogue system, as a way of making conversation. She briefly explained it and then asked me a little about myself.

'I'm a doctor,' I told her, 'preparing for missionary service overseas.'

After this short conversation, I turned away and was instantly struck by the most powerful thumping of my heart I've ever experienced. I knew at once that the Lord was confirming what I already believed; that this was the girl he had chosen for me in answer to all my prayers and yearnings over the years. I watched her with interest during the next few weeks and slowly gathered relevant information. This was not easy with the restrictions on male and female students chatting with each other. However, when I felt certain that she was also drawn to me, I handed her a letter in which I enquired whether she felt it consistent with the Lord's leading for her, to consider serving him in Yemen. A day or two later, she gave me a brief note in which, to my absolute horror and mortification, she turned me down.

For the next two months I lived a nightmare, thinking that it was probable that she had told others of my letter, and that they were secretly mocking me. (In fact, she hadn't told anyone at all about our letters. She didn't have a special boyfriend, and had recently been reading a book by Amy Carmichael, an unmarried missionary in India in the first half of the twentieth century. Adele had told her father and a group at her church that she planned to serve the Lord overseas as a single missionary.) Thinking it over, I took this shock to be of the Lord. He was testing me to see if I was willing for him to give, and then to take away; so that he would know if he was absolutely everything to me or not. How *deeply* I sank during those weeks, avoiding Dell at all costs, ashamed and shocked that I of all people, usually so reserved where girls were concerned, had now had the ground cut away completely from under my feet!

I needed to talk to someone, so I went privately to see the Rev Arthur Deane, the College Principal. He was sympathetic and gave me some helpful advice. I also shared it all with my mother when I went home one weekend. She knew that at 27, I'd never had a girlfriend, and the years were slipping away. I've sometimes jokingly said that once I'd told my mother and she contacted some of her praying friends, Dell didn't stand a chance!

Eventually, Adele started to reconsider the whole matter. She'd felt God calling her to serve him in the Middle East after hearing a visiting missionary speak at College, but she thought it was to be with the Lebanon Evangelical Mission. However, the Lord seemed to be blocking her way forward with them. At the same time, she could see the struggle I was going through. Then one evening she decided to visit Barbara Hunter, a nursing sister I had been in a Bible study group with at Newcastle Hospital, and now a fellow student at the College. Dell shared it all with her in confidence and Barb spoke up strongly for me.

The next morning, a Thursday, I was walking to lectures alone when Dell caught up to me.

'Perhaps we ought to talk things over together,' she said.

We decided to go out for a picnic on the coming Saturday and I arrived at her home as planned on May 29, 1971, driving my little blue, humpback Morris Oxford. Adele's youngest sister Louella opened the door and then, having been welcomed by Mrs Dwight, who I liked at once, I sat down at the dining room table while Dell finished packing the picnic basket. Mr Dwight had gone out to play golf, apparently.

Strangely enough, without having told Adele, I'd planned that we'd go to picturesque Wiseman's Ferry. There before me on the dining room table was a painting which Mrs Dwight had done only a few days before—of that spot! I couldn't help remarking on this strange coincidence.

As Adele and I drove towards Strathfield Station, I had to brake sharply to avoid a truck, and this caused the basket behind the driver's seat to tip over, spilling some milk. We stopped, and I took a cloth and wet it under a tap I saw in the front area of a block of home units and wiped up the spilt milk to prevent it smelling the car out later. After that little incident, we both felt relaxed and at ease. I chatted away almost non-stop (especially about the humorous hospital revues I'd been involved in), all the way to Wiseman's. There we got out and went for a walk beside the river. We still didn't feel like lunch, so we decided to walk up the hill, but as we were just setting out, Dell said, 'Michael, I think the Lord is leading us together.'

I felt weak in the knees. 'Really?' I said. 'Can we sit down?'

I led her to a nearby park seat and asked her to tell me everything, starting at the beginning. It turned out that Dell had already accepted in her heart that the Lord intended for us to be together but hadn't known when to tell me. I sat listening, dazed, yet praising God that he had not failed me, and that I hadn't mistaken his leading.

We talked till late, having eaten by dribs and drabs, and having watched the sunset from our car, now parked at the lookout beside the road, up near the top of the ridge.

'There's something I ought to tell you straight away,' I said to her, and described what had happened three years before when I was baptised in the Holy Spirit. As I told her, I hoped against hope that this wouldn't immediately end our friendship and was so relieved when she straight away set my heart at rest. She herself had become interested in the gifts of the Holy Spirit through reading *The Cross and the Switchblade* by David Wilkerson, some months before. That possible obstacle was out of the way.

I turned to her and said, 'Will you marry me?'

She said, 'Yes'.

We were late driving home, so I stopped at the first public phone box we came to so that we could ring our parents and let them know that we were okay. We then called in at Epping so that I could introduce Dell to my mother. Mum knew we were going on the picnic, of course, which must have been a wonder to her, as I'd hardly ever taken a girl out before, let alone been in love. Also, I'd rarely shared my deepest thoughts with her or with anyone else. Dell and I perched close together on stools in the kitchen and ate our dinner, much to Mum's secret delight and joy. 'At last it's happened!' she must have thought, as we chatted away about the day.

What a day it had been, and our first outing together! I drove Dell home and left her outside her back door, after giving her a kiss on the cheek!

There would be many more happy visits to the Dwights' home in Greenacre over the years ahead. Adele's father and mother were both committed Christians. Mr Dwight rose through the ranks of Telecom to be a training technician and on his retirement, was head of all Telecom (later called Telstra) training facilities in NSW. Adele had given her life to the Lord when she was just six years of age, kneeling beside her bed with her mother. She grew up in the Bankstown Open Brethren Assembly, and was an enthusiastic participant in many Christian activities, both within the church as well as out in the community. In her final year at Birrong Girls' High School she was both dux and school captain, and then went on to Sydney University, gaining her Science degree and a post-graduate diploma in Nutrition and Dietetics. She worked for the NSW Health Department for two years, before commencing in early 1970 the two-year diploma course at Sydney Missionary and Bible College, where the Lord brought our paths together a year later.

I love to think about how he arranged things in such unusual ways. I saw Adele in a photograph, and immediately felt sure that she was the Lord's choice for me, even before we'd met. Then, on our first outing we agreed that we were to get married. Both of us were sure about it, so why delay?

As a matter of fact, we had no time to waste. I knew that we had to move quickly if Dell was to be accepted by the Red Sea Mission Team before the end of the year. The Team had a rule that both applicants must be accepted as candidates before being given permission to become officially engaged[9].

Dell and I decided not to tell anyone of our unofficial engagement. Nevertheless, I did buy a pearl ring for her birthday on June 25, which she wore on a non-implicating finger. For my birthday in July, she bought me Young's 'Analytical Concordance to the Bible', which I still use to this day. Except for weekends, we had to be content with limited opportunities to see each other.

Back at College, I was like a new person and got down to my studies with a light heart. My room, which I shared with John Howell and Mike Wilson, was upstairs in the old home in which the College was commenced. Because of my height, my parents had had an extended bed made for me several years previously. This I brought to College on the roof of my car, but in the dead of night to avoid attracting attention. We three fellows had a lot of fun together, but unfortunately our room was directly above the Principal's office, and I'm sorry to say that on more than one occasion, Mr Deane was forced to leave his office and call us into line when our antics made it difficult for him downstairs. We should have been quietly studying.

At the end of each year, all the College students went on a mission trip for about ten days. That year it was to Parkes, a rural town west of Sydney. On the final day, Saturday, November 20, 1971, our engagement notice appeared in the newspapers as we'd arranged. Someone must have seen it and told Mr Gibson from Open Air Campaigners, who was organising our mission trip, because he called us up to the front after breakfast and announced our engagement to everyone. We'd bought a diamond ring a few weeks before, and Dell wore it for the first time as we travelled back to

College on the bus.[10]

Having completed our studies at SMBC, I was delighted to be awarded their Diploma in Divinity and Mission (one-year course), while Dell was awarded the two-year diploma.

We sent out our first circular news and prayer letter that December, and had a card prepared with our photo on it, and the following message:

May the Lord enable us all to 'rejoice always, pray constantly, and give thanks in all circumstances; for this is the will of God in Christ Jesus for you.' And so 'brethren, pray for us.' (1 Thessalonians 5:16-18, 25).

One of these prayer cards was sent out with each copy of that first circular letter by our friend, Annette Bossley. Various friends and churches had asked to be on our mailing list, and we were thankful to have their prayer backing and financial contributions towards our support[11].

Our official farewell service was at St Philip's Anglican Church, Eastwood, on the evening after we returned from Parkes. Mr Deane preached the sermon, speaking from 1 Thessalonians 2:1-12, drawing out the points that missionary work is a high calling, a humble calling, and a holy calling.

Dr Lionel Gurney had written to me during the year, asking me if I would be willing to concentrate on eye conditions. These seemed to be prevalent around Zaidiya, the small town on the coastal plain of Yemen where, at that time, it was intended that I would be based after my Arabic language studies. I prayed carefully before I replied to him. Deep within me, I was aware of an uneasiness about my adequacy to tackle such an undertaking, and yet, I believed the Lord wanted me to press on and simply trust him in that, as in everything else. I kept my uneasiness to myself and wrote back to Dr Gurney saying that I was willing to do what he suggested.

It was then that I remembered Dr Ronnie Holland's invitation to spend a few months with him in Pakistan on my way to Yemen, so I wrote and asked him if I could take up his offer. Dr Holland was constantly dealing with eye conditions (as well as general medical and surgical cases), and this would be good experience for me. In his reply he readily agreed.

We were still waiting for Adele's official acceptance from the Field Council, and of course we weren't married, so it was decided that I would go on ahead to Pakistan for about five months, and then meet up with Adele in Yemen. In the meantime, she would tackle the newly abbreviated, six-week SIL language-learning course in Brisbane, as well as a Mothercraft and Infant Care Course, amongst other preparations.

I was originally booked to leave Sydney on December 30, but the short war at that time between Pakistan and India caused a delay in granting the visa for my stay in Pakistan. Having seen Dell off to Brisbane, she was then granted permission from the SIL staff to take a few days off from the course to fly down to Sydney for Christmas, which gave us a brief time together before our longer separation was to begin.

After all the pressure of our Bible College studies and the preparations for my departure, the unexpected delay provided a welcome time of rest for me. Then, after she had completed her six-week course and I *still* hadn't left, Dell was able to be in Sydney for when I eventually did leave, on January 26. Our final church service at St Philip's turned into a second farewell, during which Dell sang a moving solo, 'No-one understands like Jesus', accompanied on the organ by David Parsons. Another memorable incident was a visit to my home by Dr Paul White, 'The Jungle Doctor'. Although he was my father's closest friend, on this occasion he also came to see me. He gave me a farewell gift, a large book of excellent photographs depicting the Church Missionary Society's medical work in Tanzania, where he had worked. And a 'prescription'; a verse from Proverbs 4:12(a). *'As you go, step by step, I will open the way before you.'* What a wonderful promise! The Lord proved true to his word, right down to the present day.

3

Training in Pakistan

January-July 1972: Age 28

The day of departure was the Australia Day public holiday in 1972. My family were at the airport to see me off, and of course Adele, with some of her family and other friends. Though willing to part for the Lord's work, I was a little emotional as I said goodbye. It would be several years before I would be home again, and months before I would see Adele.

I arrived at the Qantas check-in counter to find I had unintentionally packed more luggage than was permitted.

'You'll have to ship it,' they told me, and I selected several items to be packed in the extra luggage that we were sending by sea. Even then I was still seven kilos overweight, but the Scotsman behind the counter kindly allowed it through without charging any fee.

I'd reached Singapore before I'd calmed down, and the next stop was Bangkok where we landed at 3am local time, after flying fifteen and a half hours from Sydney. I was exhausted but after a good sleep and a meal I felt much better. I also decided to repack my luggage to ease my conscience and sent the extra seven kilos back home by sea mail.

The Lord arranged at least two things to help me in Bangkok. Firstly, I had that repacking job to do in the hotel to keep me busy, and I was truly thankful for that. I sometimes tend to be hard on myself, thinking how stupid I am for doing this or forgetting to do that; but I've found that now and then at least, the Lord may have had a hand in it for his own purposes. Although the luggage problem was stressful at Sydney airport, it turned out to be a blessing in Bangkok.

The second encouragement was a visitor. The Red Sea Mission Team, along with other missionary organisations in Sydney, arranged flights through Ron Bailey, a Christian travel agent, who gave substantial concessions to such groups. Ron had a Chinese friend in Bangkok connected with Scripture Union, and he'd notified him of my stopover. That brother in the Lord went out of his way to visit me briefly in my hotel room, and to wish me well.

After a tearful quiet time in the morning, the rest of the day was steady. I had time to write letters to Dell and my parents before getting on a much easier and uneventful flight that evening to Pakistan.

I arrived in Karachi on Thursday night, January 27 to a terminal that had been damaged in a recent bombing, with rubble and other debris on the floor. The plane had been delayed, which meant having to stand in a long slow queue to have our passports checked. It was after 11pm before I left the airport, but I was delighted to be met by Bishop Selwyn Spence. He was from New Zealand, working with CMS and based at the Holy Trinity Cathedral, and had come to the airport at Ronnie Holland's request[12]. I was grateful to be driven to his home and given some supper, after which I got two and a half hours' sleep before he drove me to the city terminal at 5am. This was for the flight to Sukkur about 250 miles north, on a De Havilland Twin Otter turboprop, with twenty seats but only five passengers. The morning was cool and bracing, and as I walked across the tarmac towards the aircraft, I felt my first sense of exhilaration that I was in God's will and representing him. As we flew over the mostly dry country, I saw below me patches of irrigation along the Indus River, with hundreds of little quilt patterns of greens and browns.

Ronnie and Joan Holland had invited me to help and to learn from them at the hospital at Quetta, the capital of Baluchistan Province. It was winter, however, and because Quetta was usually snowed in over this period, the hospital closed for the winter months and moved the team to Shikarpur to reopen there. Shikarpur was extremely hot and humid in summer, so the team managed to avoid both extremes of weather, as well as serve and share the gospel with two groups of people.

Shikarpur was 21 miles out of Sukkur and Ronnie and Joan drove their Land Rover along the sealed but uneven road to meet my flight[13]. On the way back, we passed carts pulled by donkeys, horses, camels or bullocks. I noticed that anyone in a vehicle drove with their hand on the horn.

Ancient design of bullock cart.

I had chosen an excellent day to arrive. It was the feast which Muslims set aside to remember Abraham's sacrifice of Ishmael, and the hospital was quiet. Ronnie and Joan showed me to my room in a bungalow, built like a guest house with separate rooms, but central lounge, dining room and bath and toilet facilities. It was primitive yet comfortable, with screened windows, electricity, running water and a septic tank. My largish room had cement floor, walls and roof; a wash basin, a built-in cupboard, a chest of drawers, an overhead light and reading lamp, and, extraordinarily—a seven-foot bed! It had been used by a six-foot, seven-inch fellow who had recently worked in the hospital.

In the quiet, I was able to explore a little of my surroundings. I was struck by the dust, and surprised by the cool climate, even though I knew it was winter. Outside were birds and chipmunks, and I even saw some mongooses. It quickly became apparent that I was sharing my room with several fat, dusty-brown little lizards which fed on mosquitoes.

Shikarpur street scene, adjacent to the eye hospital.

A tour of the hospital showed me what wonderful results could be achieved even in basic conditions. I was struck by the high number of cataract operations the doctors were able to do—a dozen cataracts an hour was not unusual. Male nurses did the pre-ops and anaesthetics, and doctors, scrubbed, and wearing clean but not sterile gowns, used a non-touch technique on the patients' eyes. Dr Holland seemed to be a friendly and capable tutor, and I was confident I could learn quickly.

I enjoyed the next seven weeks; I was in good health, the days were beautiful and clear, and I had interesting hospital work. One morning when I arrived at the hospital, Dr Luther senior, a godly old man, heard me whistling happily. He smiled and quoted from Proverbs. 'He that is of a merry heart hath a continual feast.' My days were filled, and we often did enjoyable things in the evenings. I especially loved Ronnie and Joan's slides of England. On several evenings, I spent time at the hospital showing Bible film strips to patients who were able to gather in the hospital courtyard, along with their family members. I worked the projector, while Ronnie explained the pictures in Urdu, with another man translating into Sindhi.

Vegetable stall, just inside the Shikarpur hospital.

The Shikarpur period was coming to an end, however, and the team planned to leave for Quetta early on a Thursday morning, to arrive about 4.30pm. Despite only just having written to my parents about how fit and well I felt, I came down with dysentery and felt ill. What was worse, this was the day we were to travel! I was supposed to help Ronnie by sharing the driving of the Land Rover, but he had to drive the whole way himself. I was glad when we finally reached Quetta, but on pulling up at their home, he was so tired that he asked me if I would carry his wife Joan, who was paraplegic, into the house. He would normally do that himself, but the drive had been exhausting. I willingly did so but found the task embarrassing.

Around this time, I became concerned about the logistics of getting both myself and Adele to Yemen. I didn't want her to travel on her own, and if we arrived unmarried, we would have to finish our two years of language study before we'd be allowed to marry. I began to prayerfully investigate if it might be possible for me to return to Sydney to marry Adele at home, surrounded by family and friends. We could then travel together to Yemen.

Entrance (on the right) to the Christian Hospital, Quetta. Established 1886.

Unbeknown to me, one of the nurses, Florence, had the marvellous idea of the hospital inviting Dell to come and join me in Quetta. She'd be able to learn a great deal that would be helpful in the future, particularly concerning medical missionary life and work. Florence put the idea to the hospital staff who unanimously agreed, and then they put it to me. It came as a complete surprise, but as I prayed and thought it over, it seemed a wonderful plan. Adele had now been accepted by the RSMT, and they'd told her that the language school in Yemen was to begin on August 1. This scheme solved so many problems and seemed to be the Lord's answer. Also, the fact that it wasn't my idea at all seemed a good point in its favour. It hadn't even occurred to me.

Thankfully, the RSMT did agree to Adele's joining me in Quetta. Dr Gurney also wrote, asking me to try to learn a little of the Baluchi language because he was interested in that people group. (I didn't manage to learn any, but the fact that he asked me became important to us a few years later.)

Now I was waiting for Adele to arrive, but there was plenty to do in the meantime. Because the RSMT wanted me to concentrate on eye surgery, Ronnie helped me make a comprehensive list of instruments and equipment which I would need. As we added and added to the list, I wondered if it might be a little excessive, but I assumed that Ronnie thought it was better to purchase once rather than go back again and again for more. Helpfully, I was able to order and buy some things there in Pakistan, ready to take with me.

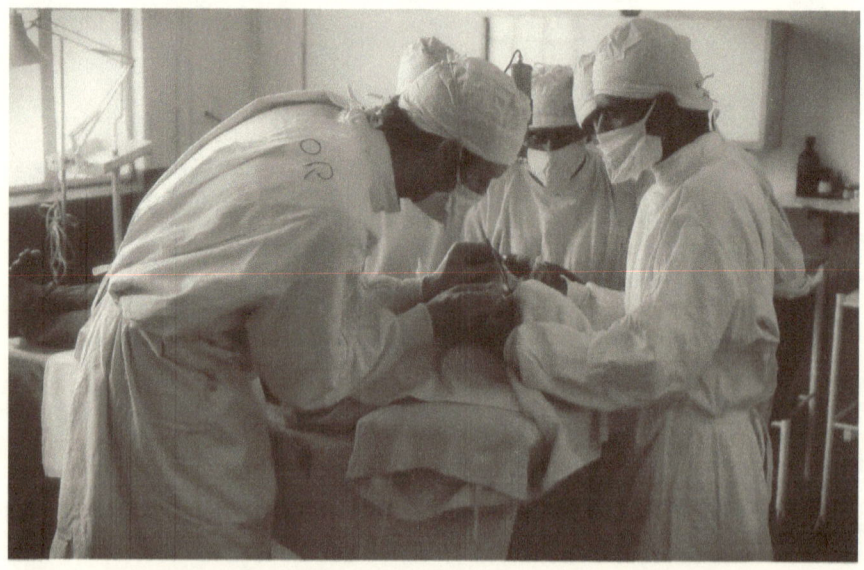

Pakistani male nurses attend to an eye patient, while I operate.

Finally, on May 27 in 1972, it was time for Adele to arrive. Ronnie and Joan drove me in their Land Rover to meet her and bring her back to the hospital. Our time together was wonderful. We were able to relax together with good music, and with nothing to organise, no rush to get anywhere, or having to drive to and fro, we had a rich time. There was a big, oblong, concrete, irrigation tank about five feet deep in the hospital compound next to the Holland's front garden, and although not full, the two of us often swam there in the evenings. Dell even got out her knitting—which I'd never seen before![14]

My hospital work kept me busy during the day. Those months in Pakistan were helpful for gathering medical and surgical experience. With the benefit of having wonderful teachers, in my time at Shikarpur and Quetta I performed 106 cataract extractions and 84 other eye operations, 219 different major surgeries and 92 smaller surgeries, not counting the numerous cases at which I was only an assistant.

I was amazed and delighted to see how the Lord blessed my surgical work. Ronnie told Adele that I had 'a good pair of hands', and I was secretly astonished to notice that of all the cataract extractions and other operations performed, whereas those tackled by experienced surgeons sometimes developed complications, mine practically never did. I could only praise the Lord for this, knowing full well that I had little experience or self-confidence. I was constantly crying out in my heart for his help and overruling, with each patient and situation. I couldn't help thinking how dreadful it would be for any of those patients if I accidentally caused them any harm. Many people around the world were praying for his blessing on the work of the hospital; and our family and friends were praying for us in particular— and he answered all these prayers. This also meant I could claim virtually no credit for good outcomes, since it was the Lord's hand that was responsible. *He* is the best physician.

Adele kept herself busy visiting girls and women of local families, Christian and Muslim. We also had children, mostly girls, dropping in to sing choruses or to learn a few words of English. She was able to learn from Florence many useful things about missionary life, and they enjoyed good fellowship together.

Not long after Adele's birthday, the most violent storm Ronnie could remember in the 32 years he'd been there hit Quetta. Stormwater channels were filled with raging torrents, 130 people died or were drowned, and I saw a dead sheep being rushed along in the flash flood. It was a reminder of how fragile life was, and how far we were from home. We waited all afternoon on two consecutive days for a phone call from our parents, but the lines may have been brought down in the storm because they never got through[15].

Adele and I join Ronnie and Joan Holland for breakfast on their front lawn.

Unknown to us, Ronnie and Joan Holland were preparing to leave Pakistan[16] and it was wonderful for Dell and me that our time coincided with their final months there. Our story would have been different if the Lord hadn't kept them in Quetta for as long as he did. The many blessings we received (and some which only came to light years later) could not have happened without Ronnie and Joan[17]. God's hand was on our time.

But our time in Quetta was ending. For seven weeks, Dell and I had been living in adjacent houses and eating together, with no travelling; having time to relax, listen to music and pray together, and so on. We were able to share things on our hearts and discuss the future, as well as beginning to work together in outreach to the patients and other Muslim contacts. On a birthday outing to the 'China café' we had a lovely meal, our chairs and tables set out on a large lawn surrounded by dim romantic lights. It was a wonderful blessing for us as an engaged couple.

Less than two weeks before we were to leave Quetta, the Lord arranged something which encouraged us. I'd had trouble finding the correct sized batteries for my cassette player. Playing cassettes, especially hymns, meant a lot to me, and I liked to send recorded messages home to family and friends. When I finally discovered a little stall selling Phillips batteries of just the right size, I was delighted to purchase some. Very quickly, however, both Dell and I went down with amoebic dysentery. While we were still in recovery, feeling terrible, a birthday card for me arrived from my sister, letting us know that she was sending us two tapes. I was miserable; I thought it was most unlikely that they'd arrive, but my verse that morning had been, 'O taste and see that the Lord is good'. I was filled with joy when, later that day, they both arrived safely. I was unable to wait to open them, so Dell and I listened together. One was music by the Celebration Singers, called 'God is so good', and the other was Beethoven's fifth piano concerto. Forty-eight years later, we still have those two cassettes. They've given us a great deal of pleasure over the years and were a reminder of how the Lord can provide everything, including needed comfort at just the right time. It was something we would need to remember in Yemen.

4

Journey to Yemen and Language Study

July-October 1972: Age 29

Our time in Pakistan was up, and Adele and I were on our way to Yemen. First, however, we had to get there.

Because the sky above Quetta is sometimes so dusty that planes are unable to land, we booked our flight to Karachi to give us two days spare, in case we needed to catch the train instead. Fortunately, on July 18 the air was clear, so we were able to fly. We were grateful for those two extra days, staying with David and Jean Penman in Karachi because Adele's amoebic dysentery had flared up again. She was quite ill, even vomiting on the plane. I was distressed because Dell was suffering so much pain, but Jean introduced us to Chlorodyne drops, taken on a teaspoon of sugar, which settled her pain wonderfully[18]. Flagyl tablets were the best treatment for amoeba. These were difficult to procure, but Jean sent her Pakistani servant to keep looking. We were relieved that he found a full course of Flagyl tablets, which Dell began immediately. Once again, we lifted our hearts to the Lord in thanksgiving and praise.

We were both much more rested the day we flew to Jeddah on the western coast of Saudi Arabia, where we had a scheduled overnight stay. At the hotel, we arranged separate but adjacent rooms. It took a moment or two to convince the man at the desk that this was what we wanted. It seemed that he hadn't previously encountered a young Western couple travelling together who insisted on separate rooms. When we explained that we weren't yet married, he was given the opportunity to see that true Christians have a different lifestyle from the culture which he had come to expect from Westerners.

The next morning, we were in for a surprise: somehow, we missed our flight! We were booked to fly south to Hodeidah in Yemen; but we'd been so delayed at the check-in counter, and the terminal was so noisy that when we arrived at the departure lounge, the once-only announcement of our flight had already been made. Despite checking with the gate attendant after every loudspeaker call, eventually it became clear that the flight to Hodeidah had gone without us. I mentioned to the airport administrators that for Saudi/Australian relations, I thought it was important that they pay for our hotel accommodation until we could catch another flight, but they weren't convinced. However, they did arrange for us to stay at a small hotel nearby, albeit at our own expense.

The next step was to retrieve our luggage, but we were slightly nonplussed to discover that one suitcase was missing. It had gone on to Hodeidah, we were told. This was interesting because nothing was supposed to be loaded onto the aircraft until the passengers had identified all their bags. These were lined up on the tarmac beside the plane to avoid putting a bomb on board —yet we hadn't *been* there to identify it. We just had to trust the Lord that we would be able to find that suitcase eventually.

There were no more flights that day, and it seemed we would have to stay for some time in Jeddah. Naturally we were disappointed at this unexpected delay, however, later we were glad when we realised that it must be in the Lord's planning. It gave us more time to rest, and more time for Dell to continue taking her Flagyl tablets.

The hotel was comfortable but had no dining room due to renovations underway, so we ate at a nearby restaurant. Wondering what to do to fill in the time, I asked the man at the reception desk if there were any picture theatres we could visit, not realising that such things were totally forbidden in Saudi Arabia. After glancing both ways to make sure that no-one else was within earshot, he whispered to me, 'I can arrange for you to see a film privately.'

Immediately we realised that this would be most unwise.

'Thank you,' we said. 'We will find something else to do.'

One of the first things we did was visit the Australian consul to explain our situation, in case we ran into difficulties. He seemed disinterested, but still introduced us to his wife, and we all had a cup of tea together. Another thing we did was to send a telegram to Sana'a to notify our team that we'd been delayed, hoping that it would reach them quickly, even though we only had the post-office box number as the address.

Finally, after three days in Jeddah, on July 24, we were notified we could fly out. Two seats were available on a small plane not listed on any of the usual flight schedules. Relieved to be on the move again, we didn't ask any questions and flew south to Hodeidah, where we were glad to be reunited with our missing suitcase. We had the address of a shipping agent there, Jacob, a good friend of the Team, and took a taxi directly to his office. He accompanied us to a restaurant for lunch, and then was helpful in assisting us as we set off on the final stage of our journey.

Because the bus to Sana'a left at 6 am, the only way now for us to reach the capital was to hire a taxi for the 240-kilometre trip. This seemed an extraordinary idea, but it was the only course open to us, and was common practice. We got into a Mercedes Benz and had a comfortable journey on a smooth road[19] although I thought the engine needed some attention; it was 'pinging' the whole way. We travelled east across the coastal plain (the Tihama), and then gradually began to climb the mountains. When the road crossed a little stream, we asked the driver to stop. This gave us the chance to 'go behind some bushes'; but it also allowed us to stand together briefly in the huge pipe through which the stream flowed under the road for a hug and kiss where no-one could see us. We didn't know how long it might be before we'd have another opportunity!

The trip from Hodeidah up to Sana'a took approximately four hours. Hot down on the coastal plain, the air grew progressively cooler the further up the winding road we drove into the mountains. As we climbed, we noticed how much greener the mountainsides were than those in Pakistan. Every slope of the usable soil was shaped into contoured terraces, on which grew a variety of grain crops and vegetables.

As we came over a ridge, we saw the city of Sana'a spread out before us on a plain, surrounded by a few mountains. An old Turkish fort held a commanding position over the plain[20].

With only a post-office box for an address, we had no idea how to find our friends—except to pray. The taxi driver took us toward the main shopping area of Sana'a and amazingly, when we stopped and spoke to a group of men beside the road, a young fellow said that he knew Wolfgang, one of our two leaders in Yemen.

'I'll come to show you the way to his house,' he offered, and obligingly got into the car. We were grateful: it turned out that there were practically no street signs in the whole country, and the houses weren't numbered, so it was always difficult directing people to an address.

We looked around us and saw that most of the houses were built of rough-hewn stone blocks, with cement floors and flat roofs. Some were made of mud bricks. Many had several storeys, with tiny, ornate wooden shutters covering the narrow windows. The upper parts of some of the windows were coloured stained glass[21].

As we drove, I remembered a verse I had shared with Bible College friends the year before: Exodus 23:20, which said, 'See, I am sending an angel ahead of you to guard you along the way and to bring you to the place I have prepared.' Out of the thousands of people living in the city, the Lord arranged for us to meet up with this young man who not only understood us but knew the house to which we needed to go. After only a few minutes we were knocking on Wolfgang's front door and being warmly welcomed.[22]

'We didn't know where you were,' Wolfgang told us. The telegram that we'd sent from Jeddah to our Team's post-office box number didn't reach them until after we arrived. They were concerned about us, of course, wondering what had happened and how we'd find them; and they were earnestly praying for our safe arrival.

ON THE WAY

When Wolfgang realised that we hadn't had any lunch, he called out to his wife Beryl to quickly bring something. Adele remembers that she opened a tin of spaghetti with little sausages in it. Everyone was relieved to see us safe and sound, and soon we were taken to our respective houses so that we could begin settling in. The next morning, we went to the office of the English communications company 'Cable and Wireless' and sent a telegram to our families in Sydney to let them know we had arrived. Because the minimum charge for telegrams was so expensive, we could only afford one. We sent it to my parents, and it reached them the next day.

Dr Gurney[23], along with Ewen, a dentist who had travelled to Singapore with Adele and then gone on to Yemen, were my housemates, sharing the bottom floor of a small, rented two-storey house. Language school was held in the top floor. Dell shared a similar stone block, flat roofed house with two other single new women, both nursing sisters; Anitra, from England and Helen who was Scottish. The other members of our team, Wolfgang and Beryl with their three little boys, occupied a third house, while Peter and Margaret with their children had another, within easy walking distance of all of us, in the newer, south-western part of the city.

Many houses were surrounded by high stone walls, but the enclosed compound of my shared house was tiny, and two sides had no compound at all. We had to pull the curtains if we didn't want people outside in the narrow, dusty lanes to look in through the barred windows on the ground floor. Peter and Margaret's enclosed compound was bigger; in it, they parked an interesting little Renault, with a gear lever coming out of the dashboard that you had to pull, twist, and push back again to change gears. We discovered that Peter brought his family with their luggage in this little car all the way up from Aden two years before.

Ewen and I were tasked with getting our own breakfast and evening meals, but had lunch at Wolfgang's home, while Adele and her housemates did all their own cooking. To begin with, I slept on a blow-up air mattress on the floor; but Dr Gurney gave me his nice, long bed when he left for a three-month trip, making things more comfortable. Our allowance of 240 Yemeni rials a month was equivalent to just over ten Australian dollars a week. We spent half on food, purchasing anything we wanted in good shops and a supermarket. With eucalyptus gum trees everywhere[24], it wasn't too difficult to imagine ourselves in some dusty, western NSW town, and it was easy to feel at home.

Adele and I were amongst five newcomers to the team, and our first week was spent in orientation lectures, prayer and marvellous fellowship. We had strong reasons to steadfastly trust God; the Red Sea Mission Team's contract with the government had not been signed yet, and it was unknown as to whether we would even be allowed to remain in the country. It was a matter for constant prayer.

Another matter for prayer came about within the first three days of Adele and I arriving in Sana'a.

'We need to have a conversation with you,' the leadership told us, and invited us to sit. 'The Team feels that you should get married soon. In early November, in fact.'

Adele and I looked at each other. 'Wow,' I said. This was far earlier than we were expecting, having been told that we'd have to wait for two years before we could marry. We were delighted, but aware that lots of extra things would need to be organised and squeezed in to the following three months, along with settling into life in Yemen and within the missionary team, and of course Arabic language study!

The reasons for the change in plan were not romantic at all, even though we were pleased about it, but instead, were entirely logistical. Dr Walker, an elderly Scottish doctor who had recently lost his wife in Yareem, where they lived and worked, would be leaving Yemen at the end of November—probably not to return—and I was needed to replace him. Accommodation for a single man was hard to find in Yareem, and with several single women missionaries there—all nursing sisters—local people were likely to believe that we were misbehaving, which could ruin our public witness[25]. I couldn't go to Yareem as a single man, but I could go as a married one.

'I guess we'd better get married then,' we said. And the wedding was on.

'Here's how we can arrange it,' they said. 'Language study is split into three sections. You can do the first section from now for the next three months, until the end of October. After you get married and have your honeymoon, you can head to Yareem, and work using the Arabic you've learned.'

They explained to us that some new team members, a Dr John and his wife Priscilla were expected to arrive from England in November. They'd do their first language learning while Adele and I were in Yareem, and then replace us while we came back to complete our second section. We'd swap back and forth until both pairs had completed their language learning and then sort things out after that.

'But we'll need permission to get married earlier than the two years, won't we?' I asked.

'Don't start planning anything until we get the okay from Mr Budd, the Team Field Secretary in Ethiopia,' they told us. 'You'll have to wait, just a little longer.'

(Happily, Wolfgang and Beryl took it upon themselves to ensure that Dell and I were supplied with coincidental reasons for being at their place for a few hours about twice a week alone in the evenings over the next few months. They were glad of the services of some baby-sitters, and of course we wished to be as helpful as possible.)

Within a week or so, Arabic language study with fifteen students from several different teams was under way, every morning except Fridays and Sundays. Wolfgang was in charge, with a pleasant Yemeni fellow teaching new sounds, words and phrases which we repeated after him. It was well-organised, but most of us still had to work hard to keep up. After a few weeks, we could see definite progress, but it was a struggle. With daily life chores of shopping, cooking, washing, and cleaning on top of the study, we were kept busy indeed, but it was good to use our growing language skills to communicate with our Yemeni neighbours, who were generally happy, friendly and open. Women mostly dressed from head to ankles in dresses and shawls, rather than favouring the one-piece burkas that we saw so much of in Pakistan and Saudi Arabia. The men wore shirts, sandals, and a wrap-around skirt, secured with a belt at the waist, the front of which was often adorned by a large, curved dagger in an ornately decorated leather sheath.

We lived comfortably, with electricity, a gas cylinder for the stove, cold running water (which was pumped from our own well by an electric motor up to a tank on the roof), and a septic tank. At one point, our nearly fifty-foot deep well almost ran dry, so we had men in to dig it deeper[26].

Inside the house, some of the concrete floors were tiled, and the interior walls were plastered and white-washed. The windows were all barred, and some had fly screens. Wolfgang and Peter had fridges in their homes, but we didn't need one. It was cool in Sana'a and we bought food mostly from day to day and used powdered milk. While almost everything we wanted was available in the shops, we were aware that in other places it might not be so easy to live.

I particularly enjoyed living with Ewen at this time. Like many of the Team members, he had a deeply spiritual outlook and a real ministry amongst locals, especially younger men. It was a joy to see such faith in action. Margaret was wonderfully calm and gentle, despite having six young children; and Beryl was thoughtful and happy. Wolfgang was enthusiastic and earnest, and the other women in the Team all had depth and gifts. Peter's patience in dealing with the government, negotiating our new contract, was an example of Christlikeness. We were all eagerly waiting to hear the good news that the contract had been signed.

In the meantime, though, there was other good news. Archbishop Marcus Loane[27] visited us all for a few days. 'I'm the bearer of good tidings,' he said when he arrived, and indeed he was, bringing the letter from Mr Budd in Ethiopia that gave us official permission to go ahead and arrange our marriage.

We immediately got into wedding planning mode and picked a date at the beginning of November. Peter and Margaret's little Hannah would be flower girl, and we'd be married in Wolfgang and Beryl's home. Our honeymoon would be in Ethiopia, near Addis Ababa, at a place called Bishoftu, run by the Sudan Interior Mission, beside a lake with a honeymoon cottage; the perfect place for a two week stay. Dell could sew, had seen some lovely material, and was confident that with a little help, she would be able to handle sorting out a wedding dress. We had everything we needed.

Then, there was more good news. Just as language school was finishing, the contract with the government was finally signed after months of negotiations, waiting, and much prayer. The timing was extraordinary. New recruits would be able to head to their various stations, and work in the town of Hajjah could begin. Even better, there was not a single negative clause in the contract now, with our leaders insisting that we be allowed unrestricted freedom in personal conversations to share the good news that the Lord Jesus Christ is the Way to heaven[28].

God consistently and gently nudged me through my days. Even when things seemed hard, there was always a purpose to his ways. One morning I went with Wolfgang in Peter's little old Renault, to get Dell's inoculation book signed after having given her a cholera booster. I had both our books with me because I'd had to show them when I'd bought our plane tickets to Asmara. The clerk stamped and signed Dell's book, and Wolfgang and I went out to the street. But no matter what we tried; we could not get Peter's little old Renault to start.

'The trouble we're having must be for some purpose in the Lord's wisdom,' I said to Wolfgang, and after about ten minutes of fruitless effort, we were interrupted by a young boy who came to the car.

'Sir, did you leave your book in the office?' he asked.

I looked in my bag and saw only Adele's inoculation book. Mine was missing! I must have left it on the desk in the clerk's office. How the young boy knew is still a mystery to me, but I hurried back inside with him. Having collected my book, I thanked the officer-in-charge and the young boy sincerely. Then, virtually as soon as I got in the car, it started normally.

'The Lord's purpose,' I remarked to Wolfgang with a smile. I would have had great trouble getting a new inoculation book, as well as all the necessary injections again, if I hadn't realised where it was. And if I *had* located it in my mind, it would have been difficult to get it back. That office was due to close for the day, and the next day was Friday, the Muslim day of worship. Being in the fasting month of Ramadan made everything less predictable as well. I overflowed with joy to the Lord and was full of gratitude that he prevented our car from starting until I'd been able to retrieve my little book.

With language study nearly out of the way, our wedding date was drawing closer. However, before we could get married, I needed to spend some time in Yareem with Dr Walker, learning as much as possible about the area and the work I'd be involved in over the following months.

On a Saturday in mid-October therefore, after language school, Ewen and I got into a taxi with twelve other people, plus everyone's luggage (mostly on the roof rack) and headed to Yareem. After several stops on the way, including a puncture, we arrived in the evening to be welcomed by the gracious, and slightly formal Dr Walker[29], in his attractive and comfortable home and garden which had most of the facilities one could wish for—except electricity. Over the next eleven days I had a useful introduction to the medical work I'd be involved with after our honeymoon. I also helped with the cooking and had my first taste of yoghurt!

Seeing Yareem was useful for me, but I was aware that Adele would not have had an introduction to the place before we came in December. However, about five days after Ewen and I arrived there, Dr Walker went to Sana'a to buy furniture for the new clinic. When he returned, he had a visitor with him—Adele! She had driven the whole way herself; three and a half hours in a Land Rover on the gravel road, without power steering. I was impressed. She stayed for two nights in another home, before travelling back to Sana'a with another missionary couple. I made the return journey a few days later in a taxi, with fourteen others this time. With only one week before the wedding, there was plenty to organise.

5

Wedding and Honeymoon

October-December 1972: Age 29

'God... has clothed me with garments of salvation and arrayed me in a robe of righteousness, as a bridegroom.' (Isaiah 61:10)

Before I left Australia, I had purchased a new suit but as I had packed, looking ahead and thinking about what I would need in Pakistan and Yemen, I'd decided to leave the new suit with my parents, bringing only an old one. When Adele and I found out that we needed to marry quickly, I'd written and asked my parents to send the new one over. They posted it by airmail on September 1, but six weeks later it still hadn't arrived. In mid-October, I started to get a little concerned, and before going to Yareem, I made arrangements with a local tailor.

'Could you make me a suit at short notice if I need it?' I'd asked him.

'Of course, sir. No problem,' came the reply.

When I came back to Sana'a after my eleven days in Yareem, I found a card in the Team's box at the post office. A parcel had arrived for someone, it said, but the relevant office upstairs was closed until Saturday morning, a couple of days later. Not being sure the parcel was my suit, I decided to err on the side of safety and went to check with the tailor.

'Could you make the suit we talked about?' I asked him and was horrified to hear him refuse.

'I can't even *consider* it,' he declared. 'I have to do a good job, so I can't start until mid-November, when Ramadan is over.'

I could have been upset, but I left his shop with real peace in my heart. I was certain that the parcel in the post office was my long-awaited suit. If it wasn't, I'd just have to get my old one dry-cleaned and be married in that. No matter what transpired, I felt certain that Jesus knew our every need, and that he had everything in hand.

On Saturday morning I was able to see the parcel in the post office, and it *was* my suit. However, I was unable to take it as the clerk had gone somewhere. When I returned at 1.30pm, the fellow still had to be found but when he came, how I rejoiced! Besides the suit I found a new white shirt and two grey ties that my parents had sent, off their own bat. I then had a hilarious time going through the suit pockets, finding eleven messages from Mum and Dad.

The parcel had taken over eight weeks to arrive by airmail. Where it had been was a mystery, but since there'd been fighting on the border between North and South Yemen in recent weeks, and a lot of other delayed mail had also arrived that day, perhaps it had been held up in Aden. I found it a marvellous demonstration of God's love, care and provision—and his perfect timing, turning up just four and a half days before the wedding.

To cap it off, our sea luggage arrived from Australia just two days before the wedding. Its departure had been delayed, and then it had to contend with border 'difficulties' with South Yemen, including all the arms and military equipment from Saudi Arabia being off-loaded at the Red Sea port of Hodeidah and other places. But we were delighted to see those four items of heavy luggage, especially because we were able to take several things on our honeymoon. We saw once again that our Heavenly Father understands perfectly all that we need, and that he's able, and in fact is delighted, to provide these things with perfect timing, and in the best possible way.[30]

Not all the news I received before the wedding was good, however. At the end of October, we were told that for October and November, because of limited funds, all RSMT missionaries would receive only a quarter of the usual adult allowances, and running expenses would have to be cut by at least 40 per cent. It was a time to soberly reflect on Deuteronomy 8:3: 'He humbled you, and let you hunger,' the passage said, yet the Lord still provided all that was needed for the Israelites. In fact, the period of limitation was for testing and discipline in preparation for all the blessings to follow in the Promised Land. How precious it was to know our God and Father; and knowing a little of what and who he is, we were able to rest in perfect confidence[31].

* * *

In the British Embassy compound, immediately after the official ceremony.

The big day, Thursday 2 November[32], dawned bright and clear, and we arrived in good time at the British Embassy for the legal ceremony a little before nine o'clock. Peter and Ewen from our Team, as well as three women and Rob from WEC (Worldwide Evangelisation Crusade) came and enjoyed the ceremony with us. Rob taped the proceedings and took most of the wedding photos. Mr Noble, the deputy ambassador, met us, and soon we were seated comfortably in his office with us facing him across the large desk. Dell wore a purple dress and looked lovely. I, of course, wore my recently arrived suit, white shirt and grey tie.

Mr Noble and his wife had gone to a lot of trouble to make his nicely furnished office look even more attractive. Gold and white zinnias and daisies from their garden had been arranged in two vases by Mrs Noble herself, and we were given white carnation corsages for our lapels. Mr Noble had obtained permission from the British Foreign Office to marry us, so we felt honoured[33]. Afterwards, when we came outside, two young English women from the Embassy threw home-made confetti over us. This was a nice surprise; it was unprocurable in the shops. Mr Noble then drove us to his home in the official white Embassy Land Rover with the British standard flying on the bonnet, where we enjoyed conversation, coffee and biscuits.

With the official part over, there was more of the wedding day to come. Dell was driven to Wolfgang's home for a 6pm service at which Dr Walker had agreed to give her away, with little Hannah as flower girl. Peter conducted the service from the Anglican Prayer Book and spoke on Isaiah 44:1–8. Verse 5 was particularly meaningful for me. *'One will say, "I belong to the Lord"; another will call himself by the name of Jacob; still another will write on his hand, 'The Lord's', and will take the name Israel.'* Years before, I'd come across those verses and had thought how good it would be to have 'The Lord's' engraved on the wedding ring, if ever he provided a wife for me. Before we left Australia, Adele and I bought her ring together and had 'The Lord's' engraved on the inner surface. I'd carried it carefully with me all the way to Yemen and was able to put it on her finger during the service.

We had the reception in the best place available, the newly opened international-standard hotel, the 'Al Hamd Palace'. This was originally the palace of one of the princes, and the name meant 'The Palace of Praise' which we thought fitting.

'As a bridegroom rejoices over his bride' (Isaiah 62.5b)

The Al Hamd Palace Hotel.

After photographs had been taken, Wolfgang drove us to several homes where some of Dell's Yemeni girlfriends lived, who were delighted to see her dressed so beautifully for her wedding. He then took us back to that same hotel, where we'd arranged to spend the rest of the night. Finally, the next morning, it was time to go to the airport, such as it was, at Sana'a. There was no proper terminal building and only a few passengers. Everything was done by just one man who sat in his Volkswagen 'beetle' with the door open. We showed him our tickets, and he stamped our passports and that was it.

We were worn out by the time we eventually landed in Asmara, and so were grateful for our stay there that night with Jack Budd, the RSMT Field Secretary, and his wife. After another early start the next morning, we finally arrived in Addis Ababa, where other RSMT friends met us, and drove us to the place where we were to spend five days. Mulu Farm was a most beautiful property on the edge of a plateau, and included some land extending 3000 feet down to the bottom of the adjacent Rift Valley. Then two and a half wonderful weeks followed at Bishoftu, the Sudan Interior Mission rest centre, with the cabins set amongst trees and flowering shrubs on a grassy slope beside the blue water of a crater lake. We were delighted to finally be married; the partnership that had begun that day at Wiseman's Ferry now was stronger than ever. We were ready for whatever was to come.

What was to come, however, would be a stressful year, and a long process of disentangling me from the eye surgery project.

* * *

I had felt uneasy about concentrating on eye conditions ever since I had written to Dr Gurney while at SMBC, but had kept my feelings to myself, believing that the Lord was asking me to trust him with it. This uneasiness resurfaced dramatically on the last day of our honeymoon, Friday, December 1, 1972.

We had flown north to Asmara on our way back to Yemen, and Mike, a RSMT colleague, met us and drove us to the Team headquarters. While there, we visited Dr Ian Lewis, who happened to be in Asmara for a few days. Dr Lewis had come out from England in 1966 with The Church Mission to the Jews to work among the Falashas, an Ethiopian tribe with

Jewish ancestry. For the previous couple of years, he'd been working in Gondar, some way south of Asmara, where he'd established a small eye unit with finance from the German organisation called the Christoffel Blinden Mission[34]. This was the group that the Team had been talking to about equipment and provisions for the eye surgery project I was intended to establish.

We had a good conversation with Dr Lewis about his work and the project I was heading to, but I was horrified when he started to talk about costs. He'd heard that the CBM estimated that the cost of our proposed eye unit in Yemen would be approximately twenty thousand pounds! I had no idea that it might cost anything like that amount. Much of that sum would have been for the purchase and delivery of the list of eye instruments, equipment and medications which Dr Holland had worked out with me, and which I had posted to Mr Budd while I was still in Quetta. I'd always felt that it was too large an order, and a little extravagant, but now I was staggered. In fact, I felt weak at the thought of the amount I was asking the CBM to pay.

For that amount of money, they would want to see a successful project emerge, and yet I felt unqualified to run anything on this sort of scale! I had no desire to over-order or be extravagant with other peoples' money and I was troubled by the thought that these donations might not be used the best way possible. At least some of the money donated to the work of the CBM would have been given by committed Christians, and probably also by some folk who were poor; none of it should be wasted[35].

Dell and I poured out the matter before the Lord when we arrived back at the RSMT headquarters later that afternoon, leaving the outcome of it all in his hands. Realising that urgent action needed to be taken, I immediately wrote two letters—one to Jack Budd, which I left for him to read when he returned a day or two later, and with it, a draft letter to the CBM, for Jack to send on. I hoped that we might be able to delay the order until it could be altered[36].

There in Asmara that evening, I did feel somewhat relieved that I'd been able to begin to rectify the whole matter and trusted that we'd be allowed to quietly begin work, and proceed step by step, as the Lord enabled—but still, my deep uneasiness hadn't left me. Was it a terrible mistake to even think that I'd be capable of establishing and running an eye surgery unit, I asked myself? What would Mr Budd and the other leaders of the Team say when they realised that I might not end up doing much at all in the way of eye work? They would be more than disappointed with me, I decided, and became stressed again at the thought of them having to face this fact, and deal with it[37].

The Lord, however, had the whole picture in mind, and he gave me comfort. My set Bible readings over the next two days spoke of peace, the Lord's care and enabling, and that he would 'teach and lead us how we should act and proceed'. I leaned on him.

I had gone to Quetta specifically to gain experience in eye work to assist us in the setting up of our own ophthalmic unit in Yemen. We'd all thought at the time that this was the main purpose of that period, and that it seemed to be the Lord's arranging and timing. I believe that it was in fact his arranging and timing, though not to ultimately establish an eye surgery work, but rather to gather experience to help in our proposed *medical* work in Yemen, as well as laying the foundation for our (at this stage unforeseen) new outreach ministry later in Pakistan.

The Three Wise Men were led unerringly to where the Lord wanted them to go, but it was only later that they could look back and rejoice as they saw how his purpose had unfolded. I've learned that we may be in the centre of his will and obediently following his leading, but having faithfully followed the star and arrived at Herod's palace in Jerusalem, we may then discover that what had seemed to be the obvious destination of our journey turned out to only be a stopover on the way to a humble carpenter's home in Bethlehem. His way is perfect.

6

Yareem, Lyndall's Visit and Andrew's Birth

December 1972-December 1973: Age 29-30

Gradually coming to realise that the Lord didn't intend for us to start an eye surgery work at all was the beginning of what would be a stressful year. I had always found change difficult to cope with, so it took me months to accept that the eye project was to be scrapped. However, I was relieved when I finally realised that we were reverting to my original calling, which included not working in a hospital, but in a simple clinic or in a mobile medical ministry, much more in keeping with my capabilities.

Despite my calling, however, I found that I now had a few qualms even about returning to the relatively straightforward clinic work in Yareem, where with my limited facility in Arabic, I would have the responsibility of being the only doctor for many miles around. But we sought to keep our eyes on the Lord, and to trust him and his promises. After we flew back into Yemen, I wrote this in my journal:

I'm praying that the Lord may equip us with all we need and enable us to be selfless for his sake and for the Yemeni people. At Asmara air terminal we saw some Yemenis and felt a real love for them. Oh, that the Lord may increase this love more and more, and enable us to be helpful and a real blessing to them by providing excellent medical and surgical care, and thus show his love in action.

We were delayed from setting out from Sana'a for Yareem by sickness. Dell came down with the 'flu and I suffered a bad attack of dysentery. More than ten days had passed before we eventually set out, but we came to see the Lord's hand in it, as Peter and I were finally able to meet the Minister of Health, a fine man, and one of genuine understanding, and we were able to share with him our thinking regarding establishing our project in the coastal half of Hajjah Province. Mike and Esther's arrival from Asmara a week after our return provided an opportunity for helpful discussions about the details of the design and layout of our proposed 'health unit'. (It had been decided not to call it a hospital, because otherwise the government would expect us to have at least 60 beds!) Mike would be building it when he and his family returned from their upcoming furlough.

Finally, however, together with Ewen, we made it out of Sana'a, heading south along the mountains to our new home in Yareem. After three days we were well settled in and working busily. In fact, that December, we treated 986 patients, 235 more than the previous month, with the weeks becoming increasingly busier as people came to realise that a doctor was back in town.

Besides the many and varied medical and obstetric cases, we were encouraged by several contacts with locals who were clearly hungry for the gospel. Three of them were young Yemeni women who had already made decisions for Christ. On Christmas Day, there in Yareem, a happy occasion, we had a morning communion service in our home, and in the afternoon, we met in the women missionaries' house with four local young women. Two were Christians, and one of them told us that she had recently led two girls to the Lord in Sana'a. Hallelujah! How we prayed for these girls, that the Lord might protect them, and use them mightily; and that they might be enabled to establish Christian homes—which of course would require Christian husbands. We were praying for one of them especially, young and recently married, that her husband, who was working in Saudi, wouldn't send for her to go to him, thus taking her from the opportunity for Christian fellowship and growth.

It was exciting for Dell to have opportunities to meet locals. One day she went out for lunch with the baker's wife and family and had an enjoyable time. They had a large radio, so we found out the times and frequencies of the Arabic Christian broadcasts from the Seychelles Islands, and 'Radio Voice of the Gospel' from Addis Ababa and suggested that they might want to tune in and listen.

Yemeni life took us a while to get used to, particularly the way they celebrated special events such as weddings, firing their weapons into the air. We often heard shooting; and usually our first thought was, 'Is today Thursday?' the day of the week when most Muslim weddings are held. At this time of year however, there was even more exuberant firing into the air from rifles and machine guns, with fireworks also going off, celebrating the men who were setting off to Mecca for the Haj. Many of the departures were from right outside our garden wall, which was disconcerting, but we never had any real cause for alarm. The women and girls also turned out, farewelling the men with a high-pitched ululation.

New Year's Eve fell on a day coinciding with our monthly day of prayer. Being a Sunday and the last day of the year, we felt that it was an excellent opportunity to set aside a whole day for thanksgiving, as well as special prayer for the year ahead. We had plenty to pray about, especially since later in the year, we hoped to have the planned medical centre functioning somewhere in the Lower Hajjah area. We would need wisdom in selecting the site, and for God to go before us, preparing the hearts of the people in that district for the coming of the gospel. I continued to be especially prayerful about the year ahead, sometimes missing breakfast and lunch to add force to my seeking the Lord's guidance, help and blessing. The day of prayer added to our regular Christian fellowship gatherings (just for us missionaries), which were small but encouraging. We met on Sunday mornings and evenings (the four missionary women happily agreed to share the leading of the Sunday evening gatherings between them), and we took it in turns to lead the Wednesday evening Bible study and prayer meeting.

Our lives were busy and full, but Dell and I had something extra to look forward to: a week-long visit from my sister Lyndall in January of that year.

ON THE WAY

Lyndall had been teaching in Scotland for a year, and it was her first time travelling in the Middle East. We made plans for various trips and outings in the times I wouldn't have to be at work, and then we committed all her travelling into the Lord's hands, little knowing just how much we would *all* need the Lord's care, protection and leading over that week.

On Thursday morning, January 11, we left Yareem in the Land Rover to drive south to Taiz. Lyndall's Yemen Airlines flight was due at 3 pm from Jeddah, so we planned to meet her at the airport, do a little shopping and then drive straight back to Yareem. However, when we reached Taiz airport, about ten miles north of the city, we learned that there was no such flight. In fact, no plane had flown from Jeddah to Taiz since December 1.

At first, we were nonplussed, but we discovered that there was a Syrian Airlines flight the next day from Jeddah to Hodeidah. A Yemen Airlines plane was supposed to connect with it and then fly up to Taiz.

'I hope she'll be on that one,' I said to Dell, naturally anxious for my sister, a young, single Western woman, travelling alone. We'd not heard a word from her since before she left England on December 23. Kidnapping and murder in the area was not uncommon and the situation could become extremely serious.

'We'd better pray about it.'

So we immediately prayed about it all, and then asked ourselves what else we could do. We were in unfamiliar territory ourselves, having never been to Taiz before. The only things we knew about it was that Brother Sammy, a Lebanese evangelist, was based here, and some Swedish missionary friends we'd met in Sana'a lived somewhere close to the President's residence.

Once again, we were to see how wonderful it is to have the Good Shepherd leading us. Over the next day and a half, we witnessed so many unmistakeable instances of his leading that I feel ashamed to admit that I've not always trusted him implicitly ever since.

Because it seemed that Lyndall wouldn't reach Taiz until the next day, we drove into the city. Almost at once we were relieved when we 'just happened' to meet Yah-yah, a chap we'd got to know in Yareem. He was a student who was gaining some income by driving a motorcycle taxi; and with his assistance we found the Yemen Airlines office to check the next day's flight details. He then led us to the President's residence, from where some locals directed us to our Swedish friends' home[38]. These friends were so helpful and invited us to use their guest flat.

After lunch and a rest, we went down to the post office to arrange a phone call to Wolfgang in Sana'a to see if he'd heard any news from Lyndall. As we were learning, phone calls were uncertain in those early days. For one thing, there was only a single line stretching the approximately 250 kilometres from Taiz to Sana'a, strung on rough wooden poles beside the road. The same telephone line was used for telegrams. (I'd watched the Yareem telegraph operator tap out a message with the Morse code key they were still using.) That evening the call came through to our friends' home, but there was no news. Wolfgang hadn't heard anything from Lyndall.

Next morning, we went again to the Yemen Airlines office, to be told that there would be no plane from Hodeidah after all; the passengers would be brought to Taiz in taxis or buses. This was a new problem and meant that we would have to wait some hours for Lyndall's potential arrival. Deciding to use our time well, we did all our shopping that morning, helped by Brother Sammy, and then had lunch at his home.

But it was Friday, and the Yemen Airlines office was now closed, which posed another problem: if Lyndall was arriving by taxi or bus (and we still didn't know *if* she was arriving at all) where would she be brought to? She obviously wouldn't be dropped off at the Airlines office, so in the early afternoon, we began going to the Hodeidah and Sana'a taxi stations to check if they'd seen Lyndall or heard anything of her. At each place we left a note for her with the Swedish friends' phone number, should she arrive there. We then started driving around to the different hotels, continuing to search for her. The chap behind the desk at the first hotel that we visited rang all the others for us. When he got off the phone with the last hotel, he had some news.

'It is definitely her. Tall and fair, he described her,' said the receptionist. 'She has gone in a taxi to Sana'a.'

This was promising. We knew that Lyndall had our Sana'a post-office box number; she also knew some names, and of course the British Embassy was there.

'It's probably her,' I said. 'But I want to be sure.'

We drove over to the hotel and found that the young woman had sensibly left a note—and certainly wasn't Lyndall! She was someone working with the World Health Organisation; and her description was short and dark now. It was another disappointment.

'What will we do now?' Dell asked.

'Our only hope is to go to the remaining hotels, yes, even the ones they've already rung, and leave notes for Lyndall, just in case she should arrive some time, some day.'

Just before 3.30 pm we drove up to the Plaza, our last hotel. Who should I see sitting in the lobby, but Lyndall! She looked terribly wind-blown, hot and weary, but she was overjoyed at laying eyes upon her brother. There with her, to our great surprise, was Malcolm, an Irishman living in Yareem[39], and his wife. Unbeknown to us, Malcolm and his family were off to Aden the following morning for a short holiday. When the bus from Hodeidah dropped Lyndall at the front entrance to that hotel in Taiz, a city in Arabia where she knew nobody, there in the lobby were Malcolm and his wife who not only immediately took care of her, but who already knew Adele and me personally. He'd just given Lyndall a one hundred rial note for a hotel meal, and the key to their room so that she could freshen up. He had even offered her his own car and driver to take her on the several hours' journey to Yareem the next day if we hadn't arrived. Also, if she'd had to stay the night in the hotel, they would have been in a nearby room.

Of course, the Lord knew that we were coming, but so that Lyndall would be met by friends, and so that she wouldn't consider setting out for Yareem on her own, he'd arranged for Malcolm and his wife to be there in the lobby when she walked in.

'Things like this have happened all along the way,' Lyndall told us. As she'd travelled through the Middle East, the Lord had proved to her how wonderful he is. On her way from Jeddah, several of the passengers had been kind and helpful when her flight had unexpectedly taken her to Hodeidah[40], and when they all had to travel on to Taiz by bus. We could only marvel at how he had arranged everything so perfectly, and with impeccable timing.

We thanked Malcolm and his wife profusely, returned his hundred rials and room key, and then drove Lyndall to our Swedish friends' home for a good wash and a bit of a rest. We had our evening meal, and then called in on another missionary couple who had been helping, to let them know that all was well. They tried to dissuade us from heading off to Yareem that night as it was about 9 pm before we got away, but we were keen to go. We introduced Lyndall to unsealed Yemeni roads and bumped our way into Yareem at 11.30 pm, having only stopped once on the journey to enjoy the coffee and rolls which we'd brought with us from Taiz, and then flopped into bed, glad indeed to be home at last.

The remainder of Lyndall's visit was uneventful, and her onward flights from there to Sydney were straightforward. We were glad to hear later that she'd arrived home safely.

Lyndall with two local girls, in our front garden at Yareem.

Old Turkish fort overlooking our picnic spot.

On our return to Yareem after dropping her at the airport, however, we weren't so glad when we heard that there'd been a robbery at the new clinic. There had been robberies of drugs and equipment previously, and fortunately the thieves hadn't got into the storeroom this time either. However, the stolen midwifery bag and Ewen's dental instruments were valuable, and a great loss. Dr Gurney came down from Sana'a to help us sort matters out and to arrange for a night watchman.

It would be untruthful to suggest that everything in the life of a missionary was happy and exciting. Not only was a considerable amount of time taken up with sheer hard work or what often seemed to be dreary duty, but there were also times of real fatigue, trial and sorrow. In the first year and a half after Adele and I had arrived in Yemen, in Sana'a and Yareem alone, there had been seven separate robberies of goods belonging to our Team or to individual members. Two of the robberies had involved Adele's and my own personal belongings, despite our care and caution. Some of the things weren't essential, while others we'd been able to replace. But, as I wrote at the time,

'The important issue as we see it is not the loss of our goods, valuable or otherwise but our attitude to the loss. There are many things that the Lord has to deal with in a Christian's life before we begin to approach Christlikeness, and the matter of possessions is one of them.

If we long for Christ to be here amongst these people, working out his purposes for their blessing, then we can see to it that he is here by allowing him to fill us to overflowing with himself and all that he is.

We long to know him more and more; but in straining forward for the surpassing greatness of knowing Christ Jesus our Lord, we must count all other things as if they are worthless rubbish in comparison. And we are convinced that if we do, Jesus will demonstrate himself to us by answering our prayers in such a way that we will never regret our resolve.'

Adele and I could honestly say that for the sake of the Yemeni people who needed the gospel so much and to whom the Lord had led us, we could take this spoiling of our goods joyfully; we felt that the Lord had been teaching us that if there was to be a harvest of Yemenis, then those who had been led to be concerned for them must be prepared to surrender everything to him for their sake.

Of course, material things weren't the most valuable possessions. Our health and that of our loved ones, and even our lives were valuable. Nowadays, with modern medicine and advances in surgery, we tend to feel that the events recorded in missionary biographies of yesteryear—of illness and loss of life—are no longer applicable. It goes without saying of course, that no-one would wish to return to such circumstances; but they do highlight the extent to which those missionaries cast their lives upon the Lord and set out to serve him, whatever the cost. In many places around the world, wonderful blessings were seen in the form of people saved as a result.

We and our missionary colleagues had been earnestly praying that many more Yemenis would soon join those whom the Lord had already called out of Islam. Perhaps it was understandable that very soon he would decide to test our faith and whether our surrender was all-inclusive, before answering those prayers.

The clinic was becoming ever increasingly busy. Over the next month, despite one week having been quieter due to the Muslim festival of Eid and a Team retreat in Sana'a, we still saw 1,081 patients. Most were in the clinic, but a few of that number were home visits. We also usually had one or two obstetric cases each week, which were sometimes difficult.

The real joy came from having opportunities to share the gospel in small ways—including using a memorable and eye-catching poster which had been left in our living room by Dr Walker. It depicted a line of people heading towards the edge of a cliff, and with the first man falling off. Others were turning aside at the cross where their load of sin dropped from their shoulders, and they then began climbing the steep steps up to golden glory. On the poster were two clearly printed texts in Arabic. Firstly: 'I take no pleasure in the death of the wicked, but rather that they turn from their ways and live. Turn! Turn from your evil ways! Why will you die?' The second was: 'Jesus said, "I am the way and the truth and the life. No one comes to the Father except through me."' Dell heard one of the Christian Yemeni girls explaining it all simply to the woman who was Dell's language helper; she was moved by it[41].

There were other encouragements. We'd been delighted to hear from Peter the amazing story of the conversion of several men in one Yemeni city, and how others were now interested in the gospel message through the witness of these believers. Two whole families had also been saved, and Peter was in contact with some of them, and able to supply them with Arabic Bibles and other Christian literature. The Lord had been working in the hearts of at least two of the men for possibly 30 years, giving them a longing for truth and light; and then over those years, his plan to deliver them from darkness gradually unfolded through circumstances in which they found themselves. It was a wonderful story and encouraging for us all.

One of those believers felt that he would like to gather some of his interested friends together in his home for Bible studies. Peter believed that this was the time for Brother Sammy to be introduced to him, which he organised. Sammy had been living and working in that city for some months, and the Lord had wonderfully blessed and protected him in his outreach. We were also delighted to hear of the growth of some believers in another city as well. It was clear that the Lord was quietly establishing his church in Yemen.

Despite these joys, being so busy took its toll, and in June, after I had felt deeply weary for several days, I felt prompted to dig out of our trunk the second volume of Hudson Taylor's biography, *The Growth of a Work of God*. When I began reading it, I rejoiced to notice how the bitterness and burdens slipped away as I was again immersed in this book, saturated as it is with examples of the Lord's goodness, provision and unfailing love in all circumstances.

While reading, I saw the map of Yemen on the wall above my desk, with Hajjah Province up in the north-western corner. That was where it was intended that Adele and I were to begin our new work. As I looked, I was overcome by a feeling of weakness. Why had the Lord chosen me for such a responsible task? Surely someone who was more capable as a doctor, a leader or administrator would be better suited to it. Maybe a great thinker or speaker, perhaps? I thought of missionary people in important places and positions, past and present—Hudson Taylor, Samuel Zvemer, Ion Keith-Faulkoner, Henry Martin, Dr Gurney, our local leader Peter—all men with real gifts and intellect. How dwarfed I felt as I considered those men, and many others beside.

At least I could say that I loved the Lord deeply, I decided. I knew that *he* certainly was enough for all that lay ahead, even if I most certainly was not. I recalled how I'd seen him use me in the past for his kingdom, and I gradually came to accept that he could no doubt do the same again, even in these vastly different circumstances. As I poured out my heart before him, the stress and burden seemed to quietly dissolve. I knew that he understood my longings, yearnings and intentions, well before I could even marshal them into thoughts. So once again, I placed the future into his hands; and as I considered these things, it became clear that if any glory were to ensue, it could only belong to him alone.

* * *

In April, Peter, Ewen and I set out in the Land Rover to make a survey trip of the coastal section of Hajjah Province, or Lower Hajjah[42], searching for a suitable site to establish our medical work. This was the region that the Ministry of Health had allocated to us. We visited a few sites and settled on a general location[43], a small village called Muharraq, almost in the centre of the province, at the western foot of the mountain range which runs north-south through the whole country. It was busy on Saturdays when people came together from the surrounding districts for a weekly market.

In early July, after Adele and I had completed the third part of our Arabic studies, Peter and I set out to visit Muharraq again. We spent an important three days there, talking with local authorities who were cooperative, and we were able to agree on a suitable area of gently-sloping, terraced land for our medical building and housing. All the stress we'd gone through over the previous twelve months began to fade now. It was decided to leave the eye work to one side; we would commence with general medical clinics with some outreach into the surrounding districts (chiefly for preventative measures and immunisation of children). Since we didn't have a builder at that time, we decided to erect local-style stick and thatch huts: one for the clinic, one as a house for the single women nursing sisters, and one for Adele and myself.

Dell and I then returned to Yareem for our final three months of work there. The clinic was becoming even busier; during July 1,717 patient visits were recorded. I was busy, but so was Adele. Amongst other things, she helped to re-sort and re-organise the filing system for the patients' record sheets. She also prepared the midday meal for us all on clinic days and continued visiting local neighbours.

A highlight of those last busy months in Yareem was the visit in early October of Dr Hans Gruber from the Christoffel Blinden Mission in Germany. I went to Taiz to pick him up, and when we arrived home, a patient knocked on my door. He was an Indian Sikh, working with the United Nations as a tutor mechanic, teaching local fellows how to maintain heavy road-building equipment, and had cut his hand in an accident. As I stitched the patient's hand in the clinic, I discovered he came from Ludhiana in India. This was the same place that Dr Gruber had been for seventeen years, as the Professor of Pathology at the Christian Medical School.

'You should come and eat with us, and meet him,' I invited my patient, and he agreed to come and have dinner with us.

To our delight, Dr Gruber was able to speak to him plainly in his native language, pointing out his need to let Jesus be his Lord, leaving his other gods behind. This man was unusually open to the gospel, and he shared with us that he'd previously been powerfully confronted with the needs of his soul while still in India. Later he asked for, and took, a New Testament in English; and since he was stationed in Taiz I was able to arrange for another missionary to continue the contact with him. We believed that the Lord must have been working in that man's life and circumstances, and we were glad to have played a part in it.

Dr Gruber had other purposes for the visit, however, so Peter and I drove him to visit Muharraq, where he was impressed with the opportunities that the new work there would provide. He agreed with the site we'd selected; and although chiefly concerned with eye work, he showed a keen interest in all aspects of our planning, and we had warm and relaxed fellowship with him. In our discussions, however, I was astounded to hear that Dr Gruber had never seen the order of eye drugs and instruments which I'd sent off from Quetta sixteen months earlier! It had certainly been received in Germany because I had their letter of acknowledgement. I began to realise with growing relief that the Lord had heard our anxious prayers and had understood my stress and concern about that original order and had arranged for it to be lost in their filing system! Dr Gruber and I were able to sit down now to make a list much more suited to the simple clinic situation in which we would be working. Here was another example of what seemed like a mistake which the Lord had made into a blessing.

* * *

Adele and I left Yareem on November 3 for an exciting reason. The Lord had blessed us with the joy of expecting our first baby, due to arrive in mid-November! We were heading for mountainous, picturesque Jibla, specifically to the American Southern Baptist Hospital, the place we had arranged for the birth. Expecting happiness and joy, we had no idea that we were about to share in intense grief and sorrow.

A rugged and beautiful setting - though not at Jibla - with abundant crops awaiting the harvest.

But allow me to backtrack. As well as treating sick Yemenis, I often had to care for members of the missionary community. Peter and Margaret, based in Sana'a and in charge of the Team's work in Yemen, had six children who faced more than the usual likelihood of childhood and other illnesses. All of the children had 'tummy upsets' from time to time, but for some months little Lydia, who was three years old, had had recurrent and perplexing episodes of vomiting and abdominal pain. She seemed perfectly well at other times.

Lydia was a most beautiful child, and everybody loved her captivating ways. We knew her well and were 'Uncle Mike and Auntie Dell' to her. Among other things, she loved collecting her 'pretty stones'; and all who knew her would certainly agree that she herself was a precious little jewel. I had sought over recent months to diagnose and treat her illness several times and had seen Margaret in tears because of Lydia's recurrent episodes of pain. (I also thought that Margaret was distressed by my inability to prevent further episodes.)

Early in November Lydia became ill with another episode of vomiting and pain. Adele and I were far away in Taiz for three days before heading to Jibla, so Peter and Margaret took her to an excellent children's specialist, an Iraqi paediatrician who had trained in Britain and who was now working for the administrative side of the United Nations in Sana'a. He believed Lydia had tonsillitis with associated, painfully swollen lymph glands in her abdomen, a condition known as mesenteric adenitis. This is common in young children and subsides as the infection settles. However, unlike her previous episodes, this time her condition grew steadily worse.

Another doctor, working with the English Save the Children Fund, arranged an urgent barium enema examination which showed that she'd developed a blockage of the bowel known as intussusception. He recommended urgent surgery, so Peter and Margaret left their other children in the care of friends and set out with Lydia to the same hospital we were heading to—the American Southern Baptist Hospital at Jibla. Dr Young operated immediately, discovering a huge lymph gland which had triggered the telescoping of one portion of the intestine into an adjacent segment[44]. Dr Young had to remove it, and although Lydia was obviously ill, he was satisfied with the way the operation went.

Quite suddenly, however, after having been brought from the theatre, little Lydia was taken to heaven to be one of the 'bright gems for his crown', as the children's hymn puts it. It was exactly three years and five months since she'd entered the world in that same hospital.

Adele and I had no inkling of what had happened until we reached Jibla on the evening of November 6 to prepare for the arrival of our own baby. When we were told that little Lydia had died a couple of hours before, I, like everybody else, was deeply shocked. Now that I knew the diagnosis, I realised that Lydia had probably suffered several brief episodes of intussusception over those months, which must have settled spontaneously each time, until this final instance. Perhaps I was overreacting (as usual), but I felt terrible because I hadn't twigged to it[45].

That evening and the next morning were, without doubt, the saddest hours of my entire life to date. But I'm sure I wouldn't have suffered as I have over these years at every recollection of that calamity had I been able to keep the Lord and his purposes in the forefront of my thinking. St Paul teaches that we should be 'always giving thanks to God the Father for *everything*, in the name of our Lord Jesus Christ.' He also says, 'Give thanks *in all* circumstances, for this is God's will for you in Christ Jesus.[46]'

Lydia had been carried gently to heaven, and now we who were missing her so much had to prepare to bury her little body. Early next morning, in the cool freshness of the new day, we gathered at the top of the hospital grounds, shadowed by the higher slopes of the hill. This quiet corner was the only Christian cemetery this land had known for about 1300 years, and Mrs Walker's the only grave. We sang 'Jesus loves me', 'When He cometh, when He cometh, to make up His jewels', and 'When peace, like a river'. I wept freely and was so overcome with grief that I could hardly sing a note. I was able to help by being one of the four who carried the coffin, made in the hospital workshop.

'Since she was such a precious little jewel,' Peter said in his sermon, in both English and Arabic, because quite a number of Yemenis had gathered nearby, 'should we mind if our Heavenly Father wishes her to be with him, at home in heaven? Of course not. She would be far safer and happier there than here on earth; and Jesus himself could fill the gap that her departure would leave in our lives. This would be a joy, for us to have more of him than would otherwise be the case.'

As we laid her to rest, Peter read Psalm 23.

Fear not little flock, He goeth ahead:
Your Shepherd selecteth the path you must tread.

What a comfort it was to realise that it was the Lord who was leading our steps. Dell and I were deeply moved by the strength of Peter and Margaret's faith and courage, and their unshakeable conviction that our loving Heavenly

Father did all things in tenderness; and that all things worked together for good in the lives of his children[47].

Moving away from the little grave shortly after, we could see the many terraces stretched out before us in the shallow valley below, covered with grain, ready for harvesting. As the light from the rising sun shone down brightly on that scene where such careful sowing had produced the crop, I remembered that we were longing for a spiritual harvest from among the Yemeni people. The light of the gospel was shining, and the grains of wheat had been falling into the ground and dying. Now we just had to pray that the Lord would cause much fruit to be borne.

* * *

The Lord continued to demonstrate to us what a tender Father he is. Our parents had sent by air a tea chest of things for us and the baby, which reached us at Jibla after a two-month journey. It arrived at 9.30 pm so, till late that night, we had a marvellous time opening parcels, reading letters, and admiring various gifts. Some of the baby's things had been knitted by Dell's mother and it was delightful to listen to the tape recording in which our families sent their greetings and love, while we were surrounded by all the gifts.

The next morning, on Tuesday, November 20, the anniversary of our official engagement exactly two years before, Dell's labour pains began. We'd had a good rest during the fortnight we'd been waiting, but poor Dell had a hard time for two and a half days. Her pains began slowly, but they went on till Thursday evening when Dr Young discovered that the baby's forehead was coming first, in a brow presentation. This explained why her labour had been making such slow progress. It's impossible to deliver a baby presenting in this position in the normal way so Dr Young arranged for Dell to be taken straight to the operating theatre where he performed a caesarean section, and at 8.15pm Andrew Frederick was born[48].

We were in the American Southern Baptist Hospital, and when we discovered that it happened to be American Thanksgiving Day, we thought that appropriate. As a matter of fact, Dr Young had to give Dell a spinal, rather than a general anaesthetic, because she'd just eaten some Thanksgiving turkey.

Initially Dell was unable to do much herself because of the operation. The hospital was short of nurses too, so I took over the care of mother and baby from the fifth morning after the operation, while Dell regained her strength, and we began to settle into a routine as a brand new family, staying in a comfortable flat on the hospital compound.

We felt grateful, not only because the Lord brought Andrew safely into the world, but because he led us to be in Jibla, the only hospital in the country where I'd feel happy for Dell to have a caesarean section. He knew she'd need this, but we didn't expect it at all.

Our plan was to leave Jibla in December, but before that, we were able to see God graciously answering prayer. Without our asking, the Christoffel Blinden Mission had generously offered to provide all that would be needed to begin the eye work. While this was a blessing, there was still a problem; eye patients would only make up a portion of the total number of people we'd be attending to, and we had practically nothing with which to begin the general work. Without letting our needs be known beyond the members of the Team, we laid the matter before the Lord in our prayers. While at Jibla, we heard that a substantial gift, also from Germany, had reached us for the general work, and other generous gifts too—enough to send off the initial medication orders and go ahead with the building. The timing seemed perfect, as Mike and his little family had just arrived back on the field after their furlough. It seemed that the Lord had put his seal on the opening of the Muharraq station.

7

Early Days In Muharraq

1974-1975: Age 30-32

We finally left Jibla on December 6, 1973 and travelled to Sana'a. A Land Rover which the Christoffel Blinden Mission had generously donated for our work had been expected to arrive on the docks in Hodeidah by mid-December, but we now heard that it was delayed. Without the Land Rover, we were not able to travel to Muhurraq. This was providential we believed, because Dell, recovering slowly following her caesarean, was tired. She was able to take a break and focus on little Andrew. He was a delightful baby, smiling and getting excited about playing, and often distracted by his surroundings, even if he was hungry. Adele found the contrast between his little singlets and my big ones hanging on the line hilarious.

On December 22 we moved down to Hodeidah staying in the rented flat of Marion, a British nursing sister who'd previously worked with our Team but was now with the World Health Organisation, and who was away on holidays. Our task was to await the arrival of our Land Rover, which we discovered had been trans-shipped at an Ethiopian port. We rejoiced when it was finally in our possession on January 10.

Mike and Esther with their little daughter arrived down from Sana'a the following evening, and I was able to help them unload their Land Rover and settle into another flat, rented by our Team. We were moving in with them and had planned to be out of Marion's flat before she arrived from Taiz. On the day she was due back, however, all sorts of things caused us to be busy, but despite everything we had to do, Dell and I had felt that we shouldn't rush, remembering the verse, 'He that believeth shall not make haste'. It was 9 pm before we'd finally packed everything into our Land Rover ready to move, and Marion still hadn't come back. By now, I was wondering how I would get her keys to her. I'd tried to leave them with the World Health Organisation doctor, but had not found him at his home, so decided to leave a note for her with the night watchman in case she still managed to arrive that evening. I was just finishing the note when out of the darkness we heard a voice.

'Hello!'

It was Marion. She'd arrived at that moment and saw our Land Rover. Another example of the Lord's perfect timing! Now we were able to hand the keys to her personally and thank her for so kindly letting us stay in her flat. Dell and I were glad we had not rushed through the day.

Over the next three months, Mike and I made several trips to Muharraq[49], mostly to take in supplies. We had to procure almost everything we needed in Hodeidah because Muharraq was a tiny village, and practically deserted except on Saturdays, the weekly market day in that vicinity. We left for our first trip on Thursday, January 17, arriving in Muharraq at about 9.30 pm. The next morning, we unloaded the lorry full of building supplies that we had sent on ahead of us. Timber, cement, fly-screen wire netting, cube-shaped metal water tanks, hose piping and everything else was gradually transported there, while locally employed fellows helped with the labouring.

Over these months, Dell stayed with Esther in the Team flat in Hodeidah, but with their little Debbie who was eighteen months old, and our baby Andrew, it was a bit of a squeeze when Mike and I came back. However, they were happy days. By now, Dell was nearly her old self again; and she was grateful to have had Esther's help and company over those months.

On February 8, Mike and I set out again, this time with a load of timber on the enormous roof-rack which Mike had built onto the Sana'a Land Rover.

We had to stop at one point because the timber had slipped forward. While Mike was attending to the load, I began talking with three Yemeni men who were sitting nearby. One turned out to be a doctor. We had a good long chat in which I spoke about knowing the Lord personally.

'How can *I* know him?' he asked and wanted to know if I had something he could read about it. What a joy to be able to give him the John's Gospel I had in my shirt pocket, ready for just such a moment.

'This is good,' he said, as he read it out loud to the other two.

It turned out that our three new friends were stuck because they had a puncture but no spare wheel; so, we loaned them ours and followed them to the village they were heading for, where their puncture could be repaired. Then we lifted our wheel back on board, secured it, and parted company. They were grateful for our help. Opportunities to speak of the Lord with other men made being there worthwhile and helped us realise that the Lord had planned those delays to accomplish his purposes.

About a month later, while Mike and I were at Muharraq, one of the sheikhs (tribal chiefs) requested that I go and investigate an epidemic of meningococcal meningitis in his area, a remote part of the province, north from Muharraq. The WHO authorities I then notified in Hodeidah had been expecting such an epidemic following the recent Haj, the annual mass pilgrimage to the city of Mecca in Saudi Arabia, but felt that there was little they could do. They explained that in previous similar epidemics they'd just had to let it 'burn itself out'. I saw that they could hardly distribute sulphadiazine tablets to the whole population; but in case I was carrying the germ, Dell and I and little Andrew had a three-day course of medication and took other precautions as well. Then once again, I left Dell, Andrew, Esther and little Debbie in the RSMT flat there in Hodeidah and drove back to Muharraq where I shared with the sheikhs as best I could, all that the WHO personnel had told me. That trip up into the mountains took two days and a night, travelling there and back again to Muharraq, but it had been a good opportunity to serve the people, and for them to see a Christian doctor at work. I was apparently the first non-Arab person to visit that remote area and recognised that it had been an amazing privilege.

On other occasions I was asked by different men to go with them to their home districts to see patients. One of these journeys again involved climbing high into the mountains on foot, after leaving the car. Apart from the usefulness of these trips medically, they were worthwhile in other ways. A couple of times I had to spend the night in a little hamlet, and had excellent, unhurried opportunities to speak about Jesus, as well as praying with some of the patients. The best Yemeni meals that could be arranged seemed to be provided on such occasions. We all squatted or sat on the floor around the mat on which the dishes had been placed, and just dipped in with our fingers, or scooped food up with pieces of the large, flat, round bread which I loved, especially when hot and fresh. Most of the food was delicious, but I confess that I once had to gently decline a sheep's eye which was handed to me.

I did not know it then, but both the experience investigating the epidemic, and the foot journeys into the mountains would prove to be important in the future when we moved permanently to Muhurraq. Before the move, we sent our prayer partners in Australia this request:

Could we briefly outline one prayer request which will always be up-to-date and important? Whatever the reasons... our hearts do at times feel so unsteady. So often there is nobody at hand able to assist in dealing with various problems, and so we are cast upon the Lord. That is a good thing of course, and it has been wonderful to experience his enabling, protection and care. But if some wished to remember just one permanent prayer point for us, even if other points are forgotten, this is what we would ask—that our hearts may be kept steady and calmly trusting our Heavenly Father in all circumstances.

* * *

At last we were almost ready to begin our work. Mike was helping us get to Muharraq, so on April 19, he, Dell and I, with Andrew and two nursing sisters finally arrived. The move involved two heavily laden Land Rovers carrying the five adults and baby Andrew, with all our luggage and enough supplies to keep us going for some weeks. We even had a refrigerator on our roof rack[50]! We arrived late at night and found that our work commenced almost immediately; the next day the two nursing sisters and I dealt with a lengthy and difficult midwifery case which fortunately had a happy ending.

Work progresses on our home.

The two homes and the fully operational clinic hut were built in local style and were rectangles of seven and a half metres by three and a half metres wide. The walls were made of many, separate, thick bundles of sticks about two metres long, each bundle firmly held together with rope made from locally grown hemp. A shallow trench was filled in with earth around the lower end of the bundles, which were in turn held together by long, horizontal, thin bundles of only a few sticks each, all the way around the hut, inside and outside, at the top, middle and lower portions of the wall, leaving appropriate gaps for doors and windows. The internal structure of the roof was also of sticks fixed into the top of the walls and sloping up to form a ridge at the top. As with the walls, long internal and external horizontal, thin bundles firmly roped together kept the roof surprisingly strong.

Adele and I had no partitions in our house, but the nurses' hut was divided into two separate bedrooms by a woven reed mat suspended from the roof. We modified both huts by the addition of a fully fly-screened, two-metre-wide veranda all the way around, and the entire floor was cemented. There was just one access door onto the veranda from outside, opposite a curtained window. Dell entertained lady visitors on mattresses and cushions at that end of the veranda and we strung a clothesline across the other end. Part of the veranda at the back of each hut was partitioned off for both a kitchen and separate washroom. A buried plastic pipe brought gravity-fed running water from four, small cubical water tanks, set up on a platform built of rocks and earth, with a vehicle access ramp at one end.

The southern half of our home.

With no shower, we washed from a basin of water on a small table and used a bucket toilet in the washroom enclosure. I emptied our bucket each morning into the shared pit toilet about 30 yards down the slope from the nurses' hut, surrounded by matting walls with a proper door.

On the other side of a tall, straight fence made of tree branches was the clinic hut. Inside, a matting partition across the middle formed two clinic rooms, and a shady tree outside the nurses' end provided a space under which the women and children awaited their turn to be treated. We erected a temporary canvas sunshade for the men's end. This was something we'd had made in Hodeidah and under which I treated, from the back of the Land Rover, any patients who came for help during our earliest days there at Muharraq.

Nice additions to the clinic were two large earthenware water pots with lids. They made me think of jars that would have been used in Biblical times. We placed one under the tree for the women, and the other outside my clinic door. Each held five buckets of water and was kept upright by being partly set into the soil. Being porous, the evaporation kept the water cool. We left a mug with each one for passers-by to help themselves to a drink anytime.

An earthenware pot served as our 'fridge' too, while we waited for Mike to set up a generator which would run lights, fans and a proper fridge. The pot maintained the water at a sufficiently cool temperature for butter to remain firm enough to spread. We kept the various items in water-tight plastic containers. Kerosene lanterns kept our home lit at night, and our stoves ran on porta-gas cylinders. Mike had done a wonderful job in building our temporary homes. His next job was to build more permanent, Western-style buildings which the Ministry of Health insisted upon, to accommodate two little families and three nursing sisters, as well as constructing the new clinic building.

During the first five weeks, we settled in well, and learnt a good deal about the area. Now into summer the weather had grown hotter, but for a period we had almost daily afternoon rain and thunderstorms, sometimes fierce, which cooled the air down. Strong windstorms, sometimes in the middle of the night, made the matting on the roof flap frighteningly, but everything stayed together, and the huts turned out to be rain-proof.

Despite the wind at times, at other times the air was almost completely still, which didn't make it easy for baby Andrew to get to sleep in the heat.

We were grateful for a little battery-powered, hand-held fan which Sue Noble, a friend of ours from St Philip's Anglican Church at Eastwood, gave us before we left Australia. Each evening we put fresh batteries in, stood it at the foot of his little mattress and let it blow air over him for several hours until the batteries ran flat. He was kept comfortable, and it was just one more example of how the Lord was so good to us, in providing this little fan for Andrew two years before he was even born.

Within our stick hut, even on the stillest night, we didn't hear the active white ants, but we certainly heard the borers persistently gnawing away. Intermittent scuttling sounds kept us aware of the rats and lizards busy amongst the sticks of the walls and roof. After only a few weeks, we'd rigged up a canopy over the pillow end of our bed to prevent their droppings, as well as pieces of white ant tunnels, from falling on us.

The nights were filled with other sounds as well, which carried clearly across the wadi from the village; donkeys braying, grain being pounded between stones, clapping and drumming, the occasional firework exploding, the petrol-driven grain mill working late, and on Fridays, utilities and trucks arriving with goods for the Saturday market, along with numerous heavily laden camels growling angrily as their drivers kept them in order. Saturday was the noisiest day, with a constant stream of sound reaching us from donkeys, camels and the crowd, not to mention the ever-vocal dog community. The Muslim call to prayer also floated across the wadi from the stone enclosure which served as a mosque. With no electricity to amplify it[51], all we heard was the distant voice of the muezzin five times a day calling the people to prayer, no doubt sounding just the same as people would have heard over all the previous thirteen centuries.

* * *

Our three clinic days were Mondays, Wednesdays and Saturdays, but on Tuesdays and Thursdays, we packed a supply of medicines[52] in the Land Rover and drove, often several hours, to villages in the region. At first, we were invited, but soon we just began arriving in a village, where we consulted with the local sheikh or chief for permission before dealing with all the sick folk. As women and children couldn't travel long distances easily, it was helpful to be able to go and care for them in their own villages. We made a special effort to search for those with eye diseases.

Almost ready to head over to the clinic.

We arranged for some patients to come to the clinic for further care, particularly those with tuberculosis, since they required many regular visits. Sometimes a midday meal was prepared for us, which was always delicious, though often not served until about 3 pm. It was during that time, after the patients had been seen, that most of the opportunities to speak about the way of salvation seemed to present themselves, certainly much more so than in the bustle of a busy clinic day. Occasionally someone seemed genuinely interested, and as we prepared for each day in earnest prayer, we knew that the Lord was with us.

When we were able to obtain a corn/soya/milk mixture (CSM)[53] and some soya oil, Dell began a little nutrition work, teaching simple ways for the mothers to feed undernourished young children that Mary and

Elke sent over to her from the clinic. While we ate well (including the precious Vegemite which our parents sent us), unfortunately many of the local people were undernourished, especially the children. Sadly, this provided tuberculosis with suitable soil in which to settle; the disease is rare in well-nourished subjects. One little eight-month-old girl was severely malnourished and as skinny as a rake, but she wolfed down the powdered milk mixture and supplements we gave her mother, and she did well. However, a three-year-old boy, our first proper in-patient was even worse, and grossly oedematous, with retained fluid in his tissues. Because he'd lost his appetite, we had to put down a naso-gastric tube[54]. Dell mixed all his feeds of full cream milk with sugar and vitamins, and I fed him by a syringe every few hours. After only two days his swelling had noticeably subsided[55]. Not having anywhere else for him or his parents to stay, we put them up in the clinic hut, though they had to move out of course, each time we ran the regular clinics.

After some time, our base clinics were seeing 80 patients a day, and we were concentrating on vaccinating all the children under fifteen years of age against TB and smallpox on the Tuesday and Thursday village visits, rather than simply holding general medical mobile clinics. With only three of us to tackle all this, we were grateful that we had been able to surrender the major surgical aspects of the proposed eye work. Our Team's *'Principles and Practices'* stated that our aim was to avoid establishing and running fixed institutions, but that we should remain free and unrestricted, more like a commando operation. Then, if for some reason a station had to close, we would simply move somewhere else to begin again, without great loss. When Peter, our leader, reminded us of this on one visit, I was relieved and deeply grateful to the Lord that the responsibility of setting up an eye surgery unit was lifted off me. The eye instruments and most of the medications which had been sent to us could be distributed to several other Christian teams in Yemen. We knew they'd be delighted to have them.

With the adjusted thinking and altered circumstances, I began to see that at last everything was fitting in perfectly with the four points which I had felt, back in 1970, would characterise the type of missionary work into which the Lord would lead me; somewhere remote; where there hadn't been any Christian work done before; in a small, and possibly mobile type of medical work, rather than in a hospital situation; and with a faith mission[56].

* * *

Friday was the Muslim day of worship, so we set aside that day each week essentially for 'office' work, when we ordered drugs, and sent financial and other correspondence. Sundays provided a necessary rest day, as well as a chance to gather for fellowship and enjoy a tape-recorded sermon[57]. As well as regular Sunday gatherings, we also had Thursday night prayer, morning devotions, and an additional monthly day of prayer.

Attending to patients from the back of the Land Rover.

My habit was to rise early for a quiet time with the Lord before our 6am breakfast, and then open the clinic at 6.30am, preparing for the busyness ahead if it was a clinic day, or loading the car if it was a 'mobile' day. We all met at 6.50 am to pray and share the *Daily Light* reading for the day, and on clinic days had lunch about 1pm, once we finished seeing the patients. In those first weeks, we averaged about 60 patients between us in a morning. Mary and Elke, the nursing sisters, attended to the women and children, while men were seen in my 'room'. After a rest, we visited any seriously ill patients nearby who were unable to attend the clinic, and after various afternoon tasks and interruptions, Dell and I often didn't sit down to our evening meal until 8 pm. We always tried to be in bed by 9.30.

The attempt to find water by digging a well had proved unsuccessful. Therefore, on three or four afternoons a week I drove the Land Rover two miles down the wadi to the place where water came to the surface, forming a shallow stream with occasional deeper pools. One side of the wadi was formed by a sandy wall about twenty feet high, gouged out by intermittent brief torrents. Some kingfishers nested in a hole near the top, and a most enjoyable moment for me was to sometimes spot one of those beautiful little birds with their iridescent, dark blue colouring. However, bird watching was not the intention of the trip. With a couple of local young men doing most of the work, we would dig out some sand to form a pool of clean water from which to use buckets to fill a cubical metal water tank which fitted nicely into the back of the Land Rover. On our return, I reversed up the ramp and on to a platform where four identical, inter-connected water tanks stood, and then ran the fresh water into one of them. To prevent contracting schistosomiasis (bilharzia), we left the water standing for three days before using it; and even then, we also filtered and boiled our drinking water.

Invisible bugs were not the only creepy-crawlies we needed to watch out for. A two-day visit by Ron, our team treasurer, made this clear. Not only did he get the full range of weather conditions, and a fairly comprehensive impression of the whole mission station (being woken at 4.15 on Sunday morning by the arrival of a car from Abs, bringing in a fellow who had sustained a fractured leg in a fight), he also managed to have his right hand bitten by a scorpion. Ron was in agony. I was glad to be on the spot, with just one ampoule of morphine, which was enough to give him excellent relief—so much so that he was able to lead our morning gathering before he and Peter set out on their journey back to Sana'a as planned. Their return wasn't quite as planned; they had passengers. The chap with the injured leg and his companions were not able to go back to Abs in the car which had brought them. The driver had demanded a second incredibly exorbitant fare for the journey on top of what they had already paid, and they'd run out of money. The owner of the car simply drove off and left them, apparently returning to Abs with an empty car. It gave Peter the opportunity to offer them a free lift in his Land Rover since he and Ron would be passing through Abs on their way to Sana'a, and they gratefully accepted. Even just taking them as passengers was a gospel opportunity; people knew that we were Christians, and incidents like this were remembered and talked about, even years later, helping to make the gospel message attractive[58].

Ron had commented on how strikingly similar our surroundings were to those at one of the Team's stations in Ethiopia. On a clear morning after rain we could see a long distance off to the west between the hills; and apart from the mountains and the greenery, there were many coloured birds, butterflies and wildflowers, as well as guinea fowl, water birds, rabbits, hares, foxes and lizards. At the top of our wadi, where the women from the village gathered morning and evening to painstakingly fill containers from a trickle of water, I once noticed coneys, mammals like guinea pigs, but about the size of a rabbit, on the rocky slope above the cliff, scurrying for cover amongst the rocks.

And yes, we had enormous spiders and centipedes, as well as the scorpions and snakes. We tucked Andrew's mosquito net in firmly around his cot each evening. Scorpions are only lethal for little babies, and the small Australian ones are more venomous than the big fellas we met in Yemen. The camel spiders we encountered were truly enormous, but harmless. At night, numerous insects were attracted to our lights, and camel spiders made the most of it, running up and down the outside of our fly screen, scooping into their mouths with their two front legs as many insects as they could. One night I saw a massive camel spider run up the back of a man who was sitting on the ground around a village fire, and then run down his front. The man didn't turn a hair, but simply brushed it off his lap!

As the weeks passed, the intense heat and humidity made living and working more difficult. Andrew suffered from prickly heat rash. There were also the episodes of diarrhoea or dysentery with which we all had to contend, although these were unavoidable, since we willingly accepted invitations from local people to enjoy a meal in their homes.

Another feature of the weather was the intermittent, but dramatic, dust storms, when strong, hot winds blew our way after crossing the sandy, desert-like lowlands. These always necessitated an extensive clean up job afterwards. Most days, however, there was a lot of dust in the atmosphere. We would wipe the dining table clean before a meal; and then after we cleared the plates away, a thin layer of dust could be clearly seen everywhere except where our plates had been. We'd eaten that dust!

While I worked hard in the clinic, Dell managed to have considerable contact with the local women and was even able to speak to some of them about the Lord Jesus. Adjusting to some aspects of the local culture was a little difficult at times. For instance, if things were not locked away, Dell's visitors assumed they had permission to help themselves to anything they fancied[59]. The women also liked to put their fingers into Andrew's mouth, presumably so that he would suck on them; but amoebic dysentery and other maladies unfortunately resulted from such practices when people had not been taught to wash their hands. With the generator now powering our fridge, lights and roof fan, Dell also had a challenging time trying to answer questions about how the electricity from our generator could make the hot plate on which we boiled our drinking water so hot, while at the same time making the fridge so cold! The women loved to visit her, and were keenly interested in everything around the home, and in every aspect of her life, especially Andrew. Sadly, one of the most frequently asked questions about me was 'does he beat you?' All too often, that was what they expected from a husband. What a wonderful opportunity we had to demonstrate by our lives the radical difference it made, having the Lord Jesus in our hearts.

It wasn't easy for Dell to live in such a primitive situation with a little baby, so far from her mother, sisters and friends at home. The two nurses were single and busy with their work, so it wouldn't have been right to ask for their help, except in an emergency. But we could see that even though it wasn't easy, it was all extremely worthwhile because of the way her being there in Yemen as a wife and young mother enabled her to relate so well to the local women and girls. They knew Dell loved and welcomed them.

In keeping with the commitment we made to the Lord on our wedding day when we walked down the aisle together to the tune of 'For my sake and the gospel's go,' she bravely accepted it as necessary and didn't complain, although naturally she missed those at home.

Even though we were in the Northern Hemisphere, at certain times of the year we could see the Southern Cross low in the night sky. It was then we felt a gentle tug on our heartstrings and felt a little lonely, thinking of our family and friends so far away; although we never once regretted obeying the Lord's command to 'go into all the world and preach the good news to all creation'.

* * *

In August, Adele, Andrew and I, together with Mary and Elke, all piled into our Land Rover and left Muharraq for Sana'a for business and a much-needed rest. Because the rains had begun, we had a tricky drive to reach Wadi Moor; and then our hearts sank when we saw that it was in flood, and impossible to cross. Because of further rains and the condition of the road, there was no point in turning back, but we couldn't move forward either.

'You can stay with us,' said some folk from a village nearby. We had gotten to know them on previous journeys. They gave us a good meal and put us up in the village. In the middle of the night, when Dell tiptoed out of our room to go to the toilet, a young man grabbed her tightly by the wrist, and wanted her to go with him.

'My husband is here,' she said to him in Arabic, and he let her go.

It was a waiting game the next day, but the wadi was still impassable. On the third day, a lorry ventured across the wadi, and then some cars, with local young fellows wading ahead to show the best way across, up to their thighs in the flood. We couldn't help being concerned; apparently one man had already drowned, and we could see a couple of Land Rovers partly submerged which had been rolled over and over by the torrent, and then abandoned. Nevertheless, we hastily loaded the car, and prepared the engine for the drenching[60]. As the sun was setting, and after a word of prayer together, we drove gingerly into the torrent using a low, four-wheel drive gear and then emerged, rejoicing, on the other side.

Buying straw matting from a village on the way to Muharraq.

A couple of hours later, in the gathering darkness, we came to another wadi. This one hadn't flooded for twelve years, but now several cars and lorries were firmly stuck in it. What a surprise to discover that one of those cars belonged to the Yemeni doctor that Mike and I had helped on that same road exactly six months earlier[61]. He'd been stuck since the night before and was grateful for the tin of fish, bread rolls and tin of pineapple we were able to give him. While he stayed with his vehicle, we slept that night under some thorn bushes. Next morning, I helped as an Austin lorry tried unsuccessfully to pull him from the muddy riverbed. I had another good chat with him and left our tow rope for him to use later, following which, we ourselves then managed to cross the wadi a little further upstream. We finally reached Hodeidah three and a half days after setting out from Muharraq, a journey which normally takes less than eight hours[62]. Perhaps the Lord planned the delays to allow a little extra contact with our friend.

A holiday in the cooler weather of Taiz, set in dramatic mountainous terrain at about 4,500 feet above sea level was a welcome relief after our long, hot months of work, and after such an adventurous journey out. Here, at least one shower of rain was expected most afternoons, but it was only mildly humid. The mountains towered up steeply behind us, and the clouds hovering around them hid the houses perched on the top of the ridges. What we liked best were the two gum trees with straggly, peeling bark outside the front door of our little flat, because they reminded us so much of home.

ON THE WAY

Adele and Andrew.

8

Encouragements, Dangers and Provision

In October 1974, after our holiday in Taiz and the Team's area conference in Sana'a, those of us heading for Muharraq travelled down to Hodeidah to prepare for our return, this time for a seven-month stint.

Mike and two nurses went off first in his Land Rover in the hope of finding thatching for our three rooves, and to get the place tidied up a bit before we arrived. A third nurse joining us meant that their hut now had to be divided into three little bedrooms. Our task was to bring the third nurse with us, a fridge, building materials and enough provisions for four months.

We left Hodeidah on a Wednesday in a heavily laden Land Rover and made our way along the dirt track through the coastal plain. After nightfall, there were no streetlights or road signs, and no more than an occasional faint gleam of light from a hurricane lamp in a tiny hamlet of stick huts along the way. There'd been a good deal of rain, and at one point, we became stuck in some deep mud. We praised the Lord when he arranged for a big Austin lorry to come along, with enough men to pull us out. They'd almost run out of oil, so we let them have all they needed from our spare can. One of the men sat on our front mudguard and directed us for a mile or so through the puddles.

We didn't risk crossing Wadi Moor at 10.30pm, so spent the night at the 'motel' on the riverbank, settling down on some of the Yemeni-sized string beds to share the cold, starry night with the mosquitoes. In the daylight, the crossing wasn't so difficult, although a little later we nearly tipped over sideways beside a long puddle. As I tried to skirt around the water, the top-heavy vehicle teetered onto two wheels for one ghastly moment! We were glad when we arrived safely at Muharraq about mid-morning on the Thursday.

One of the first patients we saw was a sick child, the grandson of the main tribal chief (sheikh) for our region. This man lived in a stone house on a hill up behind the village. He was elderly, and had a prominent, calloused growth (seemingly always coated with a layer of brown dust), right in the centre of his forehead. Such growths were common in older men, demonstrating to everyone how religiously they had rubbed their foreheads hard into the ground five times a day for many years during the Muslim prayer ritual. The sheikh did not seem at all kindly disposed towards us and was apparently angry that the government had allowed Christians to establish a medical work in his district. (Peter had got to know him better than I had. 'Never seek his assistance for anything,' he had told me.) The sheikh's grown up son, whom we described amongst ourselves as 'the young sheikh', seemed different, in that we sensed him to be open and approachable. He lived on our side of the wadi with his wife and young children in a little hamlet, just beyond the top of the hill, directly up behind us.

The sick child was the son of the young sheikh, and was suffering from vomiting, diarrhoea, and serious dehydration. Straight away we commenced an intra-peritoneal infusion directly into his abdominal cavity. The young father's face was full of anguish as he watched me push the wide bore needle into his little son's abdomen. We usually ask parents to wait outside at times like this, but I didn't think he would have agreed to, so we let him stay, crying out in our hearts to the Lord to save this precious little life.

We were filled with thankfulness when the baby made a rapid and complete recovery, and his father was able to carry him home a few hours later. Of all the little lives needing medical care which the Lord could have chosen to bring to us from that whole district, none could have been more likely to swing opinion in our favour if there turned out to be a happy ending to such an encounter.

As with all other patients, we charged nothing for our services, but only for the medications and disposable equipment, if they could pay that small amount. (If they couldn't, we waived that cost as well.) This policy was a source of amazement for the locals, who were only too familiar with exorbitant fees being charged for such things; and we prayed that it would contribute to making the gospel message attractive for them. If asked, we explained to them that the finance for our personal needs was met by our friends and churches at home, and not by our governments. Certainly, the young sheikh thanked us, and before long we were to discover that he wasn't the only one who was truly grateful for our efforts that day. And this brings me to one of my favourite examples of how the Lord provided for us.

Dell had been making our bread most days. If she ran short of time, she would cook a batch of scones. One morning, however, she woke up in our little stick hut feeling terribly tired. We ate our breakfast cereal, and then Dell served up some baked beans which provided me with an adequate meal before I set off for the busy clinic. However, she felt guilty that she hadn't made any bread or scones.

Freshly baked scones

ON THE WAY

'If I was a real missionary,' she thought to herself, 'I would simply pray, and the Lord would send us some bread from heaven.' Lifting her eyes heavenward, she looked for a few moments at the stick roof above her. Seeing a little patch of sunlight filtering in through the straw matting, she imagined the Lord somehow sending the bread down.

Outside there was the usual noise from patients and their family members gathering near the clinic on the other side of the stick fence. Even though they knew it was too early, sometimes women would come to look at our house, or to see if Dell could help them 'jump the queue' to avoid having to wait their turn. On this morning, a little girl was standing at our front door, calling out 'Moonera, Moonera,' which was Adele's Arabic name. However, Dell wasn't feeling up to going out to meet anyone that morning. She hoped the little girl would simply go away. Meanwhile, she sadly thought how stupid she was to imagine that the Lord would send her some bread from heaven and was condemning herself that she hadn't forced herself to make the effort to get up earlier and bake the bread or scones.

'Moonera!' The little girl continued to call out, not going away.

Slightly annoyed, Dell went out onto the fly-screened verandah and walked around to the front door. There stood the young sheikh's little daughter with a pile of delicious, hot, freshly cooked, flat Yemeni bread, wrapped up in a cloth to keep it warm. Her mother was so grateful to us for saving the life of her little baby son that she'd sent this gift down for us and for the nurses, to express her heartfelt thanks. I don't need to tell you how much we enjoyed that bread and thanked the Lord for it.

Dell and I have often recalled this incident and related it to our friends. We do have a wonderfully loving Heavenly Father, who knows and understands exactly how we feel moment by moment, and what we face each day. While Dell was chiding herself for being lazy, the Lord had already provided what she desired; and in a real sense he did send her that bread from heaven.

Adele had woken up feeling worn out that morning, and we came to realise that weariness in work such as we were engaged in was not only physical. There was a constant battle raging in the unseen realm all around us; and on top of that we were establishing a beachhead in enemy territory.

Certainly the weather was often oppressive; and the added strain of having to communicate in a foreign language, and cope with living in a different culture so far from home, with the inevitable illnesses, were all sufficient to explain why we were frequently weary. But the spiritual oppression was something extra and is best understood by those who have sought to raise the banner of the Lord Jesus Christ in locations such as we found ourselves. We'd never encountered such oppression while we were still at home in Australia.

It wasn't an unrelenting struggle, because sometimes we felt ourselves more under attack than at other times; we experienced more oppression in certain Yemeni homes, hamlets, villages or towns than in others. But our energy and emotions were frequently drained, and we constantly needed the Lord's protection. Fortunately, of course, like any competent commanding officer, he has provided us with the necessary armour and weaponry to 'fight the good fight', all described in Ephesians 6:10-18. We knew it was crucial that we applied those verses to our daily lives in Yemen. I don't think it would be an exaggeration to state that our lives depended on our staying close to the Lord, and utilising his armour and weapons as intended.

How grateful we were for the many prayers our friends at home offered on our behalf, over the years. Only eternity will reveal just how vital they were; but sometimes we could sense when people were praying for us. Difficult situations would be unexpectedly resolved, or a sense of oppression weighing us down would lift and leave us. From time to time, things ran so smoothly and successfully that it was clear the Lord was answering prayer and driving the enemy and his evil forces back. On birthdays or wedding anniversaries we often noticed how light-hearted and blessed we felt, indicating the power of prayer, even from the other side of the world.

As always of course, the Lord sent encouragement when it was needed. In a letter that my father wrote to me, he mentioned Acts 26:17b and 18, believing it to be relevant to our missionary work. 'I am sending you to them to open their eyes, and turn them from darkness to light, and from the power of Satan to God, so that they may receive forgiveness of sins, and a place among those who are sanctified by faith in me.'

Another encouraging message came through one of our nurses on a prayer day during which we decided to put each of our names on a separate piece of folded paper. Everyone drew out a name and we then went off on our own to pray privately about various things, including for the colleague whose name we'd drawn. We decided to ask the Lord to give us a message to share with that colleague. Our Scottish nurse Helen had received my name, and she believed the Lord had given her the verses Luke 22:31-32a, which read, 'Simon, Simon, Satan has asked to sift you as wheat. But I have prayed for you, Simon, that your faith may not fail.' Helen said she felt the meaning was that the Lord Jesus was praying for me, so that my faith might not fail.

* * *

There were plenty of dangers to challenge our faith, living where we did. Len, the assistant administrator for the Red Sea Mission Team, knelt with me, and we had a moving time of prayer together one day, committing each other and our work to the Lord. Len's plan was to set out for Sa'ada on a solo trek through unreached areas. When he arrived back, ten days later, he told us that he had been captured by the Bedouin! He had travelled through some desolate areas; on a few sections of the journey he was able to get lifts in cars, but he often had to walk. At one remote place, Bedouin men had surrounded him and stolen all his money, his watch, camera, blanket, pullover, singlets, socks, a torch and two whistles I'd given him. It wasn't quite at gunpoint, but they were menacing enough that he didn't dare to stop them.

Praise the Lord they didn't take the compass I'd also given him. 'It's not mine,' he'd told his captors, and they had left it with him. It was certainly something he needed.

We had heard locals say that 'the Bedou aren't believers,' meaning they were not Muslims. But Len had good opportunities to chat with them about the Lord, so who knows what may have transpired. In fact, as he travelled, Len had opportunities to share the Word with many other men he met on his journey. It was often gladly received. Generally, the region was wide open for the gospel, and we were all grateful for the ways the Lord blessed and protected our friend. Three years later, we were to find that fruits of that journey led to some exciting developments. In the meantime, Len decided that for future treks in similar areas, he would go in company with others; for example, with a camel train. We knew how vulnerable we all were apart from the Lord's protection, and how much we needed his leading and blessing.

Adele and me with two local labourers, outside our home.

Other dangers weren't quite so far from home. Andrew was one year old on November 22, and we had a little party for him. We thought that he was safe on the verandah; but just a few days later, Adele called me to kill a big scorpion which she'd found under the little mattress he often sat on out there. These creatures are dangerous for children, and so while thanking the Lord for protecting him, I decided the time had come to buy some hens to try to keep down the scorpion and spider population. Soon six hens and one big rooster scratched around, producing some nice eggs as a bonus.

The chickens were good at getting rid of small threats, but they could do nothing about the snake that fell from the stick roof just in front of where I was sitting in the clinic one afternoon. I had been praying there for several hours when a clap of thunder struck. The snake was dislodged from the roof, fell to the floor and escaped into the stick wall.

Our home on the left, and Mike's work shed, with the clinic hut behind.

In December, we were told of a 'gooshwee', appearing from amongst the trees in broad daylight, and attacking two men and a little girl who quickly got themselves to the clinic for treatment. We had no idea what a 'gooshwee' was but were told that it was about the size of a donkey, and it had escaped into the scrub after the brief encounter. Later, we discovered that the creature was a striped hyena, with a different cry from the African laughing hyena. Peter had caught sight of one, while Mike and I spotted what he believed was a puma, with a tall tuft of hair on the top of its ears, trotting calmly across the track in front of us and into the scrub again, only about half a mile from our houses. These cats frequently killed sheep and goats and were known to attack anyone unwise enough to be walking alone at night, particularly without a light. (We saw ours well before sunset!) For safety from predators such as these, the men usually carried a sword, rifle or machine gun, or just the usual curved dagger, which was part of the national costume.

Weapons formerly in use were another danger. Only a few years before, the civil war had still been in full swing, and wartime relics such as burnt-out Egyptian tanks, or a transport aircraft sprawled in the scrub near Abs having failed to reach the airfield, reminded us of the action. When an unexploded bomb was discovered near Muharraq and a fire was lit on top of it, the onlookers were gratified by the most satisfactory explosion, but we were a little shaken. We stuck to the tyre tracks on the first leg of the road from Muharraq to Hodeidah, too. Even though it had been given the okay for traffic, the area had been home to plenty of land mines.

There were always dangers when it came to the roads, which were often terribly bumpy, rocky tracks. On a trip to visit two villages near Abs, we somehow managed on our way home to break a support for the Land Rover's left front spring. We could drive it temporarily, slowly and gently, so I was able to get water from the wadi, but the vehicle needed to be fixed. We sent a message to Mike to bring in a welding machine, something he'd had to do once before when part of the chassis snapped. But even sending such a message was a complicated endeavour, being sent by walkie-talkie from the sheikh's place to a telegraph operator at Maharbisha, high on the mountain ridge behind us. From there it went by Morse code to Hajjah, and probably the same way from there to Sana'a.

Another danger, although only a slight one, was that the region was volcanic. One evening, while we were gathered for prayer, the concrete floor began heaving beneath our chairs. The minor earthquake continued for about ten seconds, accompanied by a rumbling sound like a train on the mountains. However, since there were no trains in whole of Yemen, it didn't take us long to realise that that wasn't the explanation.

* * *

There were noticeable changes to our site by this time. The thatching material (stalks from the sorghum crops, six to eight feet tall) purchased for our three stick huts made the dwellings much more secure against the weather, particularly the wind. We planted a tiny vegetable garden, with some pawpaw and mango trees, and Mike planted 30 little gum trees, brought in from Yareem. Water, of course, was always the chief restricting factor, as were land negotiations—a lengthy business. As soon as these could be finalised, Mike was ready to start on the new clinic building.

Trying to negotiate more land on which to make a second attempt to dig for water also turned out to be difficult; the women would not work in the fields if they thought a man might come. The solution to the water issue was to collect rainwater from the roofs of the new buildings and store it in large storage tanks.

Every year, millions of Muslims from many countries go on 'the Haj', a simultaneous pilgrimage to the city of Mecca, in Saudi Arabia. We grew to expect some sort of epidemic from Mecca after the Haj every year; we had seen cholera in the past, and meningococcal meningitis. In 1974 it was a form of influenza, with fever, dizziness, and pneumonia accompanied by a severe cough with sputum and chest pain. When four Haj pilgrims died in a remote mountainous region that I'd visited the year before, I was called up to treat the sick. While Mike was mending our Land Rover with the welding machine, I managed to get a lift on a United Nations car taking some male teachers north. They were planning to stay in the area for about two months to assist with the taking of the national census. I was able to have a spiritual conversation with them, and even gave some scriptures out.

After I had seen and treated the influenza-suffering patients in the remote village, it was time to go home. The trouble was, there was no UN car making the same trip back. 'You could hire a donkey,' was the suggestion, but when I looked at what donkeys were available, I had to shake my head. Those that weren't going to the local market that day were far too small. It had been embarrassing when I had ridden little donkeys in the past; my legs were longer than theirs! The only alternative was to walk. Seven hours later, I arrived home, stiff and sore.

On May 3, a happy secret Dell and I had been keeping for a couple of months took a worrisome turn. A small amount of blood loss indicated that she might miscarry, and I immediately put her to bed for a week, with a 30mg tablet of Phenobarb twice a day helping her to rest. I took on most of the home duties, with assistance mainly from Esther. After the week in bed, Dell was able to gradually resume light duties, while continuing to rest a good deal, but the heat made life difficult and tended to sap our strength, with the mercury rising to well over 40 degrees Centigrade every day. As well, clinics were growing busier. One hundred and fifty patients was not an unusual number these days, and we sometimes needed to work on till 3.30 pm or even later, to treat them all, having begun at 7 am, with many other tasks to fill the remainder of the day.

But despite all of this, a most encouraging encounter was about to take place. On the morning of May 22, not long after starting the clinic in the usual summer heat, I felt inexplicably weary, so I got up and went over to the house for a quick cup of tea. I flopped down on the bed, and Dell suggested we pray. Immediately I felt refreshed, indicating that spiritual powers had been oppressing me. When I returned to the clinic, the first thing that happened was that a pleasant man in his mid-30s, almost always smiling and joking about things, who'd been coming for regular Streptomycin injections for his TB, asked me straight out in front of the other men, if he could have 'one of those little books about Jesus'. I hurried back to the house to get an Arabic gospel. When I returned, he was explaining to the other four men in the room, without any apparent fear or qualm, how Jesus is the Son of God. They were listening intently to all that was being said, and then they all wanted Gospels. I happily gave them one each, along with one or two Scripture Gift Mission booklets.

As soon as I'd treated the roomful of men, I took our new friend to the ladies' house to sit and chat with Mary, who was not working in the clinic that day, and who spoke much better Arabic than I did. The man told us that eighteen months before, he had met Ewen, who had gone on some walks while staying at Muharraq when supervising the construction of the three, local-style huts. Ewen had given him a Gospel which he read.

'I believe everything it said,' the fellow told us.

Mary and I could scarcely believe our ears, and I gave him an Arabic New Testament, which he was delighted to receive. Because he had to come back to the clinic for regular treatment, we had other opportunities to speak to him.

'I found nothing worthwhile in Islam,' he told us another day, 'but in the Gospel I discovered reality.' I then gave him World Aflame by Billy Graham (in Arabic, of course), as well as some booklets. We felt as sure as we could be that he was a true believer already, and so began praying earnestly for him and his family, as well as for those with whom he came in contact.

I purposely never once visited his village, though I believe I would have been welcome. If a foreigner like me, especially a Christian, was seen visiting him, that would have jeopardised his and his family's safety, unless there'd been some obvious reason for going, such as a medical emergency. However, before each of his scheduled visits for his injections or tablets, I prepared a little card with Bible references for him to look up at home. Each card dealt with a topic of doctrine, and I was careful to slip it to him in such a way that no-one else in the clinic would notice. I had to trust that, together with our earnest prayers for him, these cards would give him some teaching and encouragement. As soon as possible, I introduced him to Peter, who kept in touch with this brother over the years.

Because this man was so open about his faith and became widely known as a believer, and because he fearlessly shared the Good News with so many of his friends in that locality, he suffered a lot from the authorities who, of course, were all Muslims. He was fined, persecuted, imprisoned, and had some of his land confiscated; but to the best of our knowledge, he has stood firm in his faith. Praise God!

* * *

In June, while I was burning off some rubbish, a man about 40 approached.

'I would like one of your little books,' he said to me. I thought he meant a little notebook, because children often scrabbled through rubbish looking for any writing paper.

'You could buy one in the market,' I suggested, but that wasn't what he was after.

'No,' he said. 'You know, one of your little books.'

At once I realised that he wanted a gospel, and soon he was happily on his way with a copy of both John's and Luke's Gospels. I think he had heard me speaking about the Good News in one of the villages that we'd visited. The previous six months had afforded us many opportunities to tell the gospel story, especially on the village visits. (One sheikh read continually from a John's Gospel for several hours recently; and as they always seem to read out loud, this enabled other men to hear, too.)

Others saw the little gospel pamphlets in Arabic that I often purposely left on the clinic desk; some picked them up and read them, which provided the opportunity to speak a little about the matters which were so much on my heart, and then perhaps to give out a gospel or two to those in the room.

By and large, compared with most Muslim lands, Yemen (and this part particularly) seemed to be comparatively wide open for the gospel. The people often seemed genuinely interested and receptive, though more amongst the mountain people than those from the lowlands. The interest was not just amongst the men, either. We were thrilled when Mary shared with us that the young sheikh's wife had said to her that she was embarrassed to ask, but 'what does the Bible say for people who are sick in the night?' It was a simple question perhaps, but for her to ask it was staggering.

Because few Yemeni women were able to read, it was not so easy to make progress, or to leave something with them. But we were still able to testify to the Lord Jesus in word and by our actions. The woman who helped with our washing often went with the nurses on their village visits, carrying the medicine box on her head, and frequently repeating to the listening women and children what the nurses had to say. She also related everything to the young sheikh's wife on her return home, as both lived in the little hamlet on the hill up behind us.

On one village visit, the nurses were in a house in which there were pictures on the walls (taken from Western magazines) of women modelling clothing. One picture, though, was a nude. Some young fellows sitting there were glancing up at it, and then down at our ladies, who began to feel most uncomfortable. Finally, one chap got up and came forward, making some comment about the picture to Mary. She'd been praying while treating the sick, and this was the opportunity she'd been waiting for. She stood up and said, clearly, and at length, 'We are followers of Jesus and have nothing to do with impurity. Such pictures, thoughts and impurity have no place in our hearts, or in Jesus' teachings in the Bible.' She declared that they must go at once into another home. 'We'll neither eat nor drink in this house!'

'No, please,' the Yemeni ladies asked them. 'Sit down and have a cup of tea.' But Mary would not relent until all the men scrambled to their feet (including the old sheikh of that village, a nice old fellow who'd not been involved) and hurried out of the house, whereupon the village ladies shut the door and windows, and bolted them!

'Now, please, would you finish treating the sick,' the women asked. The nurses agreed to do so but not long after, Mary was amazed to hear our washer lady repeating to the village women who'd brought up the matter of refreshments with her, 'No, we'll neither eat nor drink in this house!'

As Mary was getting up to go to another house, she said to our washer lady, 'You don't have to leave with us,' but the woman got up straight away with them, showing her deep appreciation for the value Mary had publicly placed on purity, and the high place of women in Christian society by simply saying, 'Thank you so much.'

The same woman fell ill with a fever one day and had been ill for several days without our ladies knowing. On Sunday afternoon, Mary, who'd been praying at the time, felt constrained to go up the hill and visit her.

'How did you know to come?' our friend cried in wonder.

'The Lord told me,' Mary replied simply. This really impressed our washer lady. She knew that we prayed for her, and for many others; and the Spirit was clearly at work in her heart.

* * *

We rejoiced in provisions from the Lord from time to time, such as a lovely pawpaw given to us by a local family 'for Andrew', or the gift of hot, flat, round Yemeni bread, just when we'd finished all the bread that Dell had cooked. Another provision was that at eighteen weeks, Dell was quite well again since the small incident at twelve and a half weeks. After that initial week of complete rest, she was now able to do most things, although I helped as much as I could to relieve her load.

One day, a gloriously cool change accompanied a rainy thunderstorm. In such intense heat Andrew became difficult, but there was a remarkably rapid change back to his happy little self with each cool change. With the lower temperatures, we had a happy evening with a Mozart piano concerto playing, while I did the washing up. I was convinced that such relaxed happiness was related to time spent in prayer. I prayed frequently for a closer walk with him, and that my life might be a testimony to his faithfulness, depending on him entirely, in all, and for all. How good the Lord was to us; and what a joy the work was proving to be, despite difficulties.

Prayer was crucial to what we were doing, and we made it a priority. One morning in June, I took the nurses and our washer lady in the Land Rover early in the morning as far as I could on their way to the Bennie Ahmed district, after which I spent the rest of the day mostly meditating on various Bible passages, and in prayer. Not long after that, I had a request for 'a book about the Messiah' from a friend of one of the men to whom I had recently given a gospel. He said that he himself had already been given one, but his friends were reading it!

Dell and I were praying for the little hamlet up behind us, and as a clinic was finishing, a likeable teenager from up there came by. After a brief chat, he happily took a John's Gospel and a small book of parables. I got him to write his name in them, and to write that they were his; it was a precaution against my being accused of forcing our books onto people, especially youngsters. We were careful never to give any literature to children unless their parents were present and gave their consent.

Prayer affected our relationships; the watchman and his brother both seemed more cheerful and helpful in answer to prayer, and I was aware of the Lord's hand on me. It also affected the outcomes of our medical work. One Tuesday morning, I saw a desperately ill baby girl, the daughter of the sheikh in a village beyond Bennie Yusef. That afternoon I prayed earnestly and at length for her recovery, and for spiritual blessing on that village which I'd visited once before to treat two sick old men. I was so happy to hear later that the baby was well again.

When Len arrived, one Friday night in June, prepared for a walking tour out of Muhurraq, we prayed with him for rich blessing on the people he met and talked to of Jesus' love, death and resurrection. Happily, Len also brought the news that some financial straits we had found ourselves in had been relieved. At exactly the right time, the Lord had sent 50,000 DM (approximately $12,000 Australian) to cover our building costs. We had thought we had plenty of money for the buildings, but various items had proved to be more expensive than expected. We could have appealed for funds, but I was glad that the Team's policy was to not let our financial needs be made public. It was wonderful to bring our requests to the Lord in prayer, and then to see him providing in the best way, and at the time which he knew to be most suitable for his purposes. He had arranged for this large gift to go through the process of being donated, and then to reach us from Germany just when it was needed. When a gift came out of the blue like this, earmarked for our work, it confirmed to us that the blessing of the Lord was resting on this ministry, and that we were working alongside him, the Lord of the harvest, to bring salvation to Yemenis there, as well as bringing glory to his Name.

* * *

The number of patients we saw on clinic days continued to gradually increase, and towards the end of June, on a Saturday market day, we passed the total of 200 for the first time; 138 women and children seen by our three nurses, while I'd attended to 64 men.

'Each mark on this card represents one streptomycin injection.'

The work was growing, but as it was well over three years now since Adele had left Australia, and it was approaching three and a half years since I had set out, we needed to begin planning for our first furlough. Dell's pregnancy obviously was a key consideration, and it was decided that we should return to Sydney at the end of July. She had needed a caesarean section for Andrew's birth, another reason for this baby to be born in Australia.

Time and again, the Lord proved to be our perfect Heavenly Father. Adele had been wondering what she would do about warm clothes for Andrew on that first night after arriving back in wintry old Sydney. Her birthday was on June 25, and on the evening of the 23rd a birthday card from my parents arrived, all the way from Sydney. In it was the news that Mrs Norah Braga and her daughter Sheila were gathering gifts of clothing for Andrew. There was also notification of a generous gift from another special friend of ours, Stephanie Barnsdall.

This birthday card, and the gifts mentioned, made a lovely birthday present for Dell. I had searched through the local market, asking the Lord to help me find something to give her from myself, but unfortunately couldn't find anything that was suitable. On the afternoon of her birthday, after I'd finished the clinic, I told her of my predicament.

'I'm sorry,' I told her. 'I'll buy you a gift when we reach Australia.'

However, God was good. We'd invited Len to join us for the evening meal. He didn't know it was Dell's birthday and quite unexpectedly, he brought, as a thank you gift, a jar of Vegemite and two bars of chocolate! Naturally we were delighted and explained why. In the end, Dell had received several special birthday gifts, from family and friends, and from the Lord himself.

Len had a special ministry to us that night, but the Lord was using him for his own purposes. On one occasion, after he had visited us at Muharraq, he headed back to Sana'a, and had just reached Barjil, where he saw a young soldier signalling to him from the side of the road, indicating that he wanted a ride. Stopping the Land Rover, Len invited the young man to climb aboard; and then setting off, they started to chat. Naturally Len soon began to talk about the Lord, but he was in for a surprise when he offered the young soldier an Arabic translation of World Aflame by Billy Graham.

'Oh, I've already read this,' the soldier said.

Len was amazed, and even more amazed at the story that unfolded. Apparently, in each of two entirely separate, remote places in the country, a group of Christian extended families have lived for centuries, who've never become Muslims. This young man was from one of these Christian groups.

'But how did you manage to read a copy of World Aflame?' asked Len.

'My father travelled to Lebanon to buy Christian books,' the young man told him.

Lebanon was one of the few countries in the Middle East where such a book was procurable.

'But it was too dangerous to carry the books back into Yemen—his bags would be searched. My father stayed in Lebanon and copied out the books by hand into exercise books. Those do not attract attention.' The young man said that the exercise books were handed around and read by different members of the little Christian community.

In order to protect these believers, none of us in the Team, or any other Westerner, ever visited them, as that would have attracted unnecessary attention and would most definitely have jeopardised their lives and property. I don't think any of us knew exactly where they were located.

May the Lord, who down through the centuries has glorified his name amongst them, continue to guard, bless and care for these dear children of his, always.

9

Furlough, Sharon's Birth and Tropical Medicine

1975-1976: Age 32-33

In late July the time came for us to say goodbye to our friends at Muharraq and begin the long journey home to Sydney. When we reached Australia, we were struck by the spotlessly clean washrooms at Perth airport with water which we could safely drink straight from the tap; the cold July weather in Sydney after leaving the summer heat of southern Arabia; and so many homes with beautiful gardens.

It was marvellous to be home with our families again. My parents had prepared a comfortable little flat under their home at Beecroft. With the lovely gardens and pleasant surroundings, our welcome home was delightful. To cap it all, the couple who lived next door to Dell's family in Greenacre had asked if we would look after their home while they were away for six weeks from the beginning of December. Not only did this mean that we would be near Dell's family for Christmas, but we would be able to move there soon after the birth of our second child.

A moment's reflection is all that is needed to understand the deep joy and relief this was for Dell. Well over three years before, she'd left home more or less on her own, a single woman engaged to be married. Far from her family and friends, she'd bravely settled in a strange country, prepared for her wedding, been married, given birth to her first child by caesarean section, nursed and nurtured him in the most primitive of surroundings, and returned home expecting her second child. What a contrast now to have her mother on hand at last, to be surrounded by all her loved ones, and to be living right next door to her childhood home. Surely, the Lord is no man's debtor!

After arriving in Sydney, we had several weeks' rest before we began attending deputation meetings in churches and various Christian gatherings where it had been arranged for us to speak as representatives of the Red Sea Mission Team[63]. Our aim was to talk about the work of the Team and our part in it, thanking them for their prayers, while looking to the Lord to raise up more labourers for the harvest field in Yemen and other Muslim lands. Needing to care for Andrew, and with her pregnancy progressing, it was felt wisest for Dell to only participate in deputation within Sydney. I spent a week in Newcastle in early September, and Melbourne after that, and towards the end of October, I flew to Brisbane for two weeks. One meeting was a dreadful experience. Unbeknown to me, the evening was advertised as one where a 'brilliant eye surgeon' was to speak about his work in the Middle East! People were encouraged to invite their friends, and there were various medical specialists and other doctors there, including, I think, several non-Christian eye surgeons. I don't know what happened; somebody had confused me with Dr Ronnie Holland, perhaps. The fact is that I was extremely embarrassed, and explained the mistake, but it was like a nightmare. I was a very average GP addressing an august company of the medical fraternity who were clearly expecting somebody more capable. Nevertheless, the slides showed them something of our work in a remote, primitive and pioneering setting; and at least some of those present seemed genuinely interested and did their best to ease my obvious discomfort.

It's only in looking back that I believe I understand the purpose the Lord had in causing me to go through that experience. In Deuteronomy 8:2–5 we read, 'Remember how the Lord your God led you all the way in the desert these forty years, to humble you and to test you in order to know what was in your heart, whether or not you would keep his commands. He humbled you . . . to teach you . . . Know then in your heart that as a man disciplines his son, so the Lord your God disciplines you.' Only the Lord himself could do his work in and through me and make me fruitful. Since anything of lasting value will have been his doing, it was important that I didn't seek some of the glory for myself. And although I didn't realise it then, perhaps the most fruitful time of my whole life was approaching. It took place during a portion of our next term in Yemen and extended over exactly eight months. In all that had been happening, the Lord was preparing me for that time of outreach.

* * *

Dell's elective caesarean section was arranged for the morning of November 11, 1975[64], in the Poplars Private Hospital at Epping, and baby Sharon was born. The operation was successful, but my father and I were left stewing in the waiting room for an extra hour or more because the obstetrician thought that someone else had come and told us that all was well. It wasn't until after his next case that he came hurrying out to tell us. The days that followed were happy ones for me. I was glad that we now had a little girl[65].

Things were different for Adele, however. The usual policy at the Poplars in those days was for the mother and baby to remain in hospital for ten days after a caesarean birth. Although I visited her each day, Andrew was not allowed to visit, and that was hard for Dell. Also, she was exhausted, and unable to provide Sharon with the time, hugs and attention that she needed[66]. The nursing staff told Adele on at least several occasions that her baby was crying, but after feeding her, Dell had to send her back to the nursery.

Andrew was living with me beneath my parents' home, and despite missing Adele, was happy because he was lavished with attention. His grandparents had been far away when he was born, and he was twenty months old before they first saw him, though of course we'd sent them lots of colour photos and some cassette recordings.

After Dell and Sharon were discharged from hospital, we were all together again as a little family for two weeks under my parents' home. At the beginning of December, we moved to stay in the house next door to Dell's parents' home at Greenacre for six weeks. That was a good and happy time for us. When Sharon was three months old, I wrote, 'She is a joy to us; and like her father, has been putting on weight with remarkable speed.'

Our furlough was extended by six months to enable me to attend a postgraduate tropical medicine course at the University of Sydney starting in March. To get the diploma meant a full study program. Before the course began, I was also busily occupied with Arabic studies[67] and attended a course on motor maintenance, with our Land Rover in mind. To be closer to Sydney University, we moved early in the new year to Camperdown where we rented a small, two-storey terraced house. Despite Camperdown being one of the inner suburbs of Sydney, and the fact that we were close to busy Parramatta Road, our house fronted onto a quiet, dead-end street, looking out over a bowling green to large, leafy Camperdown Park and an oval, where there were swings and other things for Andrew to play on. Off the upstairs front bedroom was a balcony where he often played. From there he could see all the cars and trucks going past the end of our cul-de-sac, and like most little boys he *loved* cars and trucks. All in all, we couldn't have wished for a more pleasant or suitable location. Once again, we noticed the way the Lord provided for every need. Despite several apparent setbacks, we saw later how even those things turned out to be blessings and were all part of his perfect plan for us. There were encouragements from Yemen too; in a letter we received, we learnt that the concrete floor for our new home in Muharraq had been laid. This was wonderful, but we were even more delighted to hear that the man I'd met in the clinic, to whom Ewen had given a gospel, was going on with the Lord.

Life was harder for Adele in Camperdown; because I was attending University most days, and studying at home in the evenings, she was often alone with the children. However, her parents and youngest sister visited often, which helped. When baby Sharon was two months old and Andrew was no longer receiving the attention from his relatives he'd been enjoying, he began to object to Sharon's presence. We don't recall him hitting her or being unkind. Instead, he concentrated on attempting to distract Adele's attention away from Sharon. Even as a two-year-old, he demonstrated a measure of skill in getting his message across. Once, while Dell was feeding Sharon in the lounge room, he found a packet of flour, spread it over the linoleum floor of the kitchen, had fun skating on it, and then walked the flour over the lounge room carpet! At other times he exercised what his father regarded as spectacular athleticism, by getting up first on to the lounge beside Adele and then climbing up onto the back of the lounge, using her shoulder as support and crawling around her back.

Adding to Adele's difficulties was the fact that soon, Sharon's feeds had to be complemented with cow's milk formula. However, unbeknown to us, Sharon had an intolerance to the fat in cow's milk and probably suffered from colic most of the time, which made her unsettled, and would explain, at least partly, why she cried so much[68]. All this made life a real struggle for Adele during those fourteen months in Sydney.

Even though we were living some distance away, we continued attending St Philip's Church of England at Eastwood most Sundays. On 23 May, Rev Stan Skillicorn baptised both children during the morning service, with most members of our families able to be there. We wanted Andrew and Sharon to belong somewhere, and our St Philip's friends were prayerful and supportive.

While we'd been in Yemen, a topic I'd studied in the Bible was baptism by immersion. Having considered the matter carefully, it seemed that living at Camperdown provided a suitable opportunity to arrange it, being some distance from our home church and from anyone who might disapprove. As a baby, I was 'christened' (meaning infant baptism with the sprinkling of water) in a Church of England service, and I knew that some people might be disappointed, upset or even hostile if they heard that I had been baptised a second time. However, baptism by immersion seemed to be a matter of obedience for me. Now however, the Open Brethren chapel at Newtown was nearby. Adele had been brought up in the Bankstown Open

Brethren assembly, and I'd met some of her friends there, including some senior men. Several of them offered their support and gave approval to the elders of the Newtown assembly. The baptism was held during an evening service with a few of our close family members present. We were grateful to those Brethren friends for assisting me in obeying what I felt the Lord had directed me to do.

* * *

As soon as I'd completed the tropical medicine course and been awarded the diploma, we prepared to set out again for Yemen. On our new photo card, we had a picture of Adele and me with Andrew and Sharon, and in large letters: 'JESUS IS LORD'. In the accompanying circular I wrote:

'Naturally we both want Jesus to be Lord of our lives. Muslims don't believe that he is the Son of God, or that he died and rose again. They hold that he was a prophet who was taken up to heaven as Elijah was, and someone who looked like him died on the cross. In Romans 10:9 we read: 'If you confess with your mouth, 'Jesus is Lord', and believe in your heart that God raised him from the dead, you will be saved.' This is the message we take to our Yemeni friends. If asked about protection from danger or disease, provision for various needs, education for the children, the enemy's power over Muslim nations and his grip on their souls—to all such questions we can simply reply: "Jesus is Lord".'

We had to have the necessary vaccinations, but I was troubled about the possible risk of side effects for Sharon if she had a yellow fever injection. The literature recommended that it not be given to children less than twelve months of age, and she was only ten months old. There was no yellow fever in Yemen itself, but there was always the possibility that we might have to evacuate urgently and escape to Ethiopia for instance, where yellow fever was endemic. In Yemen we'd not been able to procure any yellow fever vaccine for Andrew, and sterility and efficacy were also concerning. Fortunately, Sharon was a chubby baby, so in the end, after consulting several medical colleagues, she was given the vaccine. Praise the Lord, she suffered no side effects or reaction.

ON THE WAY

Our departure date was September 25. After an uneventful journey we arrived safely in Sana'a, where we sent a telegram notifying our families that all was well. Once again, we had seen how the Lord himself had carried us 'on eagles' wings.

10

'How shall they hear?' and a Miracle!

1976-1977: Age 33-34

The dust in Sana'a on our arrival back in Yemen was in sharp contrast to the clean air of Sydney. We had heard that the lowlands, on the other hand, had had heavy rains, which would make driving back to Muharraq difficult. We prepared as best we could, with lots of drinking water and other things that would be helpful if we became bogged—and of course, we knew the Lord would be with us.

Adele and I, with the children, left Sana'a by midday and drove on through the afternoon and into the night[69]. Driving through the coastal plain at night was tricky because all the tracks looked alike, and there were no road signs. We often sang together the chorus, 'My Lord knows the way through the wilderness.' In the past we had lost our way many times, especially when it was completely dark, and on this trip, as we were about to cross a fast-flowing stream, we found ourselves feeling anxious that we had taken the wrong track and were in fact heading south. When we stopped and asked directions in a nearby village, two chaps kindly balanced on the bonnet of our Land Rover and guided us back to the best 'road'. At one point we noticed some dim light in the sky and looked to check that what we were seeing was moonlight. Yes, the soft glow preceding the rising moon was faintly silhouetting the mountain range, enabling us to regain our bearings. With the moon on our right as we travelled north, at least we knew we were heading in the correct direction. Whenever our headlights picked out swaying camels plodding resolutely through the darkness, we took the opportunities to check our directions from the fellows perched on top.

Another feature of driving through the coastal plain at night was that we frequently saw ahead of us a kind of bird comfortably settled on the (usually warm) sandy track. Just before we reached it, it would suddenly fly up and away through the glare of our headlights.

It was approaching midnight as we neared Muharraq. We had been driving since midday on the same tank of fuel, unable to buy petrol at Abs because they had sold out.

'We might be able to make it with what we have,' we said, and pushed on, but about a mile from our journey's end, our tank ran dry. Fortunately, we had a spare can of fuel roped to the front of the vehicle and so, leaving the headlights on to discourage hyenas, I filtered the petrol into the tank through one of Adele's handkerchiefs. Only the chirping of the crickets disturbed the stillness. I glanced up at the stars sparkling in the clear sky and saw the Southern Cross easily visible low down in the south. As always it served as a moving reminder of family and friends back in Australia, as well as the message we carried as ambassadors for Christ.

We'd only gone a short distance on our new fuel when we came to a wide expanse of mud which seemed to have no way around it. We decided to follow some previous tyre tracks, but halfway across, the Land Rover suddenly became bogged, and then tilted sideways at a precarious angle. There was nothing for it but to leave the vehicle where it was and to carry on to Muharraq on foot, which was thankfully only about four hundred yards away. After awkwardly clambering out, it was a couple of weary travellers who climbed that last little hill up out of the wadi, carrying only a torch, a few nappies and the two children.

Despite the hour, Mike and Esther happily greeted us, while four-year-old Debbie was thrilled to have Andrew to play with again. Esther provided a meal, linen and other necessities for the night, while Mike's pick-up truck made short work of pulling the Land Rover out of the mud. We had arrived safe and sound once again, praising the Lord for all his goodness.

The old clinic and the new.

Things had moved ahead in Muharraq since we had left, mostly because of Mike's gifts as an engineer and builder[70]. Our new home was nearing completion (when we arrived, it was two flats, with Mike, Esther and Debbie in one half, and ourselves in the other) and the new clinic was marvellous compared to the original stick hut. The nurses had a new home in the process of construction, and a shed built of concrete blocks now housed the original ten-kilowatt generator beside a new five-kilowatt machine. Both were British-made, self-starting, and ran on diesel fuel. There were also three 20,000-gallon tanks to collect rainwater. Only one had the guttering connected to it so far, but that one was more than three-quarters full. We also had flush toilets, and a shared washing machine. The nurses had bought two donkeys which had helped tremendously in their village visiting for the vaccination campaign, as many places were not accessible by vehicle.

Besides all these blessings, there had been remarkable evidence of the

Spirit working in the hearts of some Yemenis, although one local Christian, as previously mentioned, had been in trouble with the authorities for talking about the gospel. There'd been the possibility that he might have lost his life, but he was fined instead, which, we were told, would be tripled if he was caught visiting us. It was quite amazing what the Lord was doing in and through him, and we had practically no part in it at all.

The nurses' new home above one of our three, large, circular, rainwater tanks.

On their outings, the nurses sometimes had excellent opportunities for the gospel. We were all aware that our presence in Yemen was not assured in the long term. Mary (the senior and most experienced missionary amongst us at Muharraq, and the leader of our work there) felt that our legal status in the country was so precarious anyway, simply because we were Christians, that she would rather be thrown out of the country for sharing the Good News with Yemenis than be thrown out without having done anything at all of eternal significance.

Mike felt frustrated about how much work was still to be done to get the water tanks connected and other aspects of the houses completed. He was constantly interrupted by the local people who needed his help in fixing things or welding damaged vehicles and had to decide when to say 'no' to their pleading, so that he could finish the work on the compound.

Our half of the new house is to the right.

'Don't worry about it too much, Mike,' we told him. 'As you know, we might not be allowed to remain here for long anyway.'[71]

* * *

On our arrival in Sana'a after returning from furlough, Sharon had been ill with flu, and now, in the first three weeks in Muharraq she was teething, as well as having diarrhoea, a croupy cough, fever, and swollen glands in the front of her left armpit[72]. Andrew had similar troubles, and he and I also came down with malaria, despite conscientiously taking our anti-malarial tablets[73]. The hot days and disturbed nights attending to the children made settling in difficult. It wasn't made any easier in November, when little Sharon had an insect bite. The verandah where she played still hadn't been fly-screened, and a huge yellow bumblebee was able to fly in. Adele immediately hit it with a shoe, and thought she'd killed it. However, before Sharon could be stopped, she picked it up, and unfortunately the bee still had enough life in it to sting her hand. Screaming in pain, her thumb and hand were soon swollen, and a dusky red colour spread most of the way up her arm. I gave her antihistamine syrup and aspirin, and the following day she was much improved, though her hand and arm were still swollen. This incident placed our flyscreening at the top of the priority list.

Although nasty, that incident was almost insignificant in comparison with what came about in the middle of December. Sharon, now thirteen months old, had suffered with gradually worsening diarrhoea and then vomiting for six weeks. I searched for the cause under the microscope and tried every appropriate remedy available, but all to no avail. In the meantime, she continued to get worse.

Late one night after she'd been vomiting for about five days, I could see she was dehydrated. 'If she vomits once more, we're going to Jibla[74],' I said. When she did vomit again soon after, and her eyes rolled back in her head, I could see that she was dying. Despite the distance and the state of the roads, we set about preparing immediately for the journey. Before we left, at 2.30 in the morning, our nurses were able to skilfully put a fine, plastic naso-gastric tube down into her stomach, via her nostril. This enabled Dell to use a syringe to intermittently give her a solution of water containing sugar and salt, just a few millilitres at a time, as we drove through the night. (To our enormous relief, her vomiting stopped; however, it made no difference to her diarrhoea.)

Seventeen and a half hours later, on 17 December, Adele and I, with the two children, arrived in Taiz. I was too exhausted to drive any further, and some friends in that city from the Swedish Pentecostal Mission gave us the key to an unoccupied flat, intended for Jibla Hospital staff, in which we could stay the night. Before morning, although Sharon had managed to pull her naso-gastric tube out, she'd begun taking her bottle again, alternating milk with the sugar/salt solution. Another two hours' drive that morning brought us to the hospital and, as always, the folk there were warm and welcoming. Due to the shortage of available accommodation, we were only able to stay there a few days, but in that time, they discovered Sharon's intolerance to the fat in cows' milk. To our great relief, she was on her way back to health, and a couple of weeks later she was completely settled on a brand of powdered milk in which the animal fat was replaced by vegetable fat. Praising the Lord for this, we soon set about attempting to desensitise her by adding one drop of full-cream powdered cows' milk to her bottle of modified milk the first day, two drops the next, three drops the third, and so on until she was able to drink undiluted cows' milk without any problem[75].

* * *

Back in Jibla, Dr Young had kindly suggested we stay again in the hospital flat in Taiz for a couple more days while Sharon recovered. While there, we were able to spend some time with Don and Morag McPhail, a Pentecostal couple from Scotland who had had a visit from the author, Jean Darnall, some months before. This woman had been on a private prayer retreat in a monastery at Mt. Sinai, where she had a vision in which she saw a map with Yemen clearly marked. Above the map was a hand holding a sword dripping with blood. She was told that brother would rise against brother, and during that time of bloodshed, the believers would become manifest on the mountains of Yemen; in her vision she could see many little tongues of fire dotted along the mountain ridges. Because Jean didn't know where Yemen was, she went to the monastery library and found out, and then decided to travel directly there so she could pass on the prophecy to any Christians to whom she might be led, eventually meeting up with Don and Morag in the city of Taiz. Never sure if our Team would be allowed to continue working in Yemen due to opposition, we listened to Jean's prophecy with prayerful interest.

All the RSMT members in Yemen planned to meet in early January for our annual conference in Sana'a, but we arrived two weeks early, having driven up from Jibla. Not only were we able to have an unscheduled but much-needed rest, it also meant that we were in Sana'a for Christmas. This allowed us to ring home to Sydney on Christmas Eve; and how good it was to be able to speak to some of our family. Besides that, an English Christian couple in Sana'a had given the Team a huge turkey, some ham, and many other surprises, so it was a wonderfully happy Christmas.

But there was an even more special gift for Adele to come. Our Team Conference had invited a visiting speaker and his wife, Robin and Celia Talbot from England, who had been OMF missionaries in Thailand, but had now established a ministry in Britain called 'Supply Line'. The conference itself was a blessing, but late on the night of January 6, Robin and Celia prayed for Adele and me in a private room with just the four of us present. In that time, Adele was baptised with the Holy Spirit, and received the gift of tongues. She'd been keen for this to happen since reading the book *The Cross and the Switchblade* by David Wilkerson, about six years before; and she knew that I spoke in tongues. After all our trials and having been away from Muharraq for a whole month, we were able to return refreshed and rejoicing.

* * *

This new period in Muhurraq would turn out to be the beginning of two new ventures—one of which, I believed, was the main reason for which God took me to Yemen.

We were back in Muharraq with different people this time. Mike and Esther were on furlough, and Larry and Helen with Bradley (9) and Brian (6) from the USA had replaced them. John and Molly, with Nickie (3) and Suzie (2), also joined us, living in the other half of our house, which was partitioned off. John was a nurse, and an enormous help with the men's medical work. Andrew and Sharon felt fortunate to have Nickie and Suzie to play with. It was good to have these extra people because February was a busy month in the clinic. On some of the three clinic days each week we saw around 220 patients.

It was an important time for the health work, and the beginning of a new scheme for health outreach. In the second half of March, 1977,

Adele, the children and I went to Sana'a for the World Health Organisation conference at which I presented a report concerning our work in Muharraq. The scheme I outlined was one to train primary health workers. This received warm encouragement from the Ministry of Health and WHO representatives. It seemed that I was pioneering this type of training in Yemen, even though we hadn't yet found a suitable man to send for training.

Chatting on a non-clinic day outside the clinic hut.

This time in Sana'a was also the beginning of what would become a new ministry for me. I shared in our Sana'a Sunday evening service something that I believed the Lord had laid on my heart. It was a special burden to reach out to the region around Muharraq with the gospel message. For several weeks I'd felt increasingly burdened concerning the eternal welfare of the people living in the villages and hamlets I could see from Muharraq, dotted along the top of the ridges, on the mountain slopes, and out on the lowlands. However, I had no strategy to tackle the task of reaching them with the Good News. What I did have, however, was a time frame: I had the strong impression that whatever I did, it had to be completed within the next seventy weeks, or by mid-July 1978.

We returned to Muharraq with no certainty about any of it, except the knowledge that the Lord had both the health training plan, and the burden I felt to share the gospel, firmly in his hands.

It was back to work at the clinics, which were becoming busier, with 260 patients between us one day, and about 3,000 each month for two months. One morning in early June, a patient, a man about 35 asked us for some books. Someone had given him a Gospel of John a year ago, and he knew our Yemeni brother well, living high on the mountains behind his valley.

'I want *World Aflame* by Billy Graham,' he told us. When he saw a few other booklets we had, and a New Testament, he decided he wanted those as well.

Knowing that there were two other believers on that mountainside, we felt that the fellow was probably also a believer, so open and friendly.

I wrote home to my parents:

This work into which the Lord has led us is wonderful. We plod along, while wrestling in prayer for people to be saved, and the Lord is working spiritual miracles. We are barely involved at all directly, and that's the way it must be here. We don't go chasing after the believers either (much as we'd love to meet them), because our visiting them could jeopardise their safety. The Lord can care for his children without our interference. There are others who have gospels, but these two or three that we know more personally are the ones over whom we feel the most joy.

Fairly quickly, the WHO-approved health program began as well, with the local 'chemist' taking on our training. Over the course of our discussions, we looked at the possibility of altering the whole community situation, by encouraging improvements in water supply, animal husbandry, agriculture; and by widening the 'streets' in the market and encouraging better ventilation in the houses. We discussed the mechanism of illness, including germs, and the way the white blood cells fight against them and produce fever. We talked about vaccinations, and how they work to give protection; how germs enter the body, and ways to protect ourselves against them; and what to do if someone has a fever.

I was soon able to make the 20.6 kilometre drive all the way up to Maharbisha, the track having recently been widened for vehicles. (The distance may have been short, but it still took an hour and 20 minutes to get there, up a steep mountain road.) I went through the same things with the 'chemists' there, spending about four hours with them, and working from an excellent manual put out by the WHO for training village health workers. Unfortunately, there were no Arabic copies of the manual available, but there were helpful diagrams and sketches in it to show our learners. I dictated the things I wanted the men to learn, and then on each visit gave them an oral 'test' on the previous week's work. Best of all, I had lunch with one of them, and was able to explain the gospel message to him.

The clinic hut, with thatched shelter for men waiting to be treated.

Thursdays were my days to go to Maharbisha and I had a good time whenever I drove up there, teaching and sharing the gospel message with ones and twos. Other tracks up the mountains were similarly widened in the months ahead, one of them going right up to the top of the mountain ridge behind our village, and a couple of others climbing the mountainsides further to the north of us. What a privilege and joy it was to realise that the Lord had seen to it that we were already established, and widely known throughout this previously remote and inaccessible region, before he arranged for it to be opened in this way. Not only were we widely known, but because it was more than three years since we'd begun our regular clinics, people had had time to ascertain that we were trustworthy and dependable, with no hint of corruption or interest in bribery.

We were happy to look after any member of the community, even the most vulnerable. One tragic case was that of a twelve-year old orphan girl who was unwillingly married to a young teenager. In order to make her 'co-operate' with the marriage, her father-in-law tortured her horribly. Finally, in despair, the girl poured kerosene over herself and set it alight. For weeks Anitra and Helen spent two hours every afternoon dressing her terrible burns. Despite her need to go to Jibla Hospital for skin grafting, no-one was willing to pay or arrange for her transport. Finally, despite the cultural, moral and ethical difficulties with the situation, we made the decision to take her ourselves. At 10 p.m. one Wednesday night, after the heat of the day had subsided, Larry and I with the girl, along with her brother and father-in-law, set out in the Land Rover via Taiz for the American Southern Baptist Hospital at Jibla. We had to drive gently and slowly for her sake, but Larry had devised a way to make her journey more comfortable by cleverly suspending her bed in the back of the Land Rover so that it wasn't touching the floor. One small mercy was that while having to wait four hours to cross the flood in Wadi Moor, we managed to snatch a few hours' sleep. After 27 hours on the road, we finally reached Jibla at 1 a.m. on the Friday morning. Larry and I were exhausted, but we had made it[76]. After four hours' sleep, we set out for home, but decided to go through Sana'a, rather than back through Taiz.

On our way to Sana'a, we came across an accident. The British Ambassador and his family, travelling in their beautiful Jaguar with a Yemeni driver at the wheel, had smashed into the back of a covered utility. Fortunately, no-one was hurt. I couldn't help smiling when, in true British fashion, the Ambassador's wife said, 'Well, let's have our picnic here, shall we?' There and then, they spread out the picnic things away from the road and sat down. Larry and I were invited to join them, and I've never seen such a feast at a picnic before! We seemed to have far better appetites than anyone else at the banquet (understandably perhaps), and must have made the hostess feel a good deal happier than might otherwise have been the case, judging by the amount of chicken, ham and other odds and ends she 'forced' us to take care of. Later we were able to give them a lift to Sana'a in our Land Rover for which they were grateful, leaving the Yemeni driver with the Jaguar. We felt that in his mercy the Lord had arranged the circumstances to enable us to meet and help them, and to show them a little of his love and care. Of course, we explained to them that we were members of the Red Sea Mission Team.

Whether we were with the Ambassador, a young, injured girl, or with village leaders, we sought to make the gospel message attractive by the way we lived, praying that the Lord would shine through us so that the fruit of the Holy Spirit would be evident. Various things that were said and done by people from the local community demonstrated to us that our prayers were being answered. For instance, one day a man drove his enormous truck up onto our property and asked me if he could leave it there for a week or two. (See photo on page 173.) I think he was going on the Haj to Mecca in Saudi Arabia. Giving me the keys, he asked if I would start the engine and let it idle for a few minutes every couple of days to keep the battery charged. I gladly agreed and lifted Andrew and Sharon up into the cabin to sit beside me while I performed my duty over the days ahead. It's true that we had a night watchman who was also present most days; and although I think the driver could have left his truck near the government representative's building or the sheikh's home, he came to us. I felt honoured that he entrusted us with such a responsibility, knowing of course, that we were Christians. In ways like this, I believe that the Lord was setting the stage for a time of special outreach.

More and more I found myself looking up at the mountain ridge towering behind us, especially in the evenings. Dotted along the top, and up the mountainside, little lights revealed the location of dozens of hamlets, and I knew that there was ridge after ridge away to the east beyond the one we could see. Out to the west on the coastal plain were many villages. I believe I was the only doctor for possibly 3,000 square kilometres[77]; and we were certainly the only missionaries. This was a huge responsibility medically; I felt that there was a great need to teach and warn the leaders in those areas about several serious communicable diseases and explain to them the procedure to follow in the event of an epidemic. Mostly that would need to be done on foot and would require several treks.

Even more important than the medical responsibility was the spiritual responsibility. There were hundreds of thousands of Yemenis living in that region, and if they didn't hear the gospel message from us, from whom would they hear it? People from the more remote parts of the region had told us that they'd never had a foreigner come their way—not even Egyptians during the civil war in the 1960s. Surely we were the only ones who could share the gospel message with them? Admittedly, there were excellent Christian short-wave radio programmes broadcast in Arabic morning and evening from the Seychelles Islands; but even if people happened to be able to afford a radio, and tuned to the correct frequency at the right time, batteries which had not already been rendered at least partly ineffective by the heat and humidity were hard to come by. And how were they going to get Scriptures? They would be risking getting into serious trouble if they attempted to write and request Scriptures from the Seychelles mailing address because mail entering or leaving the country was sometimes opened and checked in the central post offices.

It was now two years since Len had stayed with us for a few days and gone on walks up into the mountains and out into the lowland areas nearby. Since I continued to feel increasingly burdened for all those around us who were not heading for heaven, I wrote to Sana'a and asked Len if he might be able to come and do some more evangelistic trips. It seemed a perfectly reasonable thing to me; I was snowed under with medical work, and I knew that he enjoyed such outreach, despite it being arduous. I, on the other hand, didn't enjoy mountain climbing. Besides that, such trips would almost certainly have to be done alone since the Team would not be able to spare two missionaries to go together, and it did not seem best to go with a Yemeni. (In order to avoid hindering spiritual discussions, any companion would have to be a Christian, and a Yemeni believer would be risking his life if he participated in such outreach.) To put it frankly, I was nervous about going on evangelistic trips because I was afraid of being murdered! I continued to pray that Len would come and was disappointed when he wrote back to say that unfortunately he was not able to, due to the pressure of other commitments.

It was now nineteen weeks since, in March, I'd felt that the Lord was laying it on my heart to see that our region was reached with the gospel before seventy weeks had passed. More than a quarter of those weeks had already ticked by, and I was no wiser about what to do.

* * *

The Team gathered us all together twice each year for spiritual refreshment and to discuss Mission business. Having worked through the summer heat on the Arabian lowlands[78], we were all looking forward to our annual holidays on the cooler mountains, following which we would attend the September conference.

The heat had been made worse by a time of water shortage. The rainwater we'd been able to collect earlier in the year almost lasted to the August rainy season, but with four households to supply, it couldn't quite stretch the distance. Then Larry and Helen, and John and Molly, had to go to Sana'a and Hajjah respectively, so that when we did run out, as the only man on the station, I was responsible for getting more water. The stream two miles from Muharraq was polluted, so we decided to fetch the water from a spring in another spot. Over the next couple of weeks, I drove there nine times to fill up the tank in the back of the Land Rover, with each round trip measuring sixteen kilometres over rough tracks.

Early in August, we were well and truly ready for a break. Having closed

ON THE WAY

the clinic, on Tuesday August 2, Adele and I with Andrew, Sharon and two British nursing sisters, Anitra and Helen, all set out in the Land Rover for Sana'a.

The ladies' fridge that needed repairs went on the roof rack, along with four foam mattresses, two empty gas cylinders, Andrew's dinky car and tractor, a five-gallon tank of petrol, and the spare tyre, all covered over with a tarpaulin and canvas canopy, with three tent poles lashed on. The inside was also chock-a-block with the six of us and our luggage, plus sleeping bags, and plenty of drinking water and food in preparation for any possible stops beside flooded wadis. Our departure had been delayed by my having been requested to remove the head of one of the generators so we could take it to Sana'a for servicing. This had to be done last thing before we left and proved to be an interesting exercise. First, I had to decide exactly what the head was, and then I had to remove it!

The journey, though rough, passed without incident for the four hours until we reached Wadi Moor. We were relieved to find that although it was in flood, cars were managing to get across. Immediately I set to work removing the fan belt and covering all the electrical wiring with grease and plastic sheeting, secured by string. Then, after a word of prayer together, I engaged low ratio and four-wheel drive, and we made our way across, driving partly down current so that the flow assisted us over. On the other side, the plastic and string had to be removed, and the fan belt replaced.

Whenever we had to make a crossing like this, I constantly reminded myself that if your engine stopped in mid-stream, you'd 'had it'—for two reasons. Firstly, with no headway, the current could easily tip the car right over—and we passed two overturned cars as we crossed. Secondly, with the engine stopped, water could flow up the exhaust pipe and into the engine. Another car there had been pulled out of the water, and it was from these men that I borrowed a wrench needed to tighten the fan belt. (You lie under the vehicle to do this.) Water had flowed along their exhaust pipe, and they were waiting for a mechanic to come all the way from Sana'a to pull the entire engine apart, clean and dry it, and put it together again. They were going to be sitting there for a few days and so would have plenty of time to think over our brief chat together and read the couple of Arabic Gospels and a copy of *Way of Salvation* that I left with them.

Sometime after nightfall as we continued heading south, a rainstorm crossed our way. Inside the Land Rover was nice and dry, but suddenly we heard and felt the thump-thump-thump of a flat tyre[79]. With the weight of our load and the position of our car on the rough road, the jack was unable to lift the wheel sufficiently. However, the driver of a small Toyota Landcruiser stopped and assisted us with his jack. Before the job was completed (not easy in the dark) we were both drenched with rain. (This friendship on the roads was a feature of Yemeni men, and we were grateful for their kindness. We in our turn shared our grease, tools and petrol.) Fortunately, in the car I had a dry shirt and footah (Yemeni skirt which men wear). The flip-flops on my feet didn't need changing.

The rain soon stopped, but shortly afterwards we came to another flooded wadi. Unfortunately, we were still about ten miles north of the sealed Hodeidah to Sana'a road. In the reflection of the headlights from the opposite bank, we could see the water swirling along through the night and realised that it was impossible to cross. A large gathering of assorted cars and trucks were spread out along either side of the wadi, and the occupants were settling down for the night. Despite our disappointment, there was nothing for it but to drive off to one side a little way, unpack the mattresses, sleeping bags and other necessities, and try to get some sleep on the ground beside the car. From previous experience we had learned to be prepared; we even had the canvas canopy with poles to set up as protection from the sun if needed. It was 11 p.m. before Sharon finally settled, and then all was quiet, apart from the roaring torrent nearby.

At first light we were up and about again, eating, repacking and preparing the engine for the fresh dunking. An hour later, to our relief, we joined the sealed main road, ready for the remaining six hours or so driving up the winding mountain road to Sana'a. Our flagging spirits were revived when we stopped to have the puncture repaired at a tiny little tyre place with a nearby roadside 'restaurant', where we had a delicious Yemeni breakfast of fizzy drinks, followed by scrambled eggs with tomatoes, onions and spices mixed in, scooped into the mouth on pieces of bread roll. We also enjoyed sweet, white tea, always served in glass tumblers.

While the others were finishing their meal, I walked along and found that the job was not finished on the spare wheel. The repair place was a typical little establishment with discarded tyres lying everywhere, old bits of paper and flattened cigarette boxes in the mud, and everything disorderly. I sat down on an old, large tractor tyre, and leant back wearily against the wall, watching the two boys put our tyre back on the wheel. In a minute or two their father arrived and sat down. As is frequently the case, he was surprised and pleased to see a European in Yemeni dress and was especially pleased when he heard me doing my best to speak Arabic.

'Where have you come from?' he enquired.

'Muharraq, below Maharbisha.'

There was a pause. 'What work do you do?' he asked.

'I have two jobs,' I said. 'The first is that I'm a doctor. We have a clinic at Muharraq.' I left another pause.

'And what's your other job?' he asked.

'I'm an ambassador.'

'Oh. For what country?'

'I'm a Christian,' I said. 'I'm an ambassador for Christ.'[80]

After the night's events and all the driving, I was simply too tired to proceed building on this theme any further, but after a minute or two of silence he said straight out: 'Do you have any books?'

'Yes,' I said. I knew he meant Arabic Gospels, so I went to the car and got a Luke's Gospel, a John's Gospel, and a *Way of Salvation*, and gave them to him. He was clearly delighted and couldn't do enough for me in return. He even wanted to get up on the roof rack and rope down the spare wheel himself, but I talked him out of it. For one thing, he had good clean clothes on. Also, I had to insist on his taking the money for the job since he didn't want to charge me. It seemed to me that he'd been hoping for a long time to somehow find and read a gospel, and now he had his own copies! Although it had been inconvenient to have a puncture, we believed that the Lord had prepared that man's heart and had led us to him in this way.

When we finally reached Sana'a, we were able to stay in a lovely home that belonged to a friend, furnished and beautifully equipped, for the three days before we were due to set off to Yareem for our holiday. Even better, being on our own, we didn't have to keep the children quiet. We flopped into bed that first night and woke wonderfully refreshed the next morning to find that one of the verses in *Daily Light* for that day was: 'We went through fire and through water: but thou broughtest us out into a wealthy place.'

In Yareem we had a magnificent holiday staying in one of the comfortable little houses built for the German/British road-building company. The camp had a tennis court as well as a swimming pool. It was a refreshing break. Once again, we felt how good the Lord was—as always!

After our holiday at Yareem, we returned to Sana'a for the Team's twice-yearly conference, where one of the main matters to deal with was working out how we could fit in to the Yemen government's five-year health plan for the nation. I continued to feel burdened about the hundreds of thousands of people in the Lower Hajjah region. I'd agonised about their need to hear the gospel message and wondered how it might be possible for any who desired Scriptures to obtain them. This burden was steadily increasing with the deadline I believed the Lord had given me for the task to be accomplished, now only ten months away.

However, I had something else to think about for the moment. While in Sana'a, I had swabs taken from both of my ears, to be examined in a laboratory. For months, I had been having trouble with some otitis externa. This infection, while almost painless, was a nuisance, and interfered somewhat with my hearing. The discharge from the ears had persisted for many weeks, and no treatment I'd tried had made any difference. The laboratory result showed that a bacterium called pseudomonas was the cause of the infection. Unfortunately for me, it was resistant to all antibiotics except Colistin. Thankfully, this was available in Sana'a and John, the other doctor with our Team, began at once to irrigate my ears with a Colistin solution. Perhaps more disquieting was that he could see that my right ear drum was perforated. The infection had spread more deeply, and now involved the middle ear as well.

'If it spreads more deeply still, there's a real possibility of meningitis,' he told me. 'You might have to consider flying to Nairobi in Kenya for treatment by an ear, nose and throat specialist.'

The problem, though it had seemed mild, now clearly needed to be tackled urgently. If I went back to work in the clinic at Muharraq, there would be no doctor anywhere near to treat the infection, which would be aggravated by the heat and humidity of the lowlands. (The air in the mountains was much cooler and drier.) It was decided that as a family we should return to the house at Yareem for a further two weeks where John could give me intramuscular injections of Colistin, as well as continuing with the irrigations.

Providentially, those weeks away from the constant pressure and busyness of the work in Muharraq provided me with unhurried time for thinking and prayer about my ongoing burden for the people of the region. I'd already begun to consider going on some hiking trips, but my thinking was vague; and the two serious obstacles—the effort of mountain climbing, and my fear of being murdered[81]—remained. If I was killed, what would such a calamity mean for Adele and the two little children? Besides, there was still the medical work which needed all the staff possible.

Now, however, as I prayed, a plan began to gradually crystallise in my thinking. With a map of Lower Hajjah before me, I worked out that if I was able to go on eight trips in the mountains and four in the lowlands, I could pass through the entire region for which I felt we were responsible. I knew that it was the Lord's purpose for the people there to hear the message about Jesus, and how he had opened the way into heaven for anyone who will come to him and believe this good news. I could also see that it was probable that he'd placed me in Muharraq so that he could reach them through me. He would be preparing certain hearts to willingly receive the good news, and I knew that he could easily guide my steps so that those men's paths and mine would cross, if only I would trust him and go. Then, having passed on the gospel message to those few individuals (even if only during a brief encounter), the Lord could then work through them to reach others in their localities, whether I myself ever went that way again or not.

I already knew that the mountain trips would have to be undertaken largely on foot and would usually require spending one or more nights on the way; but the lowland ones could be done in the Land Rover and would probably only need single-day journeys. In each area there were one or more tribal chiefs (sheikhs) who lived there permanently, as well as a government representative (armal) who was appointed to that district for perhaps two years before being sent somewhere else. My plan would be to talk with these leaders about medical matters, particularly what we'd all have to do if an epidemic broke out. I would also carry some basic medicines with me, as inevitably on every trip I'd meet sick people needing treatment. Because the sheikhs resided there permanently, if I had to stay overnight anywhere, I would aim to stay with them rather than with the armal. The sheikhs were able to read, and also had a home big enough to provide somewhere for a guest to sleep. More importantly, however, if *they* became interested in the gospel, it would be less of a risk for anyone else in their district (and therefore under their authority) to also show interest.

As I could see from the map, most of the hiking trips would be reasonably close to Muharraq; but one of them would take me much further north and would require some days to complete. Since our regular clinics were held on Mondays, Wednesdays and Saturdays, it would be possible to undertake most of the journeys by leaving late Wednesday afternoon if necessary, and I'd not have to be back until Friday evening, thus still being present for the clinics. The longer journey would take at least a week, as far as I could judge, and I'd therefore have to miss some clinics. I considered our staffing and personnel situation for a moment. John and Molly were now back at Muharraq, so if I could get back there before they were due to leave for furlough, I'd have time to tackle that long trip while he was still there to run the men's clinics. Afterwards I'd be able to fit in all the other, shorter, trips around the regular clinic routine.

Working out all these details and becoming more and more certain that this was the Lord's plan for me, I gradually found that the considerable effort required for mountain climbing became inconsequential in my thinking. Also, amazingly, the Lord took away my fear of being murdered. I recalled reading in various biographies how he'd protected missionaries in other countries, and I became convinced that he could lead and protect me in a similar manner. Almost five years before, I'd had the music from the hymn 'For My sake and the Gospel's, go' played at the conclusion of our wedding service. Here was a chance to continue to obey that command, and I was now eager to begin without delay. Many people were praying for us, and this was the kind of ministry for which we'd come to Yemen.

There was still one major obstacle preventing my returning to Muharraq and getting under way with this outreach—my ear infections. Of course, there had been much earnest prayer over this period for the Lord to heal me. However, we were shocked to discover that after two weeks of intensive treatment, the follow-up lab swabs revealed the bacterium had now become resistant to *all* available antibiotics, even Colistin. The situation was serious. We could only cast ourselves upon the mercy of God while seeking his guidance.

On Wednesday evening, October 19, one of our Team members, Anita, a Swedish nursing sister who was stationed nearby in Yareem, came to visit us in the little house we were staying in at the road camp. As we chatted together, she mentioned that the Holy Spirit had given her the gift of healing.

'Would you like me to pray about your ear infections?' she asked. We were delighted, and readily agreed. While I sat on a chair, she and Adele stood on either side, placed their hands on my head and shoulders, and prayed for my healing. I didn't feel any different; but from then on, whenever the thought of my infections came to mind, I said, 'Thank you Lord, that you are healing me now.'[82]

The morning after Anita's visit, the usual discharge which had come from my ears during the night was obvious on my pillowcase, but we continued to trust the Lord, and to remind ourselves of his goodness and promises. The morning after that, however, my pillowcase was perfectly clean.

'Your ears are virtually clear,' said the missionary doctor who came to check me over that day. 'Only a small amount of dried matter remains. And the perforation in the eardrum has healed over.'

This was obviously a miracle! As I considered what had happened, I realised that the Lord could see that I didn't *need* to be ill any longer. He'd either planned or permitted my ear infections so that I'd have the necessary time to pray and work out the details of the various trips which would enable me to pass through each part of the territory for which I felt burdened. In that time, he also dealt with my aversion to mountain climbing, as well as my fear of possibly being killed. Over the years, Adele and I have seen instances where it was obvious that the Lord had used sickness to accomplish some purpose. None, however, was clearer than this example of my ear infections, which persisted for four months but which were then healed miraculously *when I didn't need to be sick anymore*. That illness had now accomplished its purpose. To witness a miracle was amazing, but it was truly awesome to experience one myself!

* * *

On Monday, October 24, since I was now healed, we moved to Sana'a as the first step towards returning to Muharraq. I shared my vision for the twelve treks with Peter, and he arranged for an official letter of introduction in Arabic to be prepared for me by the Ministry of Health. It explained that I was the doctor based at Muharraq, and that I wished to discuss medical matters with the various local authorities. It also requested that they assist me in any way necessary. I made several photocopies of that letter and planned to carry two or three with me on each of the journeys. Looking back, I believe that it may well have been a key factor in securing my safe passage, since it gave me government authority to be visiting those different localities. I was fortunate to get it too. Just two weeks before this, on October 11, the President of Yemen had been assassinated. Considerable turmoil in government circles ensued, and I can't help wondering if such a letter would have been so forthcoming if it hadn't been for the enormous distraction of the political events which were engrossing everyone's attention, and which resulted in a chaotic situation in government offices. Be that as it may, we can always rest assured that the Lord is in ultimate control of everything that happens.

The day after we arrived in Sana'a, Adele developed a pain in the right side of her lower abdomen. One of the doctors from the American Southern Baptist Hospital in Jibla happened to be visiting Sana'a at the time, and I asked him to see Adele. He felt that although she was not nauseated or feverish, she probably had acute appendicitis, and I agreed with him. How grateful we were that we hadn't already returned to Muharraq, which was so far from Jibla, the only hospital in the whole country to which I felt confident taking her. Also, the roads were so rough in the lowlands that it would have been a slow and painful journey for someone with appendicitis, with the added risk that it could burst at any moment, causing a major emergency. There was nothing for it but to go back the way we'd come the day before, travelling south through Yareem, and then on to Jibla.

We spent four nights at Jibla Hospital under the care of an excellent, experienced American surgeon in his sixties, a kind, gentle and gracious man. He didn't think Adele had appendicitis, but a temporary gynaecological condition. Within a day or two, all her pain and tenderness had completely cleared, and we then headed back to the road camp for another ten days, waiting to arrange to return to Muharraq[83]. As it happened, the other doctor with our Team in Yemen, John, and his wife Cilla, had not yet visited Muharraq, and they were keen to see it. So, on November 10, at 4.30 a.m. Adele and I with our two children together with John, Cilla and their three-and-a-half year old son Richard, set out for Muharraq[84], travelling in the Yareem clinic Land Rover. Fourteen hours later we arrived safely—just after dark. The next day, November 11, was Sharon's second birthday, and Dell did the seemingly impossible by putting on a birthday party at morning tea time, with a packet cake mix her mother had sent, as well as paper streamers and balloons. The seven children present thought it was a great success. John, Cilla and Richard had to leave after lunch but before their departure, John looked in my ears, and confirmed that they were *completely* healed, with both ear drums looking perfectly normal.

Because of the delays, there were now less than three weeks before John and Molly were due to leave for furlough. It was imperative that I set out on that first trek as soon as possible. Since it would take at least a week, I had to complete it while they were still at Muharraq so that the men's clinics would continue without interruption. Peter may already have explained my plan to them, but I set it all out before them myself, anyway. Considering that I'd only just returned after having been away from the medical work for months, it must have required all the grace which the Lord could supply for them to consent to my going. I sensed that they weren't entirely in agreement (which was understandable), and they were probably concerned for my safety. But I was grateful that they *did* agree, because now the path had finally been cleared for me to go.

11

The Eight Mountain Treks

1977-1978: Age 34

I regard these twelve treks as the highlight of my missionary endeavours. The Lord had placed in my heart the urgent desire to reach the people of the region, and I believed that he would lead me to the ones he had prepared. I simply was to be his obedient servant, messenger and ambassador to explain the *Way of Salvation*, and to leave with them, if possible, the written Word.

As I prepared what I would take along on the first trek, without my asking for it, Anitra lent me her rucksack which was suitable, having several individually zippered pockets. Apart from clothing and other necessities, such as a metal water bottle and water-purification tablets, I also carried one or two small tins of mackerel flakes and a tin-opener. If I needed to use a water-purification tablet, I'd simply drop one into my one-litre bottle which I'd filled with the suspect water. The tablet would quietly fizz away, and then after thirty minutes the water was safe to drink[85]. I took medication for people I'd meet, the letter of introduction from the Ministry of Health in Sana'a, a large wall poster showing clearly what smallpox looks like compared to chickenpox, and most importantly of course, some Scriptures and other Christian literature in Arabic[86].

Considering that the location was close to the geographical heart of

Islam and thus spiritually deep in enemy territory, every piece of Christian literature which I was enabled to leave in Yemeni hands (a dangerous undertaking) was of the utmost value. Remembering that Jesus is the living Word or expression of God, and that the Bible is the written Word of God, I felt that in a real sense I was leaving something of the Lord Jesus with each of those people. With his blessing, each piece of literature was sufficient for anyone to gain the understanding to be saved; and more than that—even for tiny churches to emerge.

I took with me Arabic New Testaments in the hope that I'd meet men whose hearts the Lord had prepared, and who wanted more than just a gospel. I also prepared several packs of seven items, including two different Gospels, several Scripture Gift Mission publications such as *The Sermon on the Mount*, the *Way of Salvation*, and *Parables*, and an information leaflet describing how and when to listen to the Christian Arabic short-wave radio programmes transmitted by the Far East Broadcasting Association (FEBA) from the Seychelles Islands in the Indian Ocean[87]. I carried Gospel Recordings cassettes, as well as spare batteries in case a cassette player in a village or hamlet had flat batteries; and I began the habit of keeping a John's Gospel, a *Way of Salvation* and a Seychelles leaflet in the pocket of the short-sleeved, open-neck shirt that I wore, ready to be quietly pulled out at a moment's notice. Because it was so hot and humid, the pocket of my shirt was often wet with perspiration, so I kept them in a small plastic bag to keep them dry.

I made a special point of having a time of earnest, private prayer a day or two before each journey, asking the Lord to lead me to the men whose hearts he'd been preparing, as well as asking for deliverance from danger, sickness, accidents or Satanic attacks; and also asking for protection for Dell, the children, and the others at Muharraq.

* * *

The first trek ended up being a twelve-day journey, and the *Daily Light* readings for that first day, Monday, November 14, 1977, were appropriate and helpful. 'Be strong and of a good courage, fear not, nor be afraid of them: for the Lord thy God, he it is that doth go with thee; he will not fail thee, nor forsake thee'. I was encouraged by this and the other verses, not only for myself, but also for Dell and the children. One of the other verses read: 'In the fear of the Lord is strong confidence: and his children shall have a place of refuge.'

At a quarter past eight in the morning, Larry and Helen, with Brad, Brian and myself, set out in the Land Rover on the rough track which ran north from Muharraq. Four hours later, we reached the point I was aiming for; and after a word of prayer together and farewells, the others left to drive back while I began the climb on foot up the steep mountainside towards the government building at the top. Two hours later I arrived at the sheikh's house on the highest point of the ridge, at Wash-ha. The sheikh wasn't home, but I drank tea and talked for an hour and a quarter with the two men there. I explained that the medical reason for visiting the area was chiefly to discuss with the various authorities the course of action to take should cholera or smallpox break out in their region. They knew about the recent cholera outbreaks in Jordan and Syria, and an outbreak of smallpox reported in Somalia, and were aware that the risk was real, especially since the Yemeni pilgrims who'd travelled to Mecca for the Haj, in contact with people from these countries, would begin returning in another couple of weeks. They were genuinely grateful that I should visit them, and I was able to leave a John's Gospel with both of them.

It was half an hour's walk along the top of the ridge to reach the government building. The armal, or government representative based there was known to Peter[88], but wasn't present when I visited. I explained to the harkim, or legal advisor, my medical reason for visiting. Without my asking, he gave me a twenty rial note[89].

'I have to explain something,' I told him[90]. 'Although I have this letter from the Ministry of Health in Sana'a, I do not represent them. I have come at my own expense. This is because I feel some responsibility for the region near Muharraq. I don't want a single person to die if it can be prevented. And I think it can be prevented if we talk over any possible epidemic before it comes. I do not expect this money from you,' I told him, holding the 20 rials, 'but I am happy to accept it.'

I had the evening meal and spent the night in the home of the medical assistant[91], who was the only health worker in the area, and the only one I met on the entire trip, though there were apparently one or two in different places whom I missed meeting up with. When I left his home next morning, he took a gospel; and his children were delighted that I gave him several pamphlets for them, with gospel stories and colourful pictures.

I was farewelled from the village by the government official's son who came running after me with a gift of forty rials, 'for the road'! Fairly soon, I passed through a village where I sat down to have a brief rest. A conversation about the Lord soon struck up with a couple of men with whom I was able to leave a John's Gospel. From there the path took me right down the mountain and into a dry riverbed along which I plodded, at one point startled to see a brown snake scuttling across the sand in front of me.

This was the vicinity in which I hoped to meet a man that Len had told me about. They had met several years before when he'd passed this way and Len had given him a gospel. On the return journey, he had wanted Len to stay and teach him more, but it hadn't been possible, nor did Len have any other literature for him. I had brought a New Testament with large print especially for this man, should I meet him. I was feeling hot, tired and footsore when I noticed a man in the distance, running across the fields to meet me. It was just as Len had described what happened when he'd met this friendly fellow. We'll call him Ali; he introduced himself, was delighted when I passed on Len's greetings to him, and then led me across the fields to his home. When I showed him the New Testament I had brought for him, he was pleased with it indeed. He then went and gathered several other men from the little hamlet. They also remembered Len's visit, and all wanted literature, so I distributed various things, including colourful pamphlets to the children. Ali and his friends wanted to hear the cassettes too, but the only machine in the area was broken.

I wanted to keep going after lunch, but my feet were blistered from the climb down the mountain that morning. A solution was to hire a donkey to carry my pack for a while, which would give me some relief, as I walked in flip-flops and not my heavy boots. A woman who lived nearby was happy to give me her donkey for a period, for a fee of sixty rials—the exact sum of the two gifts I'd been given where I'd spent the previous night!

Ali accompanied me and we walked for several hours, following a shallow arc to the south, skirting right around the coastal side of the mountain. We passed many villages, but at one of them Ali stopped to chat to some men he knew. I went on ahead, but he called me back.

'They want books—big ones!' he said. I realised that this meant New Testaments[92].

I was delighted to hear that this request had come as a result of Len 'sowing' the gospel those few years before. Two sheikhs in the group took New Testaments, and one of them took my only remaining New Testament for his son. I also gave other literature to the other men who'd listened in.

We stopped in a little village for the night and chatted with the men during the evening. Although one chap was interested in the Good News, took a John's Gospel and started reading it straight away, generally this village was antagonistic. Ali saw that they had a cassette player, and suggested I play one of my tapes. I put it on, but it was not well-received.

We left that village at 6 a.m. the next day and after walking for about an hour, arrived at the road. I shaved in a nearby house, and then we all enjoyed breakfast together, squatting on the floor around the pile of fresh, flat Yemeni bread, pieces of which we broke off and dipped into a bowl of hot, melted butter. After saying goodbye to Ali, I was given a short lift in a car, free of charge, to a point where I had to get out and walk again, as the driver was going no further.

I waited at the bottom of the mountain for four hours because a car was supposed to be going from there to a large village about halfway to the town I was aiming for, close to the districts I wanted to visit. The wait initially seemed difficult, but it became worthwhile because after a long chat, I was able to leave a gospel with a fellow. Initially suspicious, he gradually became friendly, and even got me some lunch. At about 3 p.m., the vehicle I was waiting for still hadn't turned up, and it seemed to me that he and his friends hoped that I'd soon move on, so I started walking along the road. This was not the direction I wanted to go but I felt it safer to walk towards an area with which I was familiar rather than risk being caught by nightfall all alone in a barren, inhospitable region of the country.

After walking a mile or so, two cars came along, one of them driven by my friend Sheikh Yousif, from a village on the road back to Muharraq. He was on his way home after seeing to some business in the mountains and gave me a free lift to the next town, Arhem, where I got out. It was a rough journey, sitting in the back of his covered Toyota utility, and hanging on for dear life to the metal framework as we jolted over the rain-eroded track. However, I didn't mind at all because soon after I had joined them, he had said, 'I'd like some books.'

'Oh, who for?'

'Some friends of mine in the mountains; and I want a big one![93]'

As I left him in Arhem, I thanked him sincerely for the lift, and apologised that I didn't have any big books with me. (I didn't tell him that I'd given them all away!) However, I gave him a pack of seven, and six separate gospels for his friends.

With night falling, I bought food for my evening meal in a small shop, and then slept in a little 'hotel', which was simply a large, single room with beds, made by criss-crossing thin rope tightly between the four sides of a wooden bed frame, on four wooden legs. I had an uncomfortable night.

For the next leg of the journey, I joined another fellow in sharing a taxi heading for Haradth. After several hours' drive, we arrived, but I was in for a shock. As we reached the checkpoint, the policeman told me to get out.

'Let me see what's in your pack,' he told me.

I was nonplussed because I had never been asked to open my bag like that before. My main concern was that he might find the books, which might have made things more than a little awkward. It was only later that I realised that he may have thought that, as a Westerner, I might have been carrying whisky or something similar, which he would have confiscated. However, as I was unroping my bag from the back of the Toyota, I talked fast (and prayed even faster), explaining who I was, and the medical reason for my journey. Before long, we were sitting on the ground together beside the road, discussing his health. In the end, he didn't look in my bag, and afterwards I had lunch with the chief of police, a nice fellow who'd just bought a television set which received good reception from across the border in Saudi Arabia. He had it running on a twelve-volt car battery and wanted to know the meaning of the English words beside the various knobs.

I spent the night in another 'hotel', which was much the same as the one I'd stayed in the night before, except that there were no mattresses here. They also had television! I managed to wash both myself and my clothes for the first time in three days and put two of the beds together end to end to stretch out a little. I did sleep, despite the TV noise, but again it was another uncomfortable night. I was reminded of Isaiah 28:20a which says, 'The bed is too short to stretch out on.' In the morning, the flies were incredible; all over everything, including me and my breakfast of Yemeni bread, beans in brown sauce, and sweet black tea.

I tried again to arrange a ride in a taxi but had to settle for the daunting prospect of a ride on the back seat of a motorcycle, which also turned out to be expensive, at 200 rials, and long. We spent five hours heading northeast, over rough tracks. Not only was it tiring, but the driver was quite unpleasant. Admittedly, it was difficult for him because I was so heavy. My pack was also strapped on the back, making it hard for him to control the bike. We fell off at one point, grazing our legs, and it took soothing apologies to induce him to complete the journey, finally reaching our destination shortly after 3 p.m. The sheikh I visited here was friendly and helpful, and plied me with ice-cold Pepsi Cola. We talked about smallpox and other medical issues and had a meal of fish and rice. He then gave me a lift in his car to his home where we later had the evening meal and I spent the night.

There didn't seem to be an appropriate opportunity to speak about spiritual things during this visit, but since I anticipated returning that way after completing my planned circuit over the adjacent mountains, I hoped and prayed that I might be able to speak of the Lord with them then; and God willing, to also leave some scripture portions.

After a terrible night in sweltering heat, and being constantly attacked by vicious mosquitoes, I continued my journey after breakfast in the sheikh's car with his driver—whose name was Carburettor—at the wheel. However, after driving for only a couple of minutes we had a puncture. As he had no spare wheel, I set off alone on foot heading north. An hour and a half took me to the foot of the mountains, where I climbed for five hours to the top of the ridge, arriving in a village at about 4 p.m. Hot and weary, I decided not to press on any further, but stay overnight in the house of the local sheikh.

After a better night's sleep, I left a John's Gospel with the sheikh before setting out to climb to the top of the mountain. I managed to reach the home of the sheikh for that district in time for lunch. It was the Muslim Eid feast, but they invited me to stay. I felt in need of the meal and realised that the Lord had made that sheep for me to enjoy. One person was clearly not happy about a Christian eating the feast with them, and said so, but the sheikh answered him calmly, and again signalled to me to join them as they squatted around the dishes of food on the large floor mat.

It was then that something happened which many missionaries to the Muslim world dread[94]. As a sign of respect and honour, the sheikh handed me one of the sheep's eyes. For whatever reason, I was already feeling a little nauseated that day, and the thought of trying to swallow that sheep's eye was not helping. And yet, I could hardly refuse. I desperately didn't want to offend the sheikh, particularly after he'd honoured me in front of the other men (at least one of whom was opposed to my even eating with them) but vomiting at their Eid feast would be far worse. I took the eye politely and put it on my plate with the other food, and simply continued eating, urgently crying out in my heart to the Lord for wisdom. When I felt that no-one was noticing, I reached out my hand for some more food from the main meat dish, and surreptitiously slipped the eye under some of the meat and left it there[95]. This had been a distraction, but I was glad that I was still enabled to leave a John's Gospel with that sheikh, after a brief chat about the Lord Jesus. He was a nice man and a kind host, and I prayed earnestly that if he did discover that I hadn't eaten the sheep's eye, he would somehow understand; and it wouldn't prevent him from reading the gospel and hopefully being saved.

I was a week into my trek by this time. I'd heard that the government representative based near the area I was in was opposed to the gospel. Apparently, he and an English woman studying anthropological aspects of Yemen, were both visiting the next town. I prayed that I wouldn't meet either of them and was grateful that my prayer was answered. From the village where I stayed overnight, I was accompanied on my walk by a man who happily accepted a gospel after the chat we had as we walked along together.

The next place was a real little town, and after looking through it for a short while, I set off down the steep hill to the sheikh's house. I had a good chat with them[96], and was able to leave a gospel; but left hurriedly as I feared they might hand it back. I set off north again towards the government centre, reaching it about three hours later, but had lunch with the sheikh. I then visited the armal's son, the only government representative to be found, though I left as soon as I could. The men present were all lolling on mattresses on the floor, chewing gart[97] and watching television. Setting off to the north, I could only trust that I would reach a village where I could stay before night closed in. I ended up walking half by moonlight and half by the light of the fading sunset when I finally saw a little village, a good way off the track. I was loudly greeted by angry dogs, and since the men were all in the mosque for the sunset prayers, it was awkward for a little while. But they soon emerged and invited me into a home where we had the evening meal, and then I settled down for the night.

I thought of my family particularly the next day, which was Andrew's birthday. I was seeking to trust the Lord constantly to keep Dell and the children safe and healthy during my absence. Having slept well, I was delighted to be given barbecued steak on flat Yemeni bread for breakfast. After setting out once again, I walked for an hour and a half to where cars leave for Sa'ada, away to the east. After some difficulty, I eventually got a lift in a gart car for twenty rials and had a good chat with the driver and his friend, who both took John's Gospels. At the point where I had to leave them though, I was horrified to see that it was a desolate gorge. In fact, it looked particularly suited to Bedouin, the often hostile, wandering desert

Arabs. The driver refused outright to take me along the side gorge which I had to follow, and so, with vivid thoughts of Len's frightening experience of being accosted by Bedouin, I set out as quickly as I could, praying fervently for the Lord's protecting hand. I had only gone a few hundred yards, when two cars came along in opposite directions. The driver of one was going to collect a load of river sand before driving back up to the heavily populated area I was heading for. After helping him fill the back of his Toyota utility, I was delighted that he gave me a free lift to where I was going. We'd begun heading south now. It was cold and misty up there, the valley a mass of tiny villages dotted about. I was glad of my hat to keep my head warm. The cold I had caught the day before was now going down into my chest, and I planned to get to bed as soon as possible, grateful to be staying in the home of the chap who'd kindly driven me up out of the wadi. I had an excellent chat with his brother that evening and was so glad that he took a gospel. After I'd enjoyed a good sleep, the driver also took a gospel in the morning.

I then visited the armal (government representative) who pointed out the way I needed to walk. The dusty road south went down a steep hill, and a chap walking in the same direction soon caught up with me. We continued together at a good pace, and I felt that the Lord had sent him along to keep me moving quickly. After our discourse on the road, he wanted to take a gospel. He couldn't read, but someone in his village could. Before he turned off to go along a different track, he told me that a man who lived up on the mountain range to the left of us had a gospel, as well as parts of the Old Testament. There was also a sheikh with similar books. 'He uses them to cast out evil spirits,' my companion told me.

No cars came along so I walked for a couple of hours until I reached the beginning of a steep climb I would have to make to continue on my way. Just at that moment, a car going the same way as I was, caught up with me.

'Would you like a lift?' they offered and took me right to the top. I was grateful to the Lord for his perfect timing.

After looking through the Wednesday market village on the ridge, I left at mid-morning to begin the long walk down the western side of the mountains. The first quarter of the descent was misty and cool, with the path running between beautiful ferns and beside moss-covered rock faces. Native pine trees grew there, the first I'd seen anywhere in Yemen[98]. The tops of the ridges were high above sea level, and it was obvious that a lot of rain fell on the upper slopes of that western side of the mountain range. The smell of the damp earth, together with the wildflowers and small birds, made this an extremely enjoyable part of the trek. Some men were walking a little ahead of me, and once again I felt that they were helping me to keep going at a good pace. I had a midday meal with a couple of fellows who were working in a field. As I was approaching, I saw a woman bringing the food out to them; they generously shared it with me, demonstrating typical Arab hospitality. One was interested in what I had to say, and happily took a gospel. When I returned half an hour later after attending to a patient, I saw that he'd stopped work, and was reading his gospel intently. After another hour's walk, I had a brief chat with a fellow ploughing in a field. He took a gospel after we talked about the Light of the world. I pointed to the magnificent sight of rays of sunshine slanting down at an angle through dark clouds.

I finally reached the foot of the mountain at about 4 p.m. and was glad to meet some soldiers who introduced me to a simple family they knew there, with whom I spent the night. It was a tiny dwelling made up of three single-roomed huts, one of which was used partly as a shop for the surrounding hamlets. Half an hour after arriving, a rainstorm began. The walls were built of stones, but the roof was only mud trodden firmly onto a flat frame of sticks which leaked in a few places. When the rain stopped and we'd eaten, I settled down on the flat roof for a cold and uncomfortable night.

In the morning I was delighted to discover that my friendly host and his son planned to go to Mia with a load of gart on his two donkeys and was willing for me to accompany him. I was so thankful to the Lord that he roped my backpack onto one of his donkeys. I would never have been able to keep up the cracking pace they set for the next three hours otherwise. There were a few opportunities to chat to him about the Good News as we hurried along, but he couldn't read, and he wouldn't take a gospel. I was able to give him a bottle of gentian violet solution to treat a nasty wound on the back of one of his donkeys, and he was grateful for that. I in turn thanked him for the ways in which he'd helped me.

When we arrived at Mia, I was concerned that they wanted a hundred rials for a seat in a car to Arhem. This was exorbitant, and I only had ninety-seven rials with me. I decided to visit the sheikh again in whose home I'd stayed six days before at the beginning of this circuit, before settling my travel plans. Once again, the sheikh gave me cold soft drinks and was welcoming. When he heard the price that the drivers were asking, he became furious, however.

'You shouldn't have to pay a single rial,' he said. 'You can go to Arhem in my car. It is leaving after lunch.' He and his sons seemed impressed by the effort involved in my journey, and after a little while one of his sons began a discussion about religion. As we all chatted, I showed a John's Gospel to him. Then, my earnest hope and prayers over the preceding days, that I might be enabled to leave a gospel with them before departing from the area, were vastly exceeded when that same young fellow, who'd only been reading the gospel for a few minutes, asked me a question: 'Do you have any more books?'

Of course, I immediately gave him one of the packs of seven items. Even the sheikh himself said that the John's Gospel was good to read after he'd had a brief look at it; but he handed his copy back to me. I was told that the son had a reputation for being the bad one of the family, so I prayed that the Lord would accomplish a wonderful work of grace in his life.

I noticed that the sheikh's car was loaded with large cartons of washing powder and other things which I couldn't help assuming had been smuggled across the border to be sold there in Yemen for a significant profit. After travelling some way, I was transferred into another car which turned out to be faster; and I was pleased to discover that the driver was a friend of ours who was hoping to get all the way to Muharraq that evening. After a tiring trip however, we reached his home at Toof-fa at about 8.30 p.m., and decided to stay there for the night, and then complete the journey to Muharraq the following morning. I didn't get much of a chance to speak of the gospel because our discussion was largely stifled by my friend's religious father[99].

But after a welcome meal and a beautiful wash, I changed my clothes and slept well, despite my cough, which was becoming more troublesome.

It was the final day of my trek, Friday, November 25, and I was nearly home. After breakfast I visited the sheikh, and then my friend and I set out again towards Muharraq where he had to deliver his load of dates. We made good time in his little Toyota Landcruiser, reaching the clinic at about mid-morning; and what a joy it was to be reunited with Dell and the children again! After a brief hug, I got the key to the clinic, and went straight back to treat my friend's bad attack of bronchitis, without charging him, of course. I was only too glad to be able to do something in return for his kindness in driving me so far without asking for anything towards the petrol.

And so, my twelve-day journey drew to a safe and happy conclusion. When I shared with the others some details of my trip, they also were delighted by the clear indications that the Lord had directed each moment. I was so relieved to be back again at Muharraq; and grateful that the Lord had cared for Dell, the children and our colleagues while I'd been away. We all gathered to celebrate Andrew's fourth birthday that afternoon (even though it was three days late), a happy time together.

* * *

On December 21 I set out on the second trek, north to Zaytoon and then back along the mountain ridges to Muharraq again with two nights away in total. I left on a Wednesday, as soon as the last patients had been seen in the clinic, dropped off from the Land Rover on the road which climbed up towards Zaytoon, having reached the end of the road workings just as the sun was setting. Continuing from there on foot, I pressed on up to a village where I met the sheikh who kindly led me to his home and invited me to stay the night. Despite competition from the television[100], we were still able to have a good talk about 'The Way'. The sheikh's son, initially antagonistic, gradually softened; and I went to bed praying that I'd be enabled to leave a gospel and booklet with them before setting out the next morning. Before I left, they accepted the gospel and several booklets which I offered them in gratitude for their kindness to me. I took my leave and began the climb up to the government centre on the top of the Zaytoon Mountain. A man going the same way accompanied me, and after some time we met up with a young sheikh. When we sat down so that I could have a short rest, I was able to give them a gospel each and some booklets after a brief chat. It turned out that the first man had already been given a Gospel of John by one of us, several years ago! They were both friendly, and I felt thrilled at the way the Lord was leading me to particular people in this way.

When I was nearing the top, I learned that I'd missed the government representative who had left to go somewhere. This was disappointing. I had made the decision about where to go on this trek based on an invitation from this man to come and treat members of his family who were ill. I knew also, however, that he was opposed to the gospel, and not having to climb to the top of the peak now (I could not go to his house while he was away), saved a good bit of time. I did however, leave the medicines I'd brought for his sick family members with the health worker there; discussed the matter of smallpox and cholera epidemic procedure should this become an eventuality; had an early lunch with the sheikh of that village; and then left at noon to walk to Moze.

This turned out to be an easy journey, through a shallow valley running south along the top of the ridge. I passed huge banana plantations, lots of coffee, and a large swamp near Moze which was surrounded by reeds, and where many ducks and other waterfowl were much at home. About halfway there, I went through a village holding its regular Thursday market; and about an hour further south I met some friendly people beside the track. After leaving them, I'd only gone a few hundred yards when I felt sorry that I'd not spoken to them about the Lord, so I went back. One fellow had left, but three men and one young woman were still there in the field; and so, sitting down beside the path, I was enabled to have an excellent talk with them about the Way of Salvation. Two of the men took gospels and booklets.

Evening was approaching as I reached the foot of the steep climb up to Moze, and I was grateful to the Lord that at that point a friendly young man caught up with me. Taking my rucksack, he put it on his own back, and set off up the path on his donkey. I was relieved that he'd taken the load off my shoulders, but despite that, I was still footsore and weary when we finally reached what I discovered was a large township, spilling down over the steep, eastern side. The fellow who'd so kindly carried my pack took me to his home where we had a meal by the light of a little kerosene lantern. Although we had a good chat, he wouldn't take a gospel or a booklet. I didn't press him at all; that would have been most unwise.

A little later in the evening I was shown the way to the sheikh's house, where I stayed the night. I knew him well, since for some time he'd been coming to our clinic for treatment of his tuberculosis. He claimed to be 83 years old, which may have been true, but he was a vigorous and forceful man. He and his teenage son spent a lot of time preparing a mattress and bedding on the floor to ensure that I'd be comfortable, and I certainly was, stretched out full-length, and able to relax.

Early in the morning I woke to shave and avail myself of the simplest imaginable toilet facilities (in other words, totally non-existent, but just round the back of the house). I didn't need to dress, as on such journeys I only took off my belt, shoes and socks to sleep. When my host joined me for breakfast, I was delighted to discover that he already had gospels which he'd acquired in Lebanon, many years ago, when he was a sailor. Now he happily accepted a New Testament and some Christian booklets.

'A long time ago, about 1,300 years ago, there were 75,000 Christians in Yemen,' he told me.

'What happened to them?' I asked.

'All moved to Egypt, Lebanon and Jordan. Their leader lived near Jibla. A few remain,' he told me, 'to the south of Moze,' but he was vague about distances.

I set out about 9am, heading westward towards Muharraq. A pleasant nine-year-old boy decided that he was going to accompany me because he wanted his toothache attended to in the clinic the next day.

Intensively terraced mountainsides.

The terraces are constructed so rain water flows from left to right, down, then right to left.

He insisted on carrying my haversack on his back for a good part of the journey. He had such bearing, and was unlike the boys usually encountered, who tended to be bad-mannered and a nuisance. He reminded me of our Yemeni brother and his son who visited us from time to time at the clinic, and I prayed for this boy as we walked along. After a while, without any prompting from me, he announced that his father, who was now working in Jeddah, Saudi Arabia, was also a brother in Christ[101]!

Before commencing the steep descent to Muharraq, I was invited to drink tea in the home of a friendly old man who also turned out to be a patient from the clinic. He read a bit to me from the Koran after our talk about Jesus being the Shepherd, the Way, and the Son of God but he happily accepted a gospel as I left. Further to the south along the final ridge, we came to a village where I met a soldier who worked in the government centre in Muharraq. I had given him medicines for his wife, only a few days before. Now, over a tin of pineapple, I discovered that he already had a gospel which he'd been given by one of us, sometime in the past. His being a soldier led to a good chat about peace rather than war being the way of the Messiah. He asked me for a 'big book', meaning a New Testament, but since I didn't have one then, I gave him a set of seven items and promised to give him a New Testament in the clinic the next day (which he received).

The young boy and I got under way again, walking down for two hours through the area known as Benni Ay-yoob, to Muharraq. I was grateful that the Lord had arranged for a man to catch up with us for part of it, because he offered to carry my pack on his donkey right down to the Muharraq wadi. I arrived home with sore feet, but with my heart rejoicing.

I was now able to plan for the next few treks, after a break over Christmas, which was a happy time. We hosted English guests for a few days—Chris[102], with his wife June and their three teenage children. They'd previously sent a turkey to help the Murdocks with their American Thanksgiving Day celebrations, but now brought two turkeys as well as delicious seasoning, Christmas pudding and all the other trimmings, which June insisted on cooking for us all. The poor Murdocks, being from the United States, had difficulty understanding some of what we Australians and British said, or rather, what we meant when we joked around, so they may have felt a bit on the outer. Nevertheless, we'd practised a Christmas choir item together in four parts, which was good for unity, besides sounding good, too.

* * *

On Wednesday 28 December, I started on my next trek, the third one, to Maharbisha, and then back to Muharraq via Tammeer. The day before I set out, a woman had been brought down to Muharraq by car needing our help in delivering her baby. She was ill and had been in labour for some days; but the next afternoon she was well enough to be driven back to her home near Maharbisha. I was able to get a free lift with them all the way.

The patient and her family left the car at the big well in a valley a little below Maharbisha township. It was misty and cool, and they pointed out to me where the Egyptian army had been encamped during the civil war[103]. We could see the village above us where I hoped to spend the night, and the driver said he'd take me there, free of charge.

Fortunately, Ardil, the health worker I wanted to meet, was at home. When I'd been up there about six months before to lead some teaching sessions with them on various aspects of health, hygiene and treatment, he was the only one of the five local health workers with whom I'd been unable to have a proper discussion about the Lord, or to offer any Christian literature. Now, he willingly invited me in, and after a meal I settled down for an uncomfortable night, finally taking the foam mattress off the short bed, and sleeping on the floor. Ardil's wife's uncle was also staying the night with them, and in the morning, I was delighted to be able to have a good chat with both men and leave a Gospel of John and a *Way of Salvation* with each of them.

Ardil took me to a friend's house in another village, and as always, I began by showing them the letter from the Ministry of Health and discussing epidemics. They were also interested in what I had to say about the Good News, and when Ardil pulled out the gospel and booklet that I'd given him that morning, this led to further discussion. The friend's son could read, and before setting out again I was able to leave a pack of seven items with them.

When I'd been up at Maharbisha on previous visits, I'd felt led to pray for the people living in the villages I could see round about, especially those up on top of a high ridge which ran to the northeast from a point a few miles to the north of Maharbisha. I was aiming for that ridge now, and was directed to go to Burrtagarl, a village on the middle slopes at this end of the ridge. I walked on from the home where I'd stopped, having left Ardil there, and in a little while came to a large village on my way to Burrtagarl. The sheikh was away, but there was quite a group of people in his home. They were so interested that I left not only a pack of seven, but also a New Testament.

The path from there went down a little, and then up a long, steep climb to another large village. As time was slipping by and it seemed a bit off the track, I decided not to go on down to Burrtagarl after all, but instead to climb up to the point of the ridge where the path went. I would then be able to turn and continue climbing up along the top of the ridge to the northeast towards Tammeer. (Also, I'd discovered that there was no sheikh at Burrtagarl—another reason why it did not seem so necessary to visit there.) At the top of the steep climb, I stopped in that large village I'd seen, and had a good chat with the people there, about medical things first, and then about the Lord. One man took a pack of seven, and they listened happily to the Gospel Recordings cassettes I put on for them. I think they may have hoped that there would be some English pop music on it!

Again, the sheikh was not present in this village, but his son escorted me along the first part of the track leading up towards the village on the highest point of the ridge. He accepted a John's Gospel and *Way of Salvation* before we parted company. From the top of that ridge, there was a magnificent view in all directions, and I could see a populated area away to the north and northeast that I immediately decided to plan to reach on some subsequent walk. When I arrived at the village, I was invited to drink tea in one little house, and a man there accepted a John's Gospel and a *Way of Salvation*, but we did not have much of a discussion. I then went on from there to the sheikh's house which I found to be full of men chewing gart. Two who could speak a little English were from Taiz, dressed in Western clothes. They were from the Ministry of Justice, and had been checking the harkim's books, I think. After we'd spoken about epidemics, these men themselves started a relaxed discussion about the gospel, but one of them doubted that the 'common' people would be able to understand the Arabic which he read in the Gospel of John and the *Way of Salvation* which I'd shown him. It was all quite friendly, and I felt free enough to leave with the sheikh, in front of them all as I left, the gospel and the copy of the *Way of Salvation* that we'd been looking at, saying how happy I'd been to be there amongst them. The village was shrouded in mist while I was there, but the God of Light was there too; and I simply trusted that no trouble would ensue from having shared the Good News.

The ridge sloped down again before the climb up to the pinnacle called Tammeer which I was aiming to reach for the night. However, despite my concern about the fading light, I had to pause briefly at one spot because I was so moved by the beauty of the scene spread before me. In the glow of the setting sun, wave after misty wave swept up and over the saddle in the mountains from the turbulent sea of cloud which obscured from view the underlying coastal lowlands.

It was almost dark when I finally reached the government building, perched right on the top of the peak. After speaking to the armal about my trip, and then treating a sick fellow, I went down the slope a little way to the sheikh's house. He was in Hajjah; but his brothers, young men in their early twenties, and their friends welcomed me in. They'd been watching Saudi television (one segment was about mining in Australia!) when I arrived. Nevertheless, we had a good discussion, and an even better one in the morning.

The altitude and lovely clear morning allowed me to see for many miles in all directions, and I praised the Lord for the magnificent view as I resumed my journey.

It was a steep climb down the western side of the ridge into a wadi. Halfway down, a kind fellow caught up with me and offered to carry my pack on his donkey. This was an enormous help, though he set off at a cracking speed. That didn't prevent me from spotting about twenty small baboons scurrying helter-skelter down a slope amongst the scrub and trees. At the bottom of the mountain my new friend suggested that, since there were no cars there in which to get back to Muharraq, I should ride on the donkey, which I did—right back to our compound. I was grateful; those last four or five miles, although flat, were tiring because of the soft wadi sand. When we arrived at Muharraq, I gave him plenty of water and food for his donkey, as well as a good drink for himself, in gratitude for his kindness in providing me with so much free assistance.

* * *

My fourth trek from 18 to 20 January 1978, took me from Maharbisha back to Muharraq; but this time via Annanees and Manga, southwest of Maharbisha. As usual, I was grateful for the Lord's leading, particularly on one part of the walk. I had started to descend into a wadi when two pleasant fellows came along, one of whom turned out to be the postman, with the mail sack on his donkey. (Both men could read, and I was able to give the postman a John's Gospel and a *Way of Salvation*.) He was going my way initially, but after only a couple of hundred yards, he pointed out the path I had to take. I realised how the Lord had once again arranged the precise timing necessary for me to meet up with such a strategic person. If a postman became a believer, he could be of wonderful use for the Kingdom of God on his regular circuits of the area, and by being in touch with so many people.

The next day, I had reached a secluded part of the track, when a young man carrying a small business case came around the corner ahead of me. I greeted him and gave him a drink. When he started to go on his way, I began chatting about the fact that I'd come from Annanees, and the way to Manga was before us. Then I asked him, 'But where's the path to heaven?' He seemed familiar with it all, and soon said that he'd known Ulrich, a member of our Team, when the latter was teaching at a college in Sana'a. He told me that he was a Christian, and that he had various gospels and other

Christian literature. He was not afraid of dying and would go straight to heaven when he does. However, he did not seem happy, and was keen to continue with his journey, possibly afraid of the locals discovering that he was a believer.

When I approached a village, I noticed a commotion coming from a crowd of men on its outskirts.

'It's a gathering,' a man on the track told me. 'The market.'

I decided that it was a good place to avoid, as I couldn't imagine it would be a fruitful place for the gospel. However, the path led me right down past them all, and soon the crowd of men was gathering around me! There was no danger. As it turned out they were a friendly group who laughed at all my jokes, and it seemed no time at all before I had the little John's Gospel and *Way of Salvation* out of my pocket. I read to them John 14:27 about peace, and then I asked where the sheikh was because I wanted to visit him. He turned out to be the jovial man standing right in front of me and who was holding the gospel, and as we set off towards his house to talk, he slipped it into his pocket. This seemed unusual, but of course I didn't object; and we'd hardly sat down in the room when he said straight out, 'We want Christian books. Do you have some in Muharraq?'

'Yes, of course,' I told him.

He looked around to his friends and said, 'We'll drive down tomorrow, and you can give us all some.'

I tried not to show my staggered reaction and chatted away faithfully about the epidemic procedures. However, as I was leaving, I gave him a New Testament and a pack of seven items.

The same village was home to the deputy of the district government official. When I went to meet him in his house, he said he'd heard that there was cholera[104] in the area to the west. I had seen this populated ridge from the path and wondered if I'd ever be able to visit, so this was the opportunity! He wrote two letters for me to take and because it was approaching midday, I set off quickly. Before long I had handed the first letter to its recipient. To reach the second recipient, the sheikh, I set off south along the top of the ridge, passing several villages, one of which was large, with the loudspeaker blaring out the sermon from the Friday service in the mosque[105]. I pressed on, and having arrived in the sheikh's village, I waited in his house until the sermon at this mosque was over, and the men emerged. I had lunch with the sheikh, and after the medical discussion, was able to explain how Jesus is the Son of God, and to then leave with him a John's Gospel and a *Way of Salvation*! I couldn't help feeling quietly delighted. I had been able to leave the Word of Life with the sheikh of this populous ridge which I'd thought I'd have to bypass, but to which the Lord had diverted my steps. It was unlikely that any other missionary would visit that ridge in the near future, if ever, and so I believed that the Lord of the harvest intended to save people from that district through those two little booklets which were 'sown' there.

* * *

I was only away for one night on the fifth trek. It took me in a circuit on foot from the top of another road being bulldozed up the mountains north of Muharraq. I set out on 2 February 1978, and it started in a way that appeared unfruitful with a delayed beginning, some unresponsive conversations and difficulties knowing where to try to stay the night. However, I was soon to have a tremendous surprise which would radically alter my estimation of the journey's usefulness.

It was about 5 p.m. and the sun was sinking below the horizon while I was still only about halfway to the village where the next sheikh lived. As I passed a tiny hamlet, the folk offered to put me up for the night in their little mosque. However, I had resolved that, if possible, I would never enter a mosque[106]. I could see that there were only tiny, one-roomed houses in this vicinity, and so they could not put me up for the night. Finally, a fellow accepted my offer of twenty rials to lead me to the village I hoped to reach. However, several times on the way he sat down saying how exhausted he was, and how he needed another ten rials to complete the journey! I managed not to get angry with him, but took his hand and said that I'd show him the way instead; and by various similar devices, and through dint of talking about everything I could think of that would not remind him of money (largely about his own health), we eventually reached the village without my having to pay him anymore.

It was now almost completely dark. Nobody was out of doors at all, and my travelling companion had vanished. I could hear men chanting together over in one direction and realised that they must all be in the mosque, attending the last of the five daily prayer gatherings. As I sat waiting on a low wall made of rocks, a few hurricane lamps hanging in nearby huts the only light, a young boy came past.

'Could you please tell the sheikh that the doctor from Muharraq has arrived to visit him?' I said to the boy. He went off immediately, surprisingly, in the opposite direction to the chanting. I'd expected that the sheikh would be in the mosque with all the other men of the village. After a few minutes, a smallish man approached in the dim light, walking towards me as if in deep thought, with his hands held together down in front of him. At first it didn't occur to me that he could be the sheikh; I thought I'd see a man coming towards me with bearing and purpose. Nevertheless, he was the sheikh, and he shook my hand before leading me to his guest room. He struck me as being a pleasant, shy man; and I liked him immediately. After talking about our medical matters, I treated several patients who'd been brought in, and then we had a meal, after which we settled down for a chat.

'Do you study the Bible?' was his opening sentence. Soon he was turning to the first page of the copy of *Way of Salvation* I gave him and began to read it out loud, so the others there heard it all, too. When he was about halfway through, he stopped and began reading from the John's Gospel I'd also given him. By this time, it was late, and everyone except one other fellow had drifted off to their own homes. As we sat on the colourful mattresses placed around the edges of the room in the usual Arab fashion, I noticed that the sheikh, who was sitting on my right, held the booklets to his right, away from me. I sensed that he didn't want to hand them back, and he was so obviously interested that I eventually gave him a New Testament, and one of my packs of seven other items of Christian literature.

As I'd been explaining the gospel message, he and the younger man had glanced at each other and nodded from time to time, smiling slightly. The sheikh then said that much of what we'd chatted about was exactly as he'd heard on the Seychelles broadcasts many times. I could see that the younger fellow was keen too, and he was delighted with the Gospel, *Way of Salvation* and two other booklets I gave him.

'Are any Yemenis becoming Christians?' the sheikh asked.

'There are a few.'

'Is the government happy about that?' he enquired.

'No,' I answered.

'Do they have to leave the country then?' he continued.

'No', I said. 'They just become Christians quietly, without any noise or fuss.'

The sheikh went on to tell me that an armal[107] he knew is a Christian and that 'he loves the Messiah'. I felt that as he talked, he showed himself to also be a believer; or if not, to be close indeed to the kingdom; also, his young friend. I was so thankful that the Lord had enabled me to reach there for the Thursday night. If I'd arrived the next morning, it might not have been nearly so easy to chat. The next morning, the sheikh led me to the village of a friend of his whom he wanted me to meet, Sheikh Ali Hussan, but who was away. However, he came to visit me several weeks later, as I will mention soon.

* * *

While the treks were opportunities to plant the very first seeds of the gospel in communities, there were occasions where we could water and tend its growth. A few days after arriving back from my fifth trek, our Christian Yemeni brother visited us at the clinic with a friend he had been teaching about Christ. A few days after that he returned, this time with a friend who had been working in Saudi Arabia, and who was already a believer. I had arranged for some teaching tapes to give to our friend, and had prepared some cards on which I wrote a number of scripture references I selected from Berkhof's *Systematic Theology*, on a particular topic, such as 'The Unity of God'. In this way, I hoped to cover a lot of doctrine over a period of months as he visited the clinic[108].

The clinic was also a place where those who were interested could come and get more literature. Sheikh Ali Hussan, for example, came at the end of the clinic one day, later in February and asked me for books, so I took him to the verandah of our house, and discreetly gave him a New Testament, *Basic Christianity*, and a few booklets.

Of course, we constantly needed wisdom about what was appropriate or not. One afternoon, after a busy Saturday clinic, the seventeen-year-old son of the sheikh near Toof-fa came to speak to me. His father had come several times for gospels, taking a New Testament and *Basic Christianity* last time. This boy said that he'd read all the books his father had got from us and asked if he could now have some more. However, because he was young, and we didn't have any different ones left, and because our watchman was eyeing us suspiciously, I spoke quietly to the boy.

'We will return from Sana'a in a month. We plan to bring some more with us. If your father comes then, I'll give some to him.'

It was just possible this was a trap, not only to be seen giving out Christian literature (which would make some people angry), but also to be giving it to a youngster. The boy could also find himself in trouble from certain men if he was found to be in possession of such literature, and we were extremely keen to avoid that.

* * *

I was now nearly halfway through my planned twelve treks and felt very happy about what God had done, and my part in it. I wrote to my parents to say I was finally doing something that I truly enjoyed. 'The last thing which I enjoyed like this was the Scripture Union work in Newcastle, visiting the ministers and encouraging Bible reading,' I told them. Even though the treks had to be sandwiched between busy clinics and other medical tasks, these were the form of service in which Adele and I had always longed to be involved. We saw clearly that all the long years of medical training and other preparations had been vitally important and had made this time of vigorous outreach possible. Happily, there were still seven more treks to go and early on Thursday morning, February 16, 1978, I set off again from Muharraq, for a single night only. Heavy rain the day before delayed my planned start but I was still able to slip past Tammeer, high in the mountains north of Maharbisha, where I'd spent a night only seven weeks before on the third trek, without people seeing me and asking why I was back again.

I visited various villages during the day and had several good conversations with passers-by. I was glad of help from some young fellows who led me over a part of the track that crossed extensive stretches of flat rock, as I might easily have lost my way. Finally, just as the sun was setting, I arrived at the village I was headed to, footsore and weary. A couple of men who had been to the Muharraq clinic just happened to be passing the village and gave me a great welcome which acted as a helpful introduction to the sheikh. His large stone house was perched precariously on the edge of a sheer cliff. After the evening meal, we had a good chat about topics connected with Christianity, and he read a little from the John's Gospel and *Way of Salvation* but handed them back.

When it was getting late, he led me downstairs to a large storeroom which was almost filled with sacks of grain, tools and other farming supplies. Near the door was a rope bed with wooden frame and legs. I noticed a small window for ventilation, and Yemeni-style bathroom facilities. However, I was somewhat disturbed by the fact that as he left and closed the heavy wooden door, he locked me in! I looked around; I was well and truly imprisoned, with no way of escape. After thinking prayerfully about the situation and noting that I hadn't sensed any animosity, I realised that locking a traveller in for the night was most likely his custom. He could sleep peacefully without being concerned that the visitor might creep out during the night, looking for his daughters.

I felt sure that the Lord had led me to that village to spend the night, and so although the sheikh had handed the scripture booklets back to me, I prayed earnestly that I could leave some with him before I set out the next day. I slept well and was able to look out of my little window in the morning light and see the fields hundreds of feet below, where men were already working.

We ate breakfast on the flat roof of the house, and I learned that the sheikh owned all the fields which were visible so far below. I lingered a little after the meal in the hope that an opportunity might present itself to give him the booklets, but none arose. However, I was pleased when he said he would accompany me on the first part of the walk. From the front of his house, the path I had to take was 200 yards up a steeply-sloping, bare rock face. As we were setting out, the sheikh took my backpack and gave it to his nephew to carry; but then surprised me by beginning to run up the steep slope.

'He's running to get clear,' I thought. 'He's arranged for someone to shoot me from the house!'

But I was wrong. No shots rang out. I turned towards the sheikh above me, and he swung his arm quickly past himself, indicating that he wanted me to race him to the top! I'd never experienced anything like this before, but I thought that I should be able to run faster than that little old man. So off I set, sprinting as fast as I could up the slope. Unfortunately, I made no ground at all. After only covering about half the distance, I was forced to sit down for a rest. It was then I realised that we were being watched; on the flat roof below us were probably six or seven women and girls—his wives and daughters—all clad in their black outfits, clapping and cheering because the sheikh was winning!

'I'll bet they put him up to this,' I thought. I'd had occasional glimpses of women folk blending in with the shadows the previous evening as the sheikh and I sat talking in the light of the kerosene lamp. No doubt they wanted to see if their father could beat this giant from Australia who had stooped down to go through their doorways. And now here they were, laughing and clapping with delight.

'Well, that does it! I have to beat the old boy now,' I thought. Leaping to my feet, I virtually flew up the remainder of the slope, trying to ignore the sound of the shockingly biased barracking floating up from behind us.

I let him win. . . well, I couldn't catch him; and of course, he was pleased. But as he retrieved my bag from his nephew and as we reached the level track at the top, out of sight of those below, I realised what the Lord had just done, breaking down barriers, and I was glad the sheikh had won the race.

When we reached the point where he planned to leave me, he offered me 100 rials for the journey. It was a generous gift and I thanked him politely but declined his offer.

'I don't need the money,' I explained. Then, taking the little plastic bag containing the Gospel of John and the *Way of Salvation* out of my shirt pocket (as I'd done the night before), and holding them in my hand as we sat there, I was able to speak of Jesus as the Son of God. He then explained what the Koran says. After that, we stood up, shaking hands as we said goodbye, and I thanked him once again for his kind offer of the money.

'Although I don't need that money,' I told him, 'there is something that I do want.'

'Oh,' he said. 'What do you want?'

'I want with all my heart for you to take these two little books and read them.' As I said this, I held them out and he took them. He opened one and began to read it to himself. Being keen for him not to hand them back, I unobtrusively slipped my backpack on over my shoulders, and quietly moved away. After a few yards, the narrow track curved behind a large protruding rock; but just as I was about to pass out of sight, I glanced back and was thrilled to see him still standing where I'd left him, deeply engrossed in what he was reading. I went on my way rejoicing and praising God, knowing that he would continue the work he had begun in that man's heart and village.

* * *

On Thursday, March 23, 1978, I set out on the seventh trek. Working out my route proved complicated. The area I wanted to go to passed by villages I had been to before, and I didn't want to cause unhelpful enquiries into why I was there again. The only way was to drive in the Land Rover to the point where I'd be setting off on foot, and to arrive there just as the day was dawning.

Once again, Larry accompanied me while I drove north to Arhem and then up the steep mountainside to the village from where the walking track began. Having left Muharraq at 3.30 a.m., we arrived as planned at 5.45 a.m. Larry then drove the Land Rover back to Muharraq while I continued climbing on foot, reaching the saddle I was aiming for at about 8 a.m. I then turned south and made reasonable progress, even though I was feeling unwell. However, some men came running after me and asked me to come back and see a sick man. After attending to him, another fellow in the room, who with his daughter had been receiving TB treatment at our clinic, invited me to his home for breakfast. This turned out to be a friendly family. The fellow was interested in the John's Gospel and *Way of Salvation*, and happily took a pack of seven items as well, but I had to excuse myself and hurry off behind some small trees on account of the dysentery which was now making me feel weak and unwell.

My host was going in the same direction as I was and offered to accompany me most of the way to the next main village, taking my backpack and putting it on his donkey. We set off on foot at about 10.30 a.m., and sometime after our ways had parted, I arrived at the village around 1.30 p.m. Unfortunately, once again I'd been delayed by the dysentery, making one or two brief excursions into the privacy of the tall crops growing beside the path. It began to rain heavily as I reached the village, but I managed to obtain directions to the sheikh's home. After banging on his door several times, a woman's voice called from the depths, 'Who is it?' When I called back my reply, she said that the sheikh was not home, and there were no other men there either. Of course, I couldn't go in with only the womenfolk present.

With the rain pouring down and no-one else about, I looked around for somewhere to shelter, but could only find a tiny, unoccupied sheep pen at the side of the house. By squatting down, and shuffling awkwardly into the little enclosure, I found that the sheet of corrugated iron forming the roof afforded me reasonable protection from the storm. After a few minutes however, the rain eased off, and a young fellow arrived who invited me into a visitors' room. Eventually though, since it was not at all clear that the sheikh would return home that night, I decided to go on to the next village where the sheikh apparently was at home.

It was a pleasant walk through the misty fields now soaked with rain, but the mist gradually became so thick that I could only see a short distance around me. I realised that no-one could see me either; in fact, I had the distinct impression that the Lord was hiding me from view. This thought was confirmed when I reached that next village, teetering on the western edge of the plateau, because I received an unfriendly welcome. I was alarmed at the way the men suspiciously eyed my backpack and looked me up and down. I felt that they were considering robbing me, at the very least.

After explaining my medical reason for visiting them and showing the smallpox/chickenpox poster, I set off down the mountainside to the west, surprised and pleased to learn that I was only a few hours' walk from Muharraq. I had planned and intended to stay out overnight in order to be more able to share the gospel message as the Lord gave the opportunity, but because I was not asked to stay, and also felt ill, I concluded that there was no alternative but to return home.

As I was approaching Muharraq, I sat down for about twenty minutes on a low wall of rocks, allowing dusk to become darkness before passing through the market in an attempt once again to keep my journeyings as little talked about as possible. Nevertheless, a chap spotted me in the fading light from across his fields, and called out to another fellow several fields away on the other side of the track, 'What's the doctor doing, sitting over there?' The other man didn't know either; I wasn't going to enlighten them.

At no time in my life had I felt more in danger than I did in that village on the edge of the plateau, and I think it was within the realms of possibility that had I stayed there overnight, I might have been murdered. Once again, I saw how the Lord can arrange or allow for us to be ill in order to accomplish his purposes. The dysentery had caused me to not only hurry along on my journey, but also to think about getting home as soon as possible in case it worsened, and so that I could immediately start myself on the appropriate medication. The Lord, however, knowing that I'd be in danger and needed to pass through that region as quickly as possible, arranged for my dysentery to flare up. Besides that, in order not to give those villagers time to formulate a plan of attack, the Lord hid me from view with that thick cloud until I appeared unexpectedly in their midst; and then, after only a few minutes, I was on my way again, down the steep mountainside.

I had sought to share the Good News with a few other people along the way, but there was no apparent interest in any of their hearts. However, I felt that the Lord had led me, and the time I'd spent in the home where the man and his daughter lived, who'd been treated by us for TB, made the trip worthwhile.

* * *

We had not had many issues with difficult government officials, but at the end of March, a young Yemeni doctor who accompanied the new governor of Hajjah Province and chief of security on a visit to us did prove to be difficult. He had completed his training in Russia about a year before and was now in charge of medical services in the whole province. Unfortunately, he seemed intent on trying to find fault with our work. As he inspected our facility, he searched and searched along all the shelves in our medical storeroom, almost certainly looking for out-of-date medications, but not finding any[109]. The young doctor even demanded that the nurses not diagnose any illnesses: *I* had to do that, apparently. To my mind, this was contrary to the Ministry of Health, who had said they wanted to establish primary health workers and medical assistants all over the country who were to treat what they could and refer on what they couldn't handle. I didn't say that we would comply with this demand, but thanked the young doctor, and said that we would think about it together. I later found out that he had arranged for the local 'pharmacist' to visit us and see if we were doing as he'd ordered[110]. My attitude was to just go along gently. It would be okay, I felt sure.

In the meantime, I'd been thinking about the children's education. It was marvellous for Sharon and Andrew to be living in such a rural situation, surrounded by fields with sheep, goats, cattle, donkeys, camels, chickens, a pet lamb and a wide variety of wildlife, all contributing to their day-to-day experiences, but getting a formal education would be difficult. We could probably manage in Yemen through their primary years, either by correspondence courses from Sydney, or with missionary teachers. However, we'd need to return to Australia for their high schooling since we didn't feel comfortable with the thought of sending them away to boarding school. Andrew would turn twelve in November 1985, which left seven and a half years to continue with our current medical missionary work as the Lord directed, before that next phase of our lives commenced.

Andrew (on top of the big truck), and two visiting missionary children.

I thought and prayed over these matters in a concentrated way for about ten days before I shared it with Dell. When I did, she had thought in her quiet time that morning that the Lord might reveal to her that day some purpose and ministry to aim at, and for which she might prepare.

A few days later, I sensed that the Lord was impressing on my heart that he wanted us to plan and prepare for a new work in a new country. This thought was partly triggered by the constant uncertainty about the Team's being allowed to remain in Yemen. From the first day that Adele and I arrived in the country, there was the definite possibility that we would all have to leave at short notice. Sometimes our visas took many months to be renewed, and I began to think, 'Where would the Lord be likely to send Adele and me if we ever did have to leave Yemen?'

As I saw it, our specific work in the Muharraq region was ending. After only five more treks the campaign of twelve trips would be completed. And although I was a doctor, my main love and purpose, I believed, was to be a colporteur, carrying the gospel message and Arabic scriptures to prepared hearts, even if they were in the remotest corners of that portion of the Hajjah Province. All our medical work was worthwhile, but it set the scene for evangelism. The Lord Jesus was able to shine out to those around us, making the teaching about himself attractive and the gospel message that we shared with them more readily acceptable.

When my twelve treks had been completed, as far as I could foresee, there would not be any obvious medical reason for systematically visiting every section of our region again as I was now doing. People could always come to the clinic at Muharraq and request scriptures, but others could exercise that ministry. I could leave the country after handing over to another doctor. And even without a doctor, our male nurse John had cared for the men while I'd been away. We'd heard that one (and possibly two) new missionary doctors were soon to join the work of the Team in Yemen, so it seemed to Adele and me that *our* time of 'sowing the seed' was almost over.

Six months before this, while we'd been delayed for those weeks at the German road camp, a thought had begun to crystallise. We recalled how the Lord had sent us to Pakistan on our way to Yemen in 1972, and we began to realise that there was a faint possibility that he might send us back there sometime in the future. We felt led to begin turning our eyes towards Baluchistan, in Pakistan[111]. While I was in Pakistan, Dr Gurney, who had had the Baluchi people on his heart for many years, asked me in a letter to try to learn a little of the Baluchi language if I could. I didn't learn more than a word or two, but it seemed that the Lord wanted us to now carry out that directive. In prayer, on Tuesday April 18, 1978, I surrendered all these plans to the Lord, and 'laid them on the altar'. In my journal, I wrote:

As Abraham was directed to offer up Isaac, his most precious and important possession, with all the accompanying promises and blessings, so I felt led today to do the same with my calling, coming to the point of being willing for the Lord to take away these tasks, plans and promises, and to give them to someone else, if he chooses to do so. I need to be careful so that I don't turn out to be seeking great things for myself. It must be his work, and any glory must be his.

Over the next few days, I prayed and thought about the Crowe family. This was a family we had never met, but we had heard that the Lord was leading them to Pakistan. They had two children, who, I thought, would be good companions for Andrew and Sharon if the Lord sent us to Pakistan. Then, out of the blue, Helen, one of our nurses, without knowing anything about our growing interest in Baluchistan, gave me a copy of the Crowe's prayer letter which described their call to Pakistan. We had never laid eyes on one of their prayer letters before and I couldn't help feeling that this surprising incident constituted a confirmation of our call from the Lord to leave Yemen, go to Pakistan to learn the Baluchi language, and work amongst those people.

* * *

In the meantime, my treks were continuing. I was desperately concerned that nothing should prevent my going on the eighth trek, which was the last of the mountain hikes, covering the region between Maharbisha and Manga, to the south-west. The day before I planned to go however, on Wednesday 26 April, in the middle of the busy clinic, a patient I'd not seen before said to me, 'Don't go through Maharbisha. They're watching the city gates for you!'

What a discovery! And how kind of him to let me know. Obviously, my treks were being talked about. It seemed that I was being warned that Muslim leaders were objecting to my giving away Christian scriptures. They must have complained to the government officials, who'd instructed the soldiers at the city gate to perhaps arrest me if I passed that way again, or to at least confiscate any scriptures that I might be carrying, and to then send me back to Muharraq. But what was I to do? I was extremely keen to tackle this last hiking trip. I would then have passed through all the mountain regions for which I felt that we were spiritually responsible, and thus to have had the opportunity of meeting those men up there in whose hearts the Lord had been working.

Late that afternoon after the clinic was finished, I had to walk down the hill a little way and stand near the generator shed to supervise a delivery of diesel fuel. As the driver was filling the tank, I looked up towards the high plateau a few miles away to the south where I was hoping to go the next day. The afternoon was cloudy, and the mountains were in shadow, but I could clearly see portions of the winding, dirt road which climbed up to the township of Maharbisha, clinging to the edge of the ridge. The plateau stretched away from there to the south-west, a little lower than the ridge.

The obvious way to reach it was to drive up to Maharbisha, and then walk down onto the plateau. That was the way I went at the beginning of my fourth trek, when I travelled for some way on the path which runs south along the eastern edge of that plateau, before I turned east into the mountains again. This time, however, I planned to walk around the whole plateau, heading south initially; then turning west, and finally coming north again on my way back to Muharraq. But if they were now watching the city gates to prevent my passing through Maharbisha, how could I even reach the plateau?

As I stood there by the generators, earnestly praying to the Lord for guidance, a gap appeared in the clouds out to the west allowing a beam of sunlight to shine down on the mountainside. The strip of light stretched from where I could see the road, about two-thirds of the way up towards Maharbisha, and then ran slightly upwards and to the right, across to the edge of the plateau. On the darkened mountainside, this strip stood out distinctly like a path of light for about a minute until the gap in the clouds closed, and the entire scene was once again plunged into shadow.

Every time I recount this incident, I am totally convinced all over again that that day, the Lord showed me the way to safely reach the plateau. He was not only blessing the whole outreach and protecting me from harm as I undertook these trips, but he was also providing his divine strategy for the best way to proceed. He showed me that I should drive in the Land Rover up as far as that point on the road, and then get out and simply climb on foot from there up the side of the mountain and onto the plateau, bypassing the town of Maharbisha altogether! And that's exactly what I did.

At 4.30 a.m. on Thursday, April 27, Larry and I set out in the Land Rover. Because he was feeling unwell, Larry had crept out an hour or two beforehand and had lain down on the back seat of the car in case he didn't wake up at the right time. It was good of him to accompany me so that he could drive the car back to Muharraq, and I was extremely grateful to him.

At about 5.30 a.m., at first light and about two-thirds of the way up the road to Maharbisha, I got out and, after a word of prayer together, left Larry to drive back to Muharraq. I climbed down the short slope to a small wadi which I crossed, and then set off up the long and steep northern side of the mountain towards the plateau. Most of the way was up indistinct shepherd paths or rabbit tracks. It was so steep at times that I had to climb those sections using my hands as well as my feet. At one point, about three quarters of the way up, I saw a village ahead and purposely avoided it. A narrow path coming from the village skirted around the side of the mountain, and then led up to Maharbisha; but I crossed straight over it.

This higher section of the mountainside which I'd now reached was covered with small trees and scrubby undergrowth. Being hungry and ready for a rest, I considered sitting down beside that path; it seemed unlikely that anyone would be up and about at that early hour. To be on the safe side, however, I decided that it would be wiser to continue to climb up a little further, just in case someone did come along and see me. About twenty feet above the level of the path, I came to a large rock with a flat top which was just what I was looking for. I'd hardly sat down and opened my tin of fish when I heard the soft murmur of voices. I froze; and looking down through the trees, saw a couple of men pass below me on the path, talking quietly together as they went on their way up towards Maharbisha. Silently I praised the Lord for his timing and protection, and then enjoyed the mackerel flakes and a good drink from my water bottle.

Setting off once again, I climbed straight up the side of the mountain, and at about 7 a.m. finally reached the top. The plateau is a wide, shallow valley, and I wanted to visit the western ridge, so I got straight onto the main track leading down from Maharbisha, and quickly set off. Several men in their fields were amazed to see me pass, thinking that I must have come down from Maharbisha. 'How did you get here?' one called.

'Oh, I just came this way', I replied, waving my arm vaguely from behind me, and not stopping to give any more details. This and other incidents strengthened my belief that the soldiers at the entrance to Maharbisha had indeed been instructed not to let me through, so I was glad that I'd been led to bypass the town.

Having already been through this valley on my fourth trek, I decided to travel as quickly as I could. A Bible verse seemed impressed upon me: 'Do not greet anyone on the road', so I hurried along in silence, not even answering the occasional person who spoke to me. I went south to the end of the valley, and at the point where I'd previously turned left, I took the right turn, now heading south-west. As I neared Manga, I turned north again near the western edge of the mountain range, into the area known as Benny Durrack. This involved a long climb up to the top of a ridge, so I was hot and weary when I finally got there and was soaked with perspiration. My thought had been to stop and have lunch with the sheikh of that area before going on to stay the night with another sheikh further north. But as it turned out, there were no sheikhs in the area, so I had lunch in the home of a friendly and intelligent fellow. After a good chat, including explaining how Jesus is the Son of God, he happily accepted the New Testament from which we'd read a little, and a Way of Salvation. An old man whom I'd met on the path led me to that home. I felt that I was meant to be taken there because it seemed to me that my host was the one whom the Lord had his eye upon in that vicinity.

I went on my way rejoicing, towards the home of the sheikh who was responsible for the whole of that wide, shallow valley around which I'd skirted, as well as the western ridge. When I arrived at his home at about 3.15 p.m. I learned that he was away with a judge and four soldiers from Maharbisha, settling some disturbance. I was nervous about the possibility of them all arriving back for the night; if that happened, it would be difficult for me to speak of the gospel, so I prayed much about that. His son was also out, down in the valley working in the fields, and didn't return until sunset. In the meantime, I had a sleep; and later when the sheikh arrived, I was relieved to hear that the judge and soldiers had gone on somewhere else.

The sheikh and his son seemed friendly, and we read a little from the New Testament during the evening. After an uncomfortable night, I was pleased to be able to explain to the son, while I was getting ready to leave, how Jesus is the Son of God; and was then delighted to be able to leave literature with the sheikh himself, as I was saying goodbye. He sent a chap to accompany me down into the next region. I was glad of it, in case there was any trouble.

I eventually reached the road down which cars come from Maharbisha, and after a little while I got a lift on the back of a little Suzuki which was carrying gart to Abs. I had to hang on for dear life though, because the charioteer drove like Jehu. At the Muharraq turn-off I got down, and soon a Toyota going to Muharraq came along, and I was given another free lift home.

12

The Four Lowland Treks

1978: Age 34-35

On Thursday, June 1, 1978, I went on the ninth trek, the first of the four treks I did in the Land Rover, out on the coastal plain. My new method of transport brought with it some advantages but a fresh set of challenges as well. Leaving Muharraq at 3.20 a.m., I drove west to Abs, then south to Khamees; but soon after passing through that town, the Land Rover stopped! The accelerator pedal had become disconnected from the spring! Using the hand throttle, or choke, I was able to crawl back to a new mechanic's place just outside Khamees by 6 a.m. I woke him up and he soon had it fixed. The Lord had plans to use even breakdowns, however. While I was waiting for the repairs, I saw a taxi driver asleep on top of his car. When he woke up, he told me that he used to have a shop in Muharraq village, back in 1974 when we only had stick huts. He'd been treated for TB glands under his right armpit, which were now completely healed (he showed me the scars). I was delighted to be able to leave with both him and the mechanic a John's Gospel, *Way of Salvation* and Seychelles program sheet each, and they were able to give me the names of the sheikhs in the district I wanted to visit that day.

I drove from there to a village in which we had slept when Wadi Moor was in flood, then turned east and drove into the foothills. The hamlet in which the first sheikh lived was in sight of the wadi. He was away in Hajjah, but his brother and others were there, and after speaking of medical things and having a meal with them, I was able to speak of the Lord, and leave a New Testament and some booklets with them. A fellow accompanied me to the next sheikh's home where an early lunch was prepared for me. Although the sheikh did not want to accept the New Testament and booklet, another man took them. I prayed that the Word of the Lord would not return to him empty and drove on with a heavy heart to the home of the last sheikh I was to visit that day. He was friendly, and we had a nice lunch together. As well as a beautiful horse, he had a little Suzuki car and pigeons nesting in his guest room! After the negative experience in the previous village, I wondered if I should say anything about the Good News, but eventually began to read a little from the gospel. However, a man who arrived after I did, who'd come through the previous village, warned the others that I was speaking about the Christian religion. I knew that I must not continue the discussion there and set off for home via another road, arriving back at Muharraq at about 7.30 p.m.

* * *

Our thoughts and plans about working amongst the Baluchi people had not wavered, and shortly after this trek, Peter brought Dr Gurney to visit us all at Muharraq. Dell and I shared with him about our leading to start a work amongst the Baluchi people, and after some discussion and prayer, we felt free to let our parents know that Adele and I considered that our 'sowing' ministry was almost complete in the Muharraq region. We told them that we believed the Lord was directing us to move to Pakistan in the next year or two.

I had planned my next trip in the Land Rover for Thursday, June 15, but Larry developed an attack of vomiting and diarrhoea beginning at 2 a.m. I decided not to go, partly to care for him, and partly because I sensed that the Lord, for reasons only he knew, was using Larry's illness to prompt me to postpone this trip. I would go instead on the following Tuesday. On June 20, 1978, therefore, I set out heading north on my second lowland trip, a circular route, through the regions of Hizzarm and Benny Jambia. Leaving Muharraq at 4.55 a.m., I stopped to treat a few sick folk at the new petrol pump at Bait Al Warrada at about 6 a.m., and left a John's Gospel, *Way of Salvation* and a Seychelles program sheet with the son of the manager. Continuing north till I came to the village where the sheikh lived, I had breakfast and a good chat with him and was delighted to be able to leave the same three items with him also.

I followed the road as it began to curve westward and drove to where the most important sheikh in the region lived. He had his own water pump in a well, and extensive gardens in the wadi nearby. It was a hot summer's day, and he led the way to a little knoll, on the top of which was what could have been a circular thatched hut, except that it had no walls, just a few wooden poles supporting the thatched roof. This elevated, shady spot benefitted from even the slightest movement of the air and was obviously a favourite place where men could sit on the wooden seats and talk together. Besides the sheikh and I, three or four other men sat there in the shade, and I had an excellent discussion about who Jesus is, to which they listened intently. I felt that the Lord himself was enabling me to make it clear to them, and as I was explaining why it was necessary for him to die and to rise again, a peaceful calm descended upon us. I don't recall ever experiencing anything like it before. The faint breeze dropped completely, and there seemed to be no sound anywhere, not even from the birds or animals. For about half a minute, we all sat there in silence, and the Lord's presence seemed to be with us, confirming what I'd been saying. I feel sure that those men must have sensed the significance of that stillness, coupled with the message I'd been sharing. I was disappointed, therefore, not to be able to leave any scriptures with the sheikh, although he said that he would get some when he came to the clinic. I prayed that he would not be able to rest until he did.

At one place on this trip, I passed a man in his sixties standing beside the road. I don't know why he was there, and he didn't signal for me to stop. I hesitated momentarily, and then drove on. Over the years I've often recalled that man and have felt troubled that I didn't stop and at least attempt to share the gospel message with him. I've prayed for him and his family and friends, and I've tried to comfort myself with the thought that if the Lord had wanted me specially to speak to him in particular, he could have caused the engine to cut out, or stopped me in some other way. Perhaps sometime later, the man may have heard the message from someone else I met on that journey. Alternatively, he could have come to the clinic at Muharraq and got some scriptures for himself.

Another consideration is that maybe, for some reason, the Lord didn't want me to stop. Perhaps that man might have become violent. Only the Lord knows. And of course, Satan is busy accusing us before our God day and night, making us feel guilty when we don't need to. I was constantly asking the Lord to guide and direct me, so having asked him to forgive me if it had been his purpose for me to stop there briefly, I must now leave it with him, and even give thanks, which, of course, we're instructed to do for everything, and in all circumstances. These musings do touch on a dimension of sharing the Good News with the lost which may not be mentioned often. Do we feel that we've failed in something we were directed to do? Maybe the Lord allows such incidents to keep us humble. Otherwise we might begin to congratulate ourselves on the great job we feel we're doing for the Kingdom of God. However, he's warned us that he won't share his glory with anyone else.

Despite some negative responses on my treks, our Team did feel that we were seeing a period of openness in people's hearts around us. Our two nurses, Anitra and Sylvia, had a tremendous time in a village to the north around this time, where the men were almost fighting one another to get Scriptures so they could read the truth for themselves. They had other wonderful opportunities during their visiting, once with the women in a village near Toof-fa, and once with an ex-sheikh and his family up the wadi below Maharbisha. These folks seemed to be earnestly seeking and were most unusually interested in the gospel message. It seemed that we were having a time of absolutely unprecedented opportunity for the gospel, and we lifted up our hearts in praise and worship to the Lord for the privilege of being his ambassadors there, while wondering at the same time, how long it might last, given the political upheavals on the Arabian Peninsula at the time.

* * *

I was enabled to go on the third lowland trip on Tuesday, June 27, turning east from Khamees through territory where I hadn't been before, and on to Manga and Sook Al Ahad, both of which I'd visited on foot.

My plan was to visit the most important sheikh in the area of Khamees, so I turned off the main road and headed east into the foothills. There were large stone buildings in his village, set on the top of a high hill, plus three large water pumps down in the fields, with beautiful crops. The sheikh was welcoming, and I was delighted to be able to leave him some literature.

I discovered that the most important of the sheikhs in the Sook Al Ahad area was not at home, but on my way to his house I met a group of five men, two sheikhs and three others, all from the neighbouring lowland area, who wanted a lift up to Manga to see the government representative there and settle a land demarcation matter. It was a long journey out of my way, but it gave me the opportunity to tell them something of the Good News, and I was then able to leave a pack of my three little items with the more important of the two sheikhs; and afterwards I was glad to also be able to leave the same pieces of literature with the brother of the less important of those two sheikhs, to hand on to him later.

At the bottom of the mountain again, I visited another lesser sheikh close to Sook Al Ahad. He and his son and the others there were nice people, and friendly, and it was a joy to also be able to leave them some literature, after a chat about peace which the Lord Jesus alone can provide. Weary but grateful I arrived back at Muharraq at 7 p.m.

The watchman was angry when I returned from this, my eleventh trip. I hadn't told him that I was even going anywhere, despite his request to tell him, before I left, where I was planning to go. We took this to mean that, despite the fact that he was employed by us, the authorities had ordered him to gather that information and pass it on to them, presumably so that they could notify leaders in those areas that I was coming, and probably also to warn them not to accept any Christian literature from me. Whenever he asked me about my journeys, I answered vaguely, so as not to give anything away. He was also no doubt embarrassed because, although he'd been sleeping close to the Land Rover to guard it, I had shown him up. I'd climbed aboard so stealthily that I was already driving towards the wadi before he realised what was happening.

* * *

The fourth journey in the lowlands was all that remained now in this series of twelve planned trips. I longed to see the whole campaign finally completed and was desperate to avoid anything which might prevent my completing the twelve trips, or which might interfere with their fruitfulness. At last, Thursday, July 13, 1978, arrived, the day I planned, God willing, to tackle that final trip, which was to take me west along the northern bank of Wadi Moor, right to the coast.

I crept out of our house at 4.10 a.m., and moved as silently as possible through the darkness towards the Land Rover where, to my consternation, I could dimly see that the watchman had placed his Yemeni bed beside the driver's door, and was sleeping there! It would be impossible to open the door without having to disturb him. I'd been hoping against hope that I'd be able to leave without his causing me any difficulties, but obviously he wanted to prevent my leaving until I'd told him where I was going.

Pleading with the Lord to keep him asleep, I crept around to the front passenger's door, silently unlocked it, and was able to open it slowly and then climb in, making practically no sound at all. Without shutting the door, I managed to carefully manoeuvre myself over the gear sticks, even though it was awkward with my long legs, and, having settled into the driver's seat, I prepared to start the engine. Fortunately, it sprang to life and I was able to drive straight off, leaning over to shut the passenger's door, while in the rear-vision mirror I could make out the figure of the watchman stumbling after me, waving his arms. There was no way that he could catch up with me though. I sped away, praising the Lord.

I travelled directly to Luhayya, a town on the coast just north of where Wadi Moor enters the sea (if it's flooding), arriving at about 9 a.m. I enquired whether there was a doctor based in the town and sought him out. He turned out to be friendly and pleasant. I had a good chat with him and with an older man, to the latter of whom I gave a John's Gospel, *Way of Salvation* and Seychelles sheet. After a nice breakfast I visited the sheikh, whose baby son was ill with what I believed was malaria. After treating him (with the doctor's consent), I gave the sheikh a booklet entitled *Words of Comfort*, and other literature.

During the morning, I had a look around the town. Luhayya was in its heyday early in the 1900s during the Turkish occupation. I saw many old stone buildings, several storeys high and coated with a cream plaster, in various stages of dilapidation. The rest of the town comprised elaborate stick huts, often with private, mud-walled compounds. An inlet from the sea allowed the sailing boats to come right in beside the town to unload. The ocean-going boats are called dhows, and some were motorised. (Nearby I saw a whole pile of sacks containing sugar, marked 'Djibouti'. Since that port is on the opposite side of the Red Sea, I couldn't help wondering if that meant they were contraband). Other, much smaller boats were long and narrow, without any sail, like extended surf boats, each powered with an outboard motor. The sand was black and oily, no doubt from the innumerable ships which had plied the Red Sea and discharged unwanted oil overboard. A row of tiny stalls near the water's edge were simply a combination of something for the man to sit on, and a makeshift table on which to scale and cut up the fish ready for selling, sheltered from the sun by a piece of cloth above, attached by strings to rough poles. Quite probably, this was similar to the scenes beside the Sea of Galilee in Biblical days. The overpoweringly strong, fish-market smell was probably the same, too!

Following a good lunch with the sheikh and the doctor, I left at about 4.30 p.m. to drive back to Muharraq by a more westerly route as I travelled north, so as to pass through any villages which were on the coastal side of the main road. The doctor rode along with me for part of the way on his new Suzuki motorbike, which he'd bought that very day! Before we parted, I was delighted to be able to leave with him a gospel and other literature. Maybe the Lord had caused him to be open to the Good News by arranging for him to be feeling light-hearted because he was trying out his brand-new motorbike.

The sun was setting as I drove into the township of Zohara. I was a little concerned in case they'd already heard of me and would cause trouble. However, I didn't plan to visit the government official, and while asking directions to the sheikh's house, I came across his son who was changing the oil in his Toyota beside the roadway. He told me that his father was in Sana'a, but that his paternal uncle was present, and was praying in the mosque. It seemed that the Lord had arranged for me to meet up with this young man who wasn't praying in the mosque, so I started chatting with him and with another young fellow who came along, and other people who gathered around. It was getting dark now, so much so that it was difficult to read with them. However, I was delighted to be able to leave some literature with each of those two young men.

I then set out to drive straight back to Muharraq. The road I was on headed in a northerly direction, and met the main north-south road at Abs. I was aware that the area I was passing through contained many villages, none of which I'd ever visited; and as I drove along, I prayed for all the people living there.

At about 9 p.m. I stopped to pick up four young men wanting a lift to a big village near Abs in order to attend a funeral. I'd seen that distant village from the main road, with its colourfully painted buildings. I took the opportunity to speak with these young men about the Lord Jesus, and to give each of them some literature. What a wonderful joy and privilege to sense that the Lord of the harvest had arranged the timing of everything so perfectly, knowing that I would meet those four young representatives from that section of the country, and be able to leave with them the Word of Life!

It was 10.30 p.m. when I arrived back at Muharraq after that last trek, praising the Lord that he'd enabled me to complete all twelve trips which I'd had so much on my heart: eight over the mountains and four on the coastal plain. When I looked at the dates, I realised I had been able to finish them a week before July 21, which would be seventy weeks after the vision for the treks developed. I had shared this spiritual deadline with our colleagues in Sana'a in March 1977 the previous year, and now it had come to fruition.

* * *

It soon became clear why that deadline had been so pressing. Just nine days after completing the last of the mountain trips, an Egyptian surgeon arrived to begin work in Maharbisha, the town high up on the mountain ridge behind Muharraq. If he'd arrived earlier, it would have effectively prevented my going on about half of the mountain trips because there would have been no medical reason for me to even pass through. He would have been the doctor responsible for that whole region, and not me. Other doctors were gradually being placed in the various big towns I'd been through and for that reason it seemed unlikely that I would have a second opportunity of going to most of those areas again.

Much later, I also realised that with roads being built up into the mountains at that time, soon it would no longer have been necessary to stay out overnight on such treks. Most of the mountain villages would be reachable by day trips, within reasonable walking distance from one or another of the roads being constructed. However, I'd found that by far the best opportunities for the gospel happened during those overnight stays, and so this was probably one of the reasons the Lord had given me the deadline of July 21. After those roads were opened, the authorities would expect that any treks I went on into the mountains, where I knew the most responsive Yemenis were to be found, would be conducted in a similar way to the four lowland treks which I undertook in the Land Rover, when I didn't have to stay out overnight at all.

It was usually hot and dusty at Muharraq during summer, but that year we enjoyed some rainstorms with refreshingly cool, dust-free days, much to our surprise and relief. The atmosphere was so clear sometimes that we could see the Red Sea distinctly about forty miles away to the west. We felt prompted to pray that the rains would coincide with spiritual showers of blessing on the seed sown, as the Lord poured out his Holy Spirit, causing an ingathering of souls throughout Yemen and beyond. I liked the quote that said, 'When man works, man works. When man prays, God works.' We'd asked our friends at home to pray for the Yemeni people living in our segment of the country, and we know they faithfully did so. The outcome was that the Lord wonderfully answered their prayers, and no doubt he is still at work there today.

13

Hepatitis

1978-1979: Age 35

After four and a half months of hard work and contending with the heat of summer, we closed the clinic on Wednesday, July 26 and headed away to Jibla for a much needed break, and then to Sana'a for our Team conference, arriving back in Muhurraq in mid-September. We were very quickly back into the swing of the medical work, but faced an emergency on the night of Wednesday, October 25, when a man was brought to the clinic suffering from cholera. We hadn't seen a cholera patient before, but this scenario was exactly what I had discussed in each place I'd visited throughout the whole lower Hajjah Province, carrying my letter of introduction from the Ministry of Health. The entire medical purpose of my trips was to talk about what to do in order to prevent an epidemic of something like cholera or smallpox—and here we were having to treat someone suffering from exactly that.

    I have never seen anything like this case of full-blown cholera. Not only was the fellow vomiting profusely, but his bowel spasms caused the diarrhoea to forcefully hose out of him! We put him on one of our Yemeni beds, where the rope construction was suitable in the circumstances—the fluid went straight through the bed, and we did our best to catch most of it

HEPATITIS

in buckets placed underneath. However, despite all our efforts, plenty of his loss missed the containers, and we frequently had to mop the cement floor clean with disinfectant. We inserted an intravenous cannula, and commenced running fluids into him, aiming to keep his pulse less than a hundred beats per minute, and his systolic blood pressure above a hundred millimetres of mercury. When he got to his twenty-seventh bottle of IV fluid, he'd almost recovered. I was so glad that John and Molly had returned from furlough, and that John was there to help. He and I rostered ourselves so that one of us was always checking him and replacing the IV bottles as needed.

Our cholera case caused a flap in the area. A team of about twelve medical personnel arrived from Hajjah to vaccinate the people in the nearby villages, and the news spread far and wide that we'd treated a man with full-blown cholera in our clinic; that we'd cared for him for three days, and that he'd needed so many bottles of intravenous fluid.

Without the treatment he received, the man would most certainly have died; so naturally he and his family were grateful. We, on the other hand, were relieved that there *were* no other cholera patients.

I believe that at least one of the Lord's purposes in allowing that patient to be brought to our clinic was that it validated my medical reason for undertaking those twelve trips which I'd completed just over three months before, following the strategy which the Lord had given me, and with his blessing on every detail. Our medical work was clearly playing a vital role in improving the health of the population of the whole region, and was consequently causing the gospel message, which we endeavoured to share and to shine around, to be attractive.

* * *

Although we hadn't announced it yet, plans were in place for us to be heading to Pakistan. The Red Sea Mission Team leadership suggested that we take an early furlough from the coming August (1979), and then go to Pakistan with a whole term ahead of us. Since we were approaching the end of 1978, we expected we would serve in Muharraq for another eight months or so, before we said farewell to Yemen.

Things were not to pan out as we expected, however. The cholera case, along with other responsibilities had worn me out, and a two-week break over Christmas in Sana'a, sanctioned by our mission leadership, was exactly what our family needed. Awaiting us was correspondence school material for five-year old Andrew, and two toy tip trucks in the mail. They had been posted almost exactly a year previously, on 30 December 1977, and arrived on Christmas Eve 1978. We thought it was marvellous of the Lord to arrange that special treat for us all.

Just two days before we were due to drive back to Muhurraq, on New Year's Day, 1979, I came down with hepatitis A and was ill for nearly two weeks. At first, we were dismayed but we soon saw how good it was that we were still in Sana'a, with its medical help and laboratories, as well as the surroundings being so cool and quiet in comparison to Muharraq. However, hepatitis A was not something one recovered from quickly. With at least four weeks in bed, and then months of weariness ahead of me, we and the leadership agreed that it would be unwise to venture back to Muharraq with summer approaching, and with all the inevitable pressure and busyness of life on the station. John, our male nurse, and the three nursing sisters were to carry on the medical work at Muharraq on their own, and as soon as I was strong enough for the long journey back to Australia, Dell, I and the children would leave Yemen to enable me to convalesce in Sydney before commencing deputation work.

I wrote a letter explaining all of this to our parents and supporters, telling them not only about our leading to Pakistan, but also that we expected to be arriving home in March instead of later in the year. Even before I had posted the letter, however, the axe we had all been waiting for, finally fell. The Yemen government informed the Red Sea Mission Team that we all had to leave the country, with most of us out by the end of February.

We weren't sure what triggered our expulsion, though we heard that a Gospel Recordings cassette in Arabic had been partially recorded over by some Yemeni man, with sentences added which spoke against Islam and

Mohammed. This was not one of the cassettes which I gave anyone; but as we had reminded ourselves from time to time, if we were going to be thrown out, it was preferable that it should result from sharing the Good News rather than simply because some Muslims didn't want any Western organisations, especially Christian ones, working in Yemen. This was also exactly the situation which had been envisaged when the Red Sea Mission Team 'Principles and Practices' were formulated; if the team was told to leave any work, we would simply pack our bags and move elsewhere. Our work at Muharraq had begun in stick huts five years previously. At the time we were all told to leave, the new clinic had been fully utilised for approximately three and a half years, but we were prepared and willing to leave buildings and equipment behind if necessary, seeing that they all belonged to the Lord anyway.

Our family departure date from Yemen stayed at March, as I was still unwell, but my convalescence was progressing steadily, and I was gradually able to spend more time out of bed each day. Before we left Yemen, Peter brought our things up to Sana'a from Muharraq. Only a limited amount could be taken home with us on the plane of course, but we packed three 44-gallon drums of things that we would need in Pakistan and sent them by airfreight to Islamabad, the capital of Pakistan, to await our arrival. That was relatively close to where the Crowes had begun their work.

Our time in Yemen was ending. However, it seemed that God's work could still go ahead in some ways. About three weeks after we'd been informed of the government's decision to expel Red Sea Mission Team members from the country, the Yemeni president changed his mind. Some influential people from Yareem had insisted on our people staying, so some remained for possibly another two years, though with restricted opportunities for ministry, before finally leaving. Then, a few years later, the Team received a government request to 'please return', and some work was undertaken, but not at Muharraq. Although Adele and I have never been back to that village, over more recent years when Peter and Margaret, Wolfgang and others visited the Muharraq district, people there warmly remembered us all, and implored that we return and work amongst them again. What was even more encouraging was that it was widely known that our Yemeni brother continued to shine as a Christian.

Also, throughout that district a great desire had developed in many hearts to obtain Christian Scriptures—and their delight was obvious when they did. With his wide experience of missionary work amongst Muslims, Wolfgang later told me that he had not seen anything similar to the way the men flocked around his Land Rover in at least one village near Muharraq which he visited some years ago, all eagerly wanting to obtain scriptures. This may not seem dramatic, but it is almost unheard of in Muslim countries, to my knowledge. He particularly remembered an elderly man hobbling over to him at one place, and pleading, 'Please! Please! Could I have a Bible?' The young American brother accompanying Wolfgang on that trip fetched one for him from the vehicle, and the old man took it gratefully, and hurried away as best he could. What a *joy* it was for us to hear such reports! And may the Lord bless and encourage our faithful prayer partners! He is wonderfully answering all their earnest prayers, past and present. Unfortunately, it's impossible to follow up people in Yemen because that could jeopardise their lives, so we pray on and leave them in the Lord's hands. He is the Lord of the harvest and the Good Shepherd, and no-one else can care for his sheep as he can.

Now in 2020, I think back to Jean Darnall's 1976 words about Yemen. At the present point in time, the civil war in Yemen has been raging for five years and is certainly the worst time of bloodshed and suffering since that prophecy was received, well over 40 years ago. We've been trusting that the Lord has been bringing Yemenis to salvation over these decades; yet whereas they've had to be mostly secret believers up to this point, we've recently heard that they are now becoming increasingly manifest, especially on the mountains. Occasional snippets of news over the years encouraged us to continue trusting that the Lord was working, but news in 2018 was thrilling! It's now known that there are hundreds of believers in Yemen, and many of them are coming to faith as a result of the war! Some are boldly sharing the gospel with their families, friends and co-workers. Over recent years, the local secret believers and new converts have organised an unofficial underground church which has been growing immensely, despite suffering and persecution. They are meeting together, sometimes from different, or even opposed backgrounds. Some are former Sunni Muslims; others are former Shias. There are elderly and teenagers, women and men, and people from different tribes and ethnic groups. They have a vision to grow spiritually and to help others, regardless of their religious or ethnic backgrounds, setting an example of unity, both for Yemen and the world. In dark times, these Yemeni Christians are bold witnesses who testify that suffering for Christ is part of being a Christian.

What a privilege it is to have been enabled to sow the precious seed in that part of Yemen, and then to hear after all these years, pieces of news which demonstrate that the Lord's hand is at work there. We believe that this also carries the promise of further fruitfulness throughout that region in the years ahead, because he who began a good work in people there will carry it on to completion until the day of Christ Jesus.

14

Five Years in Pakistan, and back to Yemen

1979–1998: Age 35–54

Gradually I got over the worst of my hepatitis. After two months of rest in Sana'a, I'd recovered sufficiently to travel home to Australia, and we flew from Yemen on Thursday, March 8, 1979. I continued to convalesce in Sydney before we undertook some deputation engagements and began preparing for our new venture in Pakistan. The Lord led us, each step of the way, showing us that he intended us to live in Karachi, and to conduct our outreach to the Baluchi people there.

We arrived on January 26, 1980, exactly eight years to the day after I left Sydney to fly to Pakistan in 1972. Andrew, now six years old and Sharon, four, happily attended the British Overseas School, and after Adele's and my language study, I established two clinics, each in poor Baluchi communities, on opposite sides of Karachi. The second turned out to be where most patients were seen.

The fact that I'd worked for almost six months in Shikarpur and Quetta back in 1972 proved helpful in a number of ways. For instance, Dr Henry Luther, who'd taken over as medical director of the Quetta Christian

Hospital when Dr Ronnie Holland retired, and who knew me, kindly wrote the all-important reference letter I needed when applying to the Pakistan Medical Board for medical registration.

During our five years in Karachi, apart from the medical work, we did all we could to provide the gospel message for the Baluchi people. The majority of the two million Baluchis in Pakistan lived in the south-western Baluchistan Province, most of which was off limits for foreigners. Others lived in south-eastern Iran and southern Afghanistan, and a large number lived in the port city of Karachi, on the eastern side of the border between Baluchistan and Sind Provinces.

During 1981, apart from our other activities, Dell and I conducted a systematic private prayer campaign. Working from several maps, I listed all the villages and towns throughout the whole region where Baluchis were found. When I counted them up, there were over six hundred place names. By praying for twelve each week, we covered them all, that year.

Baluchis who could read did so in Urdu, the official language of Pakistan. This was because most education was in Urdu. Therefore, whenever we gave out scriptures, which we did whenever possible and appropriate, we used those published in Urdu. Another important contribution, however, was to arrange for Alex and Sybil, a couple from Sydney who were working with Gospel Recordings, to come in 1982 and stay with us for a couple of weeks. Assisted by a Baluchi Christian we'd got to know well, they filled two cassettes with a clear gospel presentation and some Christian teaching in the Baluchi language. One cassette was accompanied by a booklet of forty simplified pictures which the commentary explained, one by one. Alex and Sybil left many copies of the booklet with us, and we made multiple copies of the cassette. These were our most effective means of outreach as we visited different Baluchi communities throughout Karachi, and we were also able to give them to Baluchis we met in the clinics and elsewhere.

Besides that, we began preparing Christian radio programmes in the Baluchi language, but we found that it was beyond our capabilities. The Lord showed us that this was to be a task for others in the future.

As in Muharraq, we felt that our calling was to establish a 'beachhead' for others to work from. After five years, Adele and I had begun to feel that the work which the Lord had sent us to do in Pakistan was nearing completion. With the arrival of two Australian families, Rod, a nurse, and his wife Miriam from Perth, and Ian, a GP, and his wife Dorcas from Sydney, we were pleased that we were able to hand it over to others.

Just two months before we were to return to Sydney, a team of Wycliffe Bible Translators who had recently arrived in Pakistan to work in the Baluchi language, invited Adele and me to attend their team conference, especially to assist in the orientation course for their eight new arrivals. We had a great deal of useful and relevant material to give them, and information to share, which we'd gathered over the previous five years. What a marvellous joy and privilege it was for us to be able to contribute to their work in these ways as they commenced their task.

Seven years later, in November 1992, the leader of that Wycliffe team sent me a copy of the recently published Luke's Gospel in the Baluchi (or Balochi) language, and it's one of my most treasured possessions. Inside the cover he'd written, 'To Mike and Adele Babbage, from the Balochi translation team, building on the foundation you laid so well.' I understand that the New Testament and portions of the Old Testament have since been completed. A year later, in November 1993, I received a personal letter from a member of a separate group of expatriate and national workers from a variety of backgrounds who'd come together in Karachi to co-ordinate the production of regular Baluchi radio programmes, aired from the Seychelles Islands in the Indian Ocean. It wasn't the initiative of any one group or mission, and broadcasting had begun in January of that year, 1993. They'd produced and aired two programmes a week, each of fifteen minutes duration. They were also working on producing cassettes of some of the stories and of the music they had recorded. He'd heard of our previous interest in such radio programmes, so he wrote to inform us of their progress, to share how encouraged they already were, and to request our prayer support.

* * *

When the day finally came for us to say goodbye to our work and friends in Karachi, we set off for a new adventure, arriving in Sydney on March 15, 1985. What would the Lord have for us back in Australia?

Because being a doctor was stressful for me, I'd been hoping that I might be able to leave the practice of medicine and serve the Lord in some full-time Christian work. However, I soon realised that I had to continue being a doctor and was led to join a general practice at Blaxland in the lower Blue Mountains. With some money which our friend Peter Levett's mother had left us in her will, we were able to buy an excellent little second-hand car and the Lord also provided us with suitable rented accommodation in Blaxland. We were on our way.

Unfortunately, after the first day at work I collapsed with overwhelming anxiety and had to take the rest of that week off. In that time, I was able to be seen by a Christian psychiatrist, who began me on some medication. From then I pressed on with working as a GP, and gradually settled into the task. During the next twelve years I was able to serve the Lord in various ways, both through my work as a doctor, and in the wider community with Adele.

After renting a home in Blaxland for four years, we were able to get a mortgage on a beautiful home in Springwood, three suburbs further up the mountains. Andrew and Sharon attended government primary schools, and then went to John Wycliffe Christian School for their high schooling, before moving on to University.

* * *

We'd been living in Springwood for seven years when our lives took a dramatic turn.

It was a Monday evening, February 17, 1997. In my study, I was reading Interserve prayer notes[112] and came across the names of Malcolm and Audrey—friends from Karachi days in the 1980s. Malcolm, a doctor from Perth, and his wife Audrey were members of Interserve, who had lived for a time in the flat below ours with their son Michael. We'd got to know them well. Now, fourteen years later, here was an urgent prayer request for a doctor to join Malcolm and Audrey in Aden, the southern port city of Yemen, to assist him in a busy clinic where he was the only doctor. Dell walked past my study door and I showed it to her.

'Why don't *we* do this?' she exclaimed.

That night I lay awake, going over everything in my mind. Both Andrew, now 23, and Sharon, 21, had left home, so it didn't seem necessary to remain in Sydney to care for them. And we were familiar with Yemen. We could speak some Arabic, and I had the Diploma in Tropical Medicine and Hygiene from Sydney University which would stand me in good stead. We knew our parents would miss us, but they were managing well. Our brothers and sisters would be able to continue the care they were already providing for them, so in this also it didn't seem necessary for us to remain in Sydney. In the medical practice, we were all busy, but the need for doctors in Yemen was obviously far greater than in the Blue Mountains. It seemed to us that few couples anywhere would be better suited to fill this need.

Two days later was my rostered day off so Dell and I decided to begin by waiting on the Lord. After a little while we thought it would be sensible to find out whether Malcolm still *needed* a doctor to come and help. If someone had already offered to join him, that would obviate any need for us to proceed. I rang the Interserve Office in Perth, and they gave me Malcolm's phone number in Yemen. Within a few minutes, I was speaking to him; and yes, he *did* still need an assistant, urgently. We had an excellent, albeit brief, conversation, renewing the friendship we'd enjoyed in Karachi.

But now we were faced with another major decision. Back in 1971, Adele and I joined the Red Sea Mission Team[113] and served with it until 1985. Now, we chose, after seeking the Lord's wisdom and direction, to apply to join Interserve instead. Malcolm and Audrey were members of Interserve and had been granted visas to enter Yemen under the auspices of (and seconded to) the Anglican Church in Aden. The clinic was in the grounds of the church. Since *they* were members of Interserve, it would simplify matters if Adele and I also joined the same mission. I therefore rang Jeanette, the State Director of Interserve in NSW, shared with her our thoughts, and made an appointment to visit her.

That same day, after prayer, although we loved the home which the Lord had provided for us, I rang an estate agent and put the house on the market.

It was now over eleven and a half years since I'd begun working in the medical practice in Blaxland. As a partner, I'd agreed to give the practice six months' notice if I decided to leave. Not wanting to delay our departure by a single day, I sat down at my desk that evening and wrote the letter to both of the other doctors, giving notice of my intention to resign from the practice in exactly six months, on August 19, 1997.

What a day it had been! By 10 p.m. on 19 February, we could say that we were going to Yemen. Twice more in the following three years we would be given further cause to regard that date as memorable!

Six days later, a staff member from the estate agency came and took photos of the house. Our next-door neighbour happened to see her and guessed what was happening. That evening, he popped in and said that he would buy it! Five weeks later we'd been provisionally accepted by the N.S.W. Council of Interserve. Jeanette said she'd never seen applicants processed with such amazing speed. Adele also commenced Arabic language lessons on Saturday mornings to brush up her skills, and we were offered a small flat to stay in, between the time when we vacated our home and the date we'd be leaving for overseas. These facts all confirmed to us that the Lord *did* want us to serve him again in Yemen. It was encouraging to see him clearing the way for us to go.

Everything seemed to be fitting together beautifully. However, not long after, we were concerned to hear that Malcolm and Audrey had been forced to return to Perth because he'd become seriously unwell and would require complicated surgery. In fact, as the weeks passed, it gradually became clear that they would not be able to go back to Aden at all! This caused me considerable uneasiness. I'd offered to go to Aden to *assist* Malcolm. I had not thought of accepting the post of medical director, or of attempting to fill his shoes. Malcolm was gifted, and not just as a practising doctor. He was also a qualified medical administrator and had even lectured medical students in the Aden University! Besides those abilities, he was a Baptist pastor and capable preacher. There was no way that I could possibly take on any of those roles, except the one of ordinary family doctor in the clinic. Despite my misgivings, we knew that the Lord could enable us to be all that he intended us to be. We could see the amazing way that his hand had been at work in our preparations to go, and this served to confirm to us that we were on the right track, and in the centre of his will. At times like this I've sought to hold on to Isaiah 12:2, 'I will trust and not be afraid.'

One positive outcome of Malcolm and Audrey's being in Perth was that we could now speak to them less guardedly on the phone without fear of Muslim authorities listening in to our conversations. We found out about various aspects of the situation that awaited us in more detail than would have been the case, had they still been in Aden. I of course, had to carry on with my usual workload at the surgery, as well as both of us attending some speaking engagements in connection with our approaching missionary service. At times Dell felt overwhelmed, but when she realised that it was largely a grief reaction, she discovered that she was better able to deal with it. We were sad to be leaving our children, parents, friends and lovely home. The fact that Interserve agreed to our request for permission to return to Australia for our annual holidays was a big help[114]. In fact, we were pleased with all we'd experienced in our dealings with Interserve.

There was still something—a dark cloud overhead—which, although neither of us realised it at the time, would turn out to be of enormous significance.

The whole saga began during the first two weeks of June 1997, when Interserve received a fax and I was notified of its contents, though I didn't see it. It was sent by those in the Middle East responsible for the running of the clinic in Aden and revealed a potential difficulty. I had now to accept that it was necessary for me to be the Medical Director of the clinic, at least initially. This was not easy to reconcile, recalling my struggles at Muharraq and elsewhere when I was placed in a leadership role. After prayerful consideration and feeling that it should be manageable, I decided to trial the position for six months.

Secondly, more than two months before Adele and I reached Aden, we heard that the clinic work had been cut back to provide mainly preventative medicine for women and children. From the information Adele and I had, we understood that the Yemen Government had granted permission the previous year for the clinic to open under the mandate that it be restricted to providing medical care for women and children only, with an emphasis on preventative medicine. (It was much easier for men to obtain medical care in Aden than it was for women and children.) Somehow though, perhaps through misunderstandings or miscommunication, men had for some time also been receiving medical treatment at the clinic, despite the fact that presumably the wording of the Government mandate was intended to preclude this from happening. I understood that the fax directed me to assist in implementing the reversion to the original government restriction of treating women and children only. However, it wasn't until after we reached Aden that we became aware of the serious problem this was to be for us, and me in particular.

* * *

Our flights and connections on the way to Yemen were uneventful, and we arrived at Aden in the middle of the night on September 30, to be picked up by the church's administrative assistant, a Yemeni man who spoke good English. He drove us to the flat where we were to live for several months, and after briefly meeting the chaplain and his wife, Jim and Carol, who lived in the adjoining flat, we flopped into bed.

We were in Malcolm and Audrey's fully furnished flat, a single storey, semi-detached house built with small, ventilation windows near the high ceilings, which were constructed in the pre-electricity, British style. The spacious rooms with tiled floors made the flat larger than expected, but it was old and rundown, like most of Aden. Our view of the harbour showed a dozen freighters or tankers anchored at any one time, with the occasional glimpse of a passenger liner sailing by. A steep gravel path took us down to a narrow beach of gravelly sand, with three or four drab, scraggly trees and shrubs growing nearby. Being near the port, most of our neighbours were from the Yemeni port community of sea captains and harbour pilots. Generally friendly, they understood some English. It had been thirty years since the British were forced to leave Aden due to the communist takeover, and many were desperate for them to return, so they made us feel welcome.

From the house it was a six-minute, gently-sloping, downhill walk to the church, which was originally opened in 1863 but had just been totally renovated and was due to be officially re-opened in just ten days or so. Many people were coming for this important weekend, some even from overseas. The church and its facilities including the clinic were managed by an expat Anglican clergyman and his wife, with several local workers. The place was beautiful! It had air conditioning, a community centre, and accommodation for visitors or short-term workers. The brand-new clinic was modern, with six air-conditioned rooms, roof fans along the covered verandah for waiting patients, and a van we could use. From the following week, the staff would include two doctors (a Western Australian woman and myself), two female nurses from Europe, two local female nurse/translators, a receptionist, pharmacist and gatekeeper. Even the Duke of Gloucester, who was present at a function we attended at the British Consulate the day after we arrived, was impressed by the church and clinic[115]!

When we found out about the clinic hours, we weren't so pleased, however. Women and children were seen on five mornings each week, from Saturday to Wednesday; that was fine. It was the shorter men's clinics held in the late afternoon on three of those days that placed me in an awkward situation. From the fax to Interserve by the church leaders (who were based elsewhere in the Middle East), I knew that the mandate issued by the Yemeni Government when the clinic opened the previous year in 1996, was that women and children were to be cared for, with an emphasis on preventive medicine[116]. Those regionally responsible had decided that the clinic should change back to complying with this original mandate. We thought that this had already been carried out, and yet, here were three clinics for men being held each week! What was I to do? I kept the matter in prayer for some time.

There were good things about that arrival period, however, as well as the challenge. For example, we were delighted to see how our Arabic came back, and Adele found being female in Aden much easier than she had experienced in Muharraq. Rather than having to wear an 'abeiya' or overcoat, she felt it was expected that she didn't wear it at all. Her usual outfit consisted of long-sleeved thigh-length tops with slacks, and sometimes a scarf. It was also cooler than we anticipated, and not just from the sea breeze; however, we still used the air conditioners due to the humidity. Just being back amongst Yemenis was exciting; after all, we were married there[117], and had Andrew in the country. However, we found we had to tone down our enthusiasm about Muhurraq and the north of the country. In the recent civil war, it was the North that bombed and looted Aden, and then imposed Islamic law instead of British law, much to the resentment of the locals. Not unexpectedly, but sadly, there were many in Aden living in poverty. We tried to have some small apples or other food items with us when we drove around town, in order to have something to give to the beggars, especially those on our regular routes.

Over time it was clear just how different Aden was to cities and towns in the North. Because of its British heritage it seemed more like Pakistani cities such as Karachi, Islamabad, Murree and Peshawar, albeit with distressing devastation still apparent from bombs and looting. The airport, for example, was still all burnt out, with only one small section functioning.

In October, we experienced some of the fears Aden residents were familiar with when eight bombs were planted in various locations around the city, three of them exploding! Mostly targeting foreign organisations, one was discovered on the wall surrounding the church and the clinic building. The man who noticed it told our Yemeni clinic receptionist. When he went to have a look at it, he turned pale. He'd previously worked as a sapper with the Yemen army, and recognised the bomb for what it was. He knew better than most the damage it was capable of inflicting. Having shouted for everyone to be kept well clear, he rushed to the phone and called for the bomb disposal experts to come immediately with their equipment and defuse it. This they did, with only about thirty minutes remaining on the clock before it was set to explode. How relieved we were that someone had noticed it! And was it just a coincidence that a former sapper[118] was on hand at the time? We found it especially helpful for some days after this incident to remind ourselves of the promises in Psalm 91.

* * *

Memoirs are, of course, an account of one's recollections of events, happy and otherwise. I could have decided to skip over some decidedly unhappy memories of our time in Aden, except that later we were able to see that it was the Lord who'd led us through those months, and that it had all been *necessary*. So, despite the negative nature of certain incidents which occurred over our five and a half months there, it's essential to share at least part of what we went through, in order to understand what happened to us, and why. My prayer, as I write, is that the account may be encouraging to some who are or have been in a similar situation; and to point out that it was the Lord's *purpose* for us to go through that difficult time. Hopefully through reading this, others may be spared unnecessary grief and confusion if the Lord chooses to lead them along perplexing pathways, too.

We had good fellowship with Jane, the excellent young doctor from Perth, who'd come to work at the clinic for six months. She arrived in Aden in early August, about two months before we did. The morning clinics were busy, but she and the two missionary nurses weren't needed for the afternoon men's clinics which were much quieter. I conducted those on my own with just one Yemeni helper, and with Dell in the pharmacy where she was finding her niche. We'd thought she'd be helping in the church office, but because we hadn't managed to bring a laptop with us, the rude greeting she received on arrival was, 'Well, don't think that you'll be using the church computer!' making it clear that she was not welcome there.

As well as with Jane, Adele and I got on well with one of the two nursing sisters from Europe. There were also several friendly English-speaking businesspeople who came to the weekly church service each Friday morning, particularly a kind and godly German couple. However, four of the missionaries (none of whom were connected with Interserve) and an influential expatriate person who worked in the city, were difficult personalities indeed. It was almost impossible to discuss matters with them, and they didn't seem willing to pray with us—about anything! They were so unfriendly and uncooperative that we got little help from them at all. The whole atmosphere was unpleasant, despite our desire to work together with them in fellowship and unity. Somehow Adele and I were like enemies to them, and their behaviour was sometimes unchristian, to put it mildly. I won't go into detail except to say that Adele and I were both in our fifties at the time and had lived and worked with many different people and nationalities over the years, both Christian and secular. Never before had we experienced such outrageous deceit and deliberate unkindness. Part of their dislike of us may have been simply that we were Australians, but again we'd never experienced anything of that nature before, either. The whole situation was an eye-opener for us both, and those few months in Aden ended up being the most unhappy time of our lives.

Just one example of what happened was that a Christmas evening barbecue was planned for all the Christian expats connected with the church and clinic. Everyone received written invitations, except Adele and me. I don't think it could possibly have been by accident or oversight. Jane asked us if we'd been invited, and the poor thing was put in a difficult situation, but sensibly decided to attend. We were by this time settled in a nicer flat, where we had Christmas dinner by ourselves—just the two of us! It was the saddest and loneliest Christmas dinner we are ever likely to face, knowing that everyone else was meeting together, but that we'd been purposely left out. But even in that unhappiness, we couldn't help noticing the loving little touch the Lord had provided for us. It was a little Christmas pudding from Harrods. An English nurse had rented the flat before us and had left it in the back of the cupboard. Dell just happened to find it in our new flat, there in far-off southern Arabia.

Sadly, we were to lose Jane from the clinics. Just before she was due to return home, in mid-November we went with her to Jibla Hospital, a four-hour drive from Aden, where we spent two nights meeting with other Interserve members working in Yemen. While at the hospital, we shared about the difficulties we'd been encountering in connection with our work in Aden.

'You'd be most welcome to move to Jibla, and to work here, if that ever became a consideration,' some of them said.

On December 27, Dell and I flew to Cyprus for an area conference of all the Interserve workers stationed in North Africa and the Middle East. Flying with Royal Jordanian Airlines necessitated an overnight stopover in Amman, the capital of Jordan. Communications from Aden were often difficult for us, but we'd managed to arrange to stay that night with an Interserve couple and their young children. The fellow kindly came and met us at the airport and drove us to their home. It was such a blessing to be amongst friends; and while there, they took us to see the Roman amphitheatre which was still in reasonably good condition. Adele liked the city of Amman and staying there turned out to play an important part in decisions which had to be made three-and-a-half years later.

The onward flight to Larnaca in Cyprus was mostly memorable for the fact that we'd not been able to notify the Interserve office there of our arrival details. Added to this problem was the fact that all the Interserve staff members based in Cyprus were by then at the conference centre located outside the city, and we had no address or phone numbers to contact them. Try as we might, we'd not been able to find out exactly where the five-day conference was to be held, and we could only prayerfully press on with our journey, and trust that the Lord would guide and care for us. We were acutely aware as we disembarked at Larnaca and entered the airport terminal that we knew no-one there, and no-one knew us! As we and the other passengers on our flight approached the desks where the customs officers were waiting to check our passports, we noticed a young, blonde-haired woman in the queue, and wondered if she might possibly be an Interserver who was also coming to the conference. Deciding that there was no harm in at least asking, we moved in her direction and, would you believe it? Yes! She was coming to the conference! She turned out to be a Dutch doctor working at the TB hospital in a town north of Amman. Not only that, she knew where our conference was to be held, so we shared a taxi with her. We would most certainly have been in dire straits in the airport terminal without the Lord's help and guidance. I was reminded of the account of Abraham's faithful servant who travelled all the way by camel to North West Mesopotamia to find a wife for Isaac from amongst Abraham's relatives. In a wonderful way, the Lord led him to Rebekah, whereupon he said, 'As for me, the Lord has led me on the journey.' And we could say the same, with relief and gratitude.

January meant some relief from the troubles we had had. Of the four difficult personalities, one had already left, and two others had plans to leave on January 24. As well, we had developed some other friends with whom we had good fellowship and times of prayer. Also, a long weekend at the end of the month marked a Muslim religious festival, as well as a good opportunity for a break. When we heard that some friends from another mission were travelling up to Jibla, Dell was able to get a lift with them so that she could stay for a few days with an American couple, Bobbi and Marty, the leaders of all Interserve work in Yemen. Dell not only had a much-needed rest but was also able to spend time waiting on the Lord in prayer concerning our current difficulties in Aden, and our need for his help. I had decided to remain in our flat where I also could have prolonged and uninterrupted times of prayer, especially for the salvation of the people living in and around Aden.

Over the next few weeks, we were relieved to see the work beginning to run smoothly at last, with everyone apparently getting along comfortably together. However, several most unpleasant things were then said or done to us which, had I realised their significance, would have set alarm bells ringing in my mind. In fact, we were only in the calm before the storm—or the eye of the cyclone. Calamity was about to strike.

Soon after this, we heard that a leading person responsible for the church and clinic (who was also not connected with Interserve) would be visiting Aden in February. I felt that this provided the prompting for the clinic to begin complying with the mandate from the Yemen Government to only treat women and children. I naturally assumed that the fax which was sent to Interserve had been intended to inform me of that decision. If the Government learned that we were attending to men, blatantly disregarding their clear instructions, mightn't we expect them to be understandably displeased? Would it be beyond the realms of possibility that they might withdraw their permission for the clinic to treat any patients at all, and to close it completely? I had accepted the role of Medical Director of the clinic for those first six months, and so it was obviously my responsibility to act in accordance with the Government's directives. If trouble arose because men were being treated at the clinic, I might be liable to be accused of gross dereliction of duty in not putting a stop to the men's clinics, knowing that they were being held in breach of the arrangement made with the Governmental authorities.

I'd been praying and anguishing over the problem for weeks. To make changes almost immediately after arriving could have been seen as threatening certain other people's authority and leadership. It seemed impossible for Adele and me to discuss, let alone pray, with these unpleasant, dismissive people about anything. I felt inadequate, as usual, and intimidated; besides, I had only just arrived, and was settling into the routines and finding out how things worked. I had seen no alternative but to simply continue, but now decided that I had to act, despite others not being in agreement. I couldn't risk the whole clinic being closed because some people disliked the idea of stopping the men's clinics. The position of the Government and the clinic's regional leadership was clear to my mind, and so I believed that I had no alternative but to begin implementing their directives without further delay.

The men's clinic stopped, not all at once, but gradually, because some men needed repeated visits. So as not to cause more disruption or inconvenience to them than necessary, I arranged to drop the number of clinics to two each week initially; then after a fortnight a second weekly clinic was stopped; and finally, the third was also terminated.

We'd been keeping in touch with Marty, the head of Interserve in Yemen, who knew of course, that we'd been having a difficult time. When he heard that this leading regional person connected with the clinic was coming to Aden, he decided to come down and stay with us over those days so that he would be fully informed of all that transpired, and perhaps have some input as well.

The visitor arrived on Wednesday, February 18, and arranged with an assistant who'd come with him, to meet each of the staff in ones or twos the next morning. Dell and I were amongst the first to go in, together with Marty who came with us. It wasn't a long interview. The visitor said that he was concerned about what had been happening in Aden, and that he'd been kept informed of my activities. When we tried to explain the difficulties we'd faced, and gave him one or two examples of how hard things had been made—not only for Adele and myself, but also for one or two other staff members—he said that he'd think about what we'd said, and discuss it with the other staff members when interviewing them later that morning.

'Could you come back and see me later this afternoon?' he asked, and we agreed.

'I think you're going to get the chop,' said Marty, as we all drove back to our flat.

We spent the rest of the day quietly, but because I didn't want to be late for our appointment, we set out to drive back to the church with plenty of time to spare. Finding ourselves approaching the compound a little too early, we stopped beside the road, and had a time of prayer together.

When we went in for our interview, the visitor didn't waste any time.

'I've sounded out the rest of the staff,' he told me. 'I'm particularly displeased that you've stopped the men's clinics.[119]'

I had to protest. 'But I was only carrying out your wishes outlined in the letter you faxed to Sydney.'

This caught him momentarily off guard, and he paused briefly. 'That's your interpretation of it.' He said something to the effect that I wasn't the doctor they were looking for, and so we were free to leave. 'There is no need to come to work anymore, as from this afternoon.'

Naturally we were shocked. 'I do apologise for anything I've done to cause this situation,' I said. 'Is there no way we can rectify the grievances, and continue on with the work?'

'There's nothing to be done,' he said. His mind was made up.

'Well, it would be helpful for me to know what I've done wrong,' I said, 'so I might avoid similar problems in the future.'

He simply said, 'I don't like your style,' and with that, the interview was terminated.

The visitor got up and went out of the room, leaving his assistant sitting in the background. I turned to him in some desperation. 'What are we going to do? We've sold our home and cars, and I've left my medical practice to come all this way to help. Are we going to have to turn around and travel all the way back home again?' The assistant squirmed a little and mumbled awkwardly something to the effect that there was nothing he could do.

So here we were, on February 19, 1998, and I'd just been given the sack! It was exactly one year to the day since we'd rung Malcolm, made our initial contact with Interserve, put our house on the market, and written the letter to resign from the medical practice. That date had now been permanently spoiled, and every anniversary would bring to the surface of my memory the hurt and grief we felt at that time[120].

From what the visitor said, we realised that someone had been complaining about us and had kept him regularly updated on our doings. I do trust that the reader will forgive my dwelling on the shock we felt at being dismissed like this with absolutely no warning whatever, and without any attempt by the senior staff in Aden to sit down and discuss with us the things they were presumably unhappy about. In all probability these could have been simply and satisfactorily sorted out together. I also felt particularly distressed at having been so deliberately deceived and betrayed, especially by one or two whom we'd trusted and looked to for Christian fellowship, encouragement and advice. God forbid that I should ever behave in a similar manner myself, and may I be forgiven, if I ever have.

The next morning being Friday, we had our weekly service in the church. Later that day, Marty drove back to Jibla; but not before we'd had another time of fellowship together.

'You both would be welcome to come and work at Jibla Hospital, if you want to,' he assured us. We said we needed a few days to pray about it to be more certain that it was the Lord's will for us, but that we would almost certainly be taking up his kind offer. The next week we rang and notified him of our acceptance.

For several reasons, I decided that I wouldn't leave Aden immediately, but would work on at the clinic for another four weeks. For one thing, some of the patients needed a doctor rather than a nurse to treat them, and I was now the only doctor at the clinic. During the final weeks, Adele resumed working in the pharmacy, too. Also, we needed to give our friends at Jibla time to prepare things like accommodation, before we arrived. In addition, we needed at least a week to have our work visas transferred from the Aden clinic to Jibla Hospital, as well as time to pack our personal belongings. Besides this, the English nurse who'd previously lived in the flat which we were now renting was coming to visit Aden, and we wanted to meet her. As it turned out, our meeting with the nurse was a real encouragement to Adele and me, as well as to her; though the story she had to share was distressing, and extraordinarily similar to our own!

This woman was a committed Christian who'd come to Aden to work in the newly opened church clinic. She had leased the flat for a full year from March 1997, fully expecting to be staying for several years at least. Sadly however, certain personalities connected with the clinic had developed a disliking to her, and negative communications about her were sent to one or two people. Not long after that, one of those persons visited Aden. Without the slightest warning she was dismissed and told that she needn't turn up for work the next day!

The poor woman was shattered and deeply distressed but managed to secure a temporary job with the United Nations in Aden. Later, having paid several months' rent in advance for her flat, she flew home to England, leaving the fully-furnished apartment empty, and the keys with Christian friends elsewhere in the city, giving them permission to let people such as ourselves stay in it, if the need arose.

Because of the unexpected turn of events, she and her boyfriend Phillip who had planned to get married a year or two later, decided to bring their wedding forward. Now she and her husband were visiting Aden, partly to show him where she'd worked, and for him to meet her friends; but mostly to pack up her belongings, and to sign off on the terminating lease. We were only too glad to have been able to pay the rent for those final three months of her lease, and to have cared for her belongings. And how excellent it was to be able to share with her that the timing must have been the Lord's doing! Not only had her apartment been a wonderful blessing to Adele and me, but just when the lease would be expiring, we would be moving to Jibla. Despite the hurt we'd all experienced, they and we were helped and consoled through sharing our similar tales of mistreatment.

As we thought through all that had happened, it occurred to us that those senior visitors and one or two of the clinic personnel may actually have been afraid that missionaries such as ourselves might be unwise and insensitive in the way we engaged in evangelism, and so might cause the wrath of the Yemeni authorities to come down on their heads, with the church and clinic being closed down in consequence. However, I only gave out one gospel during the entire five and a half months that we were in Aden, to a taxi driver with whom I'd got talking as he was driving me somewhere.

The time in Aden was painful indeed, but I later came to realise two things. First, that it was *the Lord* who'd led us into, and through, our time there; and second, that it had all been *necessary*! Let me explain why.

The first time that Adele and I visited Jibla Baptist Hospital was in November 1973 for Andrew's birth. We stayed there several times during those early years, mostly for holidays. I knew that it was well-run and had a high standard of medical, surgical and obstetric care. Because I was a general practitioner I'd never considered working there because I was sure that I'd be medically out of my depth most of the time. It wouldn't have mattered if I'd heard that they were desperate for more doctors; I'd never have offered to work there voluntarily.

Now, however, I was being *forced* to go. I certainly didn't want to return to Sydney straight away, so we had no other option. We'd been invited to join the staff there and I accepted, though with real trepidation. I had no idea that after the initial few months of settling in, the next three years' of service which lay ahead of me at Jibla would prove to be amongst the happiest years of my whole life. Besides that, what Adele and I ended up contributing to the overall work of the hospital by filling necessary staffing positions was not only recognised by the leaders and our colleagues at Jibla, but they also made a point of telling us how much they appreciated it. Before long, it became clear that the Lord had intended all along for us both to serve him there, and the only way he could get me to go was to arrange the circumstances in such a way that I had no alternative. What a wonderful discovery this was, and how excellent to be able to share with others the blessings we'd found awaiting us after such a stormy passage through the Lord's waves and breakers.

15

The Safest Place of All

1998–2002: Age 54-59

Our four weeks remaining at Aden were up, and on Thursday, March 19, 1998 I went out early for a taxi to get to the inter-city taxi station. It was here that taxis left for Taiz, squashing twelve people including the driver into each vehicle, with four across each of the three seats. I paid for three places in the middle or back seat in order to give us enough room because of my extra-long legs. There were plenty of travellers at that time of day, and when our car was full, we set off. It was a non-stop run for a couple of hours on a good tarmac road north-west across the dry, dusty coastal plain before climbing about 3,000 feet to Taiz. This city nestles beneath tall mountain peaks which are often shrouded in mist, and its atmosphere is noticeably cooler and more pleasant than in Aden.

After some morning tea, we followed a similar taxi rank procedure, and then drove north along the mountains, reaching the outskirts of Ibb about an hour and a half later. It's a small city, and the town of Jibla is near. By this time, we were about 6,000 feet above sea level, and it felt even more cool and pleasant. A local taxi took us five kilometres west on a winding tarmac road which runs along a short valley, at the end of which is the township of Jibla occupying the northern slope, with the hospital compound on the opposite side, built on the relics of an ancient cemetery.

During the journey, Dell prayed, 'Lord, you must have something for me to do in Jibla because you are taking us there.' That evening, the nice American director of nursing at the hospital mentioned the need they had for a bookkeeper with their administrator going on furlough in April or May for nine months. When Adele offered to help, they were pleased and relieved.

The contrast between working in Aden and Jibla could not have been more complete. Compared with the coldness of our reception in Aden, Jibla gave us a warm welcome, with meals in four different homes and a larger welcome organised for the next week. Everyone was eager for us to stay long-term and we felt wanted. There were now fourteen of us Interservers at Jibla (including six children), making up about a fifth of the total expat hospital staff. I was given a comprehensive orientation programme, covering every section of the hospital and found myself working with a multinational expatriate team of nine doctors including myself, as well as nurses, technicians and other personnel, and many Yemeni workers.

Adele was delighted to assist with typing and bookkeeping. One report that she typed was by the nursing director of kitchen services, pointing out the urgent need for a consultant dietitian to assist with various problems such as naso-gastric feeds and ideas for nutritious snacks for burns patients. She was over the moon when she discovered that Adele, as a dietician, was the answer to her prayers!

'How pleasant it is to have things working out for us happily at last,' I wrote to a friend of ours soon after our arrival. 'No doubt Satan will try to upset things, but the Lord has brought us to a friendly, welcoming and appreciative fellowship, and we're being refreshed. Surely the boundary lines have fallen in pleasant places for us at present.'

Life for most Yemeni people was a financial struggle. One of the poorest countries in the world, with one of the highest fertility rates[121], it was hard to find all the necessities. For example, on the mountains, the nights got cold. Many people didn't have enough blankets and warm clothing. Over time, we were able to provide some of these things for a few of our Yemeni friends.

Jibla Hospital was widely regarded as the best in the country with patients sometimes travelling long distances to reach it. It was also known as a Christian hospital, which provided opportunities, although we had to be careful. Yemeni staff were under pressure to report us to the Muslim authorities if they heard us speaking to patients or their relatives about Christian things. Sometimes though, in answer to prayer, the Lord provided a minute or two to speak privately with interested people.

For our part, we were doing outreach in small ways. Adele and I had visited some Yemenis in their homes, which was worthwhile. We were also praying for other staff members who were finding opportunities to point people to Jesus. Scriptures in Arabic were secretly going out, and some Yemenis were able to privately view one or other of the excellent Christian Arabic videos available. Many listened in their homes to the Arabic Gospel radio broadcasts from the Seychelles Islands or from Monte Carlo; and, with satellite dishes everywhere, the new, Christian Arabic Satellite TV programmes were having a real impact.

As ever, of course, an important means of promoting the gospel message was by letting Yemenis see something of the Lord Jesus within us. All around us, people watched, weighed things up, and discussed amongst themselves what they noticed. Sometimes they commented on our lives, and the love and care we showed them.

The Jibla compound was pleasant and practical, comprising seven or eight terraced levels, with the hospital buildings at the base of the hill on the widest terrace, and with the staff accommodation further up. There was also a little library, as well as a multi-purpose building, a tennis court, and in the top corner of the compound a tiny burial ground for Christians, with five or six graves[122].

Our flat was the middle one of three little units constructed side by side in one building, and had a bedroom, small lounge, a kitchen/dining room and a bathroom. Three shared electric washing machines were located nearby in a covered, communal laundry shelter. The compound was connected to the town electricity supply, which unfortunately was far from reliable. However, the hospital had back-up generators which started automatically when there was a power failure.

The hospital had been built by the American Southern Baptists, and we were seconded to them by Interserve who provided our allowances and many other expenses. The Baptists were glad to have Interserve personnel working with them because we came as volunteers. They generously provided our accommodation free of charge, while we were only too willing to pay for our own electricity, gas, telephone, pharmacy supplies and hospital vehicle usage. Also of course, we paid for our own groceries and household necessities from our Interserve allowances. Fortunately, living expenses in Yemen were not high, so Adele and I could afford to fly home for our annual holidays, separate from our scheduled furlough every three years, which included deputation and speaking engagements. One of these annual holidays was taken in June, after nine months away in total. It had been 20 months since we had seen Andrew, and Sharon was preparing to leave for South Korea for study. We also wanted to visit our parents and obtain things like a laptop and so on.

After three and a half months in Jibla, I felt overstretched by the medical work. I arranged that after our return from Sydney, I would work solely in the out-patient department (OPD) which would be much more manageable for me.

'Do you think others might be unhappy with my decision?' I asked Marty before we left.

He helpfully pointed out that being seconded to the Baptists from Interserve, I was effectively an unpaid volunteer, and as such could legitimately stipulate where I felt able to serve. If I preferred to work only in the OPD, that would be perfectly alright.

* * *

We arrived back in Jibla on August 7 to some tragic news. Exactly a month earlier, in Hodeidah, three nuns from the Roman Catholic Order, the

Missionaries of Charity, founded by the late Mother Teresa, had been killed by machine gun fire as they left a clinic for the disabled[123]. The twenty-two-year-old gunman said he took their lives because they were 'preaching Christianity' and the attack may have been tied to the possible visit to the Vatican by the President of Yemen, who wanted to normalise relations.

Adele and I were shocked. We had met those Filipino and Indian nuns in Aden the previous November, dressed in their distinctive white habits with the bright blue strip around each hem. Things seemed more tense than usual, and two weeks after our return, we were all confined to the hospital compound. American embassies had been attacked in different countries, and the US raided Afghanistan and Sudan in retaliation. American establishments overseas—even those like Jibla Hospital—were thought to be in danger. We kept several small bags packed with essential items, ready for evacuation at short notice. When a busload of Iraqi, Afghani and Sudanese men camped in the valley a little below the hospital, we were spurred on to continue praying for protection. They were watching all the comings and goings at the hospital, and had a water tanker with them, which could hold a lot of explosives. We were perturbed to hear that they once even used the hospital water to wash before their Muslim prayers! However, one night there was a particularly heavy downpour of rain, and the next morning they were gone.

By the end of August, the restrictions had been lifted somewhat, and seven of us ventured out for lovely walk amongst the terraced grain fields in the hills above the township of Jibla. When we returned later in the morning however, the hospital people were anxiously waiting. Once again, we were all confined to the compound. This time, a local holy man[124] had caused the trouble. Either he or one of his followers publicly tore up and burnt a copy of the Koran, causing an uproar. The son of one of the hospital employees was standing nearby, and when his connection with the hospital was recognised, he was beaten up, the fury of the crowd overflowing into fresh anti-American feeling.

The crisis in Iraq heightened tensions as well. Many Yemenis held Saddam Hussein in high regard as the only leader who would stand up against

America; many had pictures of him in their homes. The President of Yemen, however, ordered the army to protect all American facilities, which meant that there were more soldiers in and around the hospital. All vehicles driven by Yemenis were searched for bombs before they were allowed through the gate. There were restrictions on us too, such as having to be back on the compound before dark. And although sometimes we may have been tempted to give way to fear, we were able to say with the psalmist, 'My flesh and my heart may fail, but God is the strength of my heart and my portion forever.' We were grateful for the many prayers of our supporters because most of the time our hearts were kept wonderfully calm and steady, enabling us to carry on with our daily work and activities.

The work of the hospital continued without interruption through the tensions. One week, our Sunday services were cancelled when for a few days it seemed unwise for too many of us expatriates to gather in the one place. We were also careful on Fridays, the Muslim 'sabbath', when mosque leaders sometimes broadcast vitriolic midday sermons over loudspeakers on the minarets. It was disconcerting to hear machine gun fire just hundreds of metres away during the wedding season. These, like fireworks, were part of the celebrations, and were fired into the air throughout the night.[125]

Despite the dangers, we had a great deal to encourage us. On the medical side of things, working only in the out-patients department drew much more on my general practice (GP) training and experience. Spiritually, there were opportunities to rejoice with the angels in heaven as people accepted the Lord as their own.

Dell stayed busy, mostly doing bookkeeping. She enjoyed visiting Yemeni families and went out a few times with American female hospital staff in a hospital car to different homes. On one such outing, they took a big, four-wheel drive vehicle and travelled for an hour and a half down a lovely green valley to visit the family of a girl who had recently been in the hospital. A young Yemeni soldier from the contingent guarding the hospital went with them, which was handy as the last stream they had to cross was flooded. Adele stumbled barefoot through the rocky torrent, with the rushing water reaching to the top of her thighs. Fortunately, she was supported by the young soldier and the girl's father, which prevented her from being washed away. The American nurse, Nickol, overbalanced on the way across, and lost one of her shoes! However, they had a good time with the family; and in answering one of the father's questions, Adele was able to explain the gospel message to them.

Of course, it was hard for Yemeni people to become believers. Those we met were often afraid. If it was discovered that they had become Christians, they were likely to be imprisoned and tortured to try to force them to return to Islam—or they could be murdered[126]. Pamphlets were distributed in Ibb and Jibla at one point, denouncing the hospital and Christians in general. With threatening wording, the local population was strongly urged not to be swayed away from Islam by Christians' 'acts of kindness'. Actually, we were encouraged by this publicity. Clearly the Lord was shining out through us in various ways, and it was having an impact.

Not long after we sent off our December letter to our friends requesting prayer, there was a violent kidnapping of sixteen tourists, including two Australians. In fact, for a month or so at the beginning of the year, on average, one Westerner was kidnapped every day. The government, making a concerted effort to bring the situation under control, asked us to give police twenty-four hours' notice of any journeys we planned to make beyond Ibb.

When Adele and four other women took a hospital car to Sana'a to spend the night and have some time out, a police car followed them through the area where a number of kidnappings had occurred. On the trip back, a police car[127] followed them most of the way, right to the hospital gates, in fact. As they drove through the township of Yareem, traffic had come to a standstill with a minor accident blocking the road. The police drove off the tarmac and onto the uneven shoulder, going on ahead past queued-up vehicles, lights flashing and siren and loudspeaker blaring, making way for Adele to drive past. They also waited while she stopped to buy petrol at another place. She was glad of the protection, but it underlined the difficulties we faced.

Another time Adele and a friend took a Yemeni family to do some shopping in Ibb. Since it was during the fasting month of Ramadan, they went at night when most of the shops were open. Adele was driving; the traffic was terrible, and people jeer at lady drivers in Yemen which made it more testing. Suddenly, a blackout made all the lights in the town go out. Then the car's brake began to seize on one of the wheels, squealing and becoming hot. Dell had no alternative but to stop the car beside the road. Fortunately, it was right in the centre of town, so they sat on the steps of a nearby shop in the semi-darkness. When some of the lights came on again, a nice old Yemeni man who was passing by took the wheel off the car for them but couldn't fix the brake problem. A big piece of rubber was wedged against the brake plate, so Adele rang the hospital from a nearby shop, and her friend's husband came in another car after about thirty minutes. Adele drove everyone home in his car, while he came back to the hospital after fixing her vehicle. It was a nerve-racking experience—and disappointing to not get much shopping done!

A friendly young soldier guarded the doorway of the emergency room in the outpatients department, sitting with his machine gun across his lap. Because the door into my consulting room was often open, directly across the narrow courtyard from him, I sometimes found that his gun pointed straight at me when I was at my desk. He was cooperative when I mentioned it to him; but sometimes he forgot, and I had to ask him to keep his weapon pointing towards the ceiling. The barred window of my consulting room looked over the high, wire fence into the car park. Once, while I was working away, a man in the car park fired his rifle four times, presumably into the air, and then made his escape behind the adjacent mosque. The Yemeni workers said he was 'a crazy man'; but that didn't diminish the danger much.

We carried on reasonably calmly with our daily duties despite the continuing threat of kidnapping and terrorist attacks. Helpful faxes and phone calls arrived from the British Embassy in Sana'a and the Australian Embassy in Riyadh (the capital of Saudi Arabia), advising us to keep 'a high level of personal security awareness and vigilance', and a low profile. What they meant was to stay on the compound as much as possible, but we did that anyway. We also left as many outside lights on at night as possible, and generally tried to be sensible and careful.

Less pleasant communications arrived too. I saw one letter the hospital received, purportedly written by students of Bin Laden in Ibb. It made shocking allegations, saying that the hospital and staff did terrible things with Yemeni babies and other patients. The basic message to us all was similar to that in Nehemiah 4:11: 'Our enemies said, "Before they know it or see us, we will be right there among them and will kill them and put an end to the work".' Like Nehemiah, we too sought the Lord's enabling and protection—and we knew that the safest place in the whole world was in the centre of God's will.

While we were upheld in prayer, Dell particularly found it stressful. As well as missing family, she found the tension and atmosphere of fear that everyone lived in took its toll. She and some others had to leave the compound frequently, simply to preserve their sanity. Others with personalities like mine were able to plod on day after day not feeling so imprisoned, nor venturing out so often.

Given that the whole reason we were in the country was for the Yemeni people, Dell found it hard not be allowed to visit local women. My work in the out-patients department brought me into contact with many Yemenis, but hers confined her mainly to her office.

Things were hard, but we did have some opportunities for relaxation. We enjoyed watching the occasional video, and Dell took a walk inside the compound most evenings. I played tennis two afternoons most weeks, and Dell sometimes led worship for expatriates, which she enjoyed.

In May, the hospital administration issued us all with a warning of an increased security risk, and just a few weeks later, the Assistant Director of Police for Ibb visited our American hospital administrator to talk about security. He came in an official capacity, but also as a friend, with the news that there were plans to kidnap or harm Europeans and/or Americans. The plans were not person specific, but nationality specific; and they were intended to cause embarrassment to the Yemen Government. They believed that Indian and Filipino staff members were not at risk; we considered that being white Australians put us in the same category as Europeans or Americans.

We were all asked to take certain extra precautionary measures, and five to seven additional soldiers were assigned to the hospital. Unfortunately, the tightened restrictions made it more difficult for Yemeni seekers and believers to meet secretly with expatriate staff, but already we had seen several instances of how the Lord enabled them to meet, despite this problem. Adele had been encouraged by teaching English weekly to a group of eight or nine Yemeni girls. I myself was encouraged when a nice old Yemeni man said to the three or four other fellows in my clinic room, 'These people have come to help us to know Jesus.' About an hour later, after his laboratory test results were available and he was preparing to leave, he said to the different group of people who were now in my room, 'Jesus is better than the other prophets.' He talked on for about fifteen seconds, almost preaching, until another man shouted angrily at him to stop, whereupon the old man simply turned and calmly walked away. I was truly delighted, though careful not to show it.

Notwithstanding the restrictions, Adele and I were able to get away for breaks in Aden several times. Our Interserve conference was the first of these, held over three nights in an air-conditioned beach resort with a private beach and shady garden. We stayed there again for three nights for a break at the end of April and had another two nights in June to celebrate both our birthdays. Again, we had a restful and refreshing time—until 3 a.m. on the second night. That was when we were woken by pistol shots; six or seven altogether, over perhaps the space of a minute. The first was loud, and we believe it was in the room next to ours; and then we heard some men shouting outside, and more shots in the garden, about ten metres from the door of our room. Adele and I prayed together and felt it best to keep out of sight. We had no idea what it was all about, or whether anyone was killed; and we couldn't see much through a crack in the curtains, but it certainly wasn't their TV turned up loudly!

We decided not to embarrass the reception staff by asking questions when we were checking out the next morning. Firstly, they probably wouldn't have told us the truth even if they knew (especially if it was bad news)[128]; and secondly, they wouldn't have wanted to talk about it. The tourist industry had been devastated by the abduction and killing of tourists the previous December, with more incidents since then[129]. Visitor numbers to Yemen had since dropped dramatically and many expatriates had left.

Just four days after we returned to Jibla, Adele was working in the kitchen-dining area of our flat when there was a sudden loud clatter and tearing sound. She thought that a large bird may have crashed into our front wire door or window, but since she could hear some Yemeni men shouting not far away, she decided to stay inside the house. A little later she saw what looked like a shiny Christmas beetle on the floor of our bedroom. Closer inspection showed that it was not a beetle—but a bullet! When she looked up, she noticed a small hole in the ceiling. When I came home from work, I found that if I looked carefully through the hole, I could see a little circular patch of daylight at one point where the bullet had come through the corrugated fibro roofing about a metre above the ceiling. From the angle, it was clear that it had simply fallen out of the sky, right at the foot of the bed. Being a Thursday, the day most weddings are held, I thought that perhaps someone had been celebrating by firing his machine gun into the air. However, the hospital maintenance worker who filled the hole in the roof said that he thought the shooting was a dispute over fields on the terraces above the compound. By firing his weapon into the air, the farmer had been forcefully suggesting to the other men that they should move off his land.

Around that time, in the out-patient clinic, I was listening to the chest of one of the security men. His pistol, which had been loosely pushed under his belt, fell onto the floor with a loud clatter, almost landing on my shoe. I was grateful that it hadn't gone off because it was pointing directly at my foot. I never had anything of that nature happen in my general practice in the Blue Mountains!

* * *

In the middle of the year, we arrived back in Sydney for Home Assignment. After a good holiday, we began our deputation speaking engagements.

Because Dell was still worn out, I undertook some of them alone, including a week in October up at Tamworth staying with our friends, Phil and Joy. However, while there I received a phone call from Sydney. It was Adele. What she had to say was a shock—but didn't come as a complete surprise. The fact was, she told me, she simply couldn't face going back to Yemen. With all the danger there, she felt that what she was contributing to the work in Jibla wasn't worth dying for.

Her thoughts had not come out of the blue. Five months previously, we'd not only discussed this possibility, but had emailed Interserve and some close family members and friends and had written to our parents to let them know that we'd probably be taking leave of absence from February 1, 2000. At the time, this was mainly because Dell had found it difficult being separated from our children and her parents for so long. The difficult security situation was another issue altogether.

At that time, Interserve had asked us not to make a final decision until November. And now, although disappointed that Dell couldn't carry on, we took it as clear leading from the Lord. We've always wanted him to close doors he doesn't want us to go through, and to open those he does, in his time and in his way.

After I drove back to Sydney, Dell and I talked and prayed over what we were to do. In December, we let our praying friends know that at the beginning of February, I'd resume working as a doctor in my old practice.

In our distress and initial confusion, the Lord continued to show us just how loving and faithful he is. This time he chose to bless us in several ways through friends who were members of the Uniting Church we attended at Springwood. For instance, after Warwick read our news, he rang me and said that a friend of his had been accepted to study at Moore College, and planned to rent out the home he owned in Hersey Street, Blaxland. Within a few days we finalised the arrangements to rent that home for at least one year.

Then another friend, Ian, told me that he knew of two used cars which were up for private sale, and which he could recommend. Again, within a few days we owned both cars for the price we'd expected to pay for one!

We couldn't help rejoicing over the way the Lord had helped us and were so grateful to those Christian friends.

At this time, Andrew, and his girlfriend Rebecca saw that it was the Lord's timing for them to announce their engagement and get married sooner than they'd been envisaging. Adele and I took this as an especially encouraging touch from the Lord. Not only were we delighted that Andrew was getting married, and to such a lovely Christian girl as Rebecca, but the date they chose, without realising its significance for us, was Saturday, February 19, 2000! On that day three years before, Adele and I had begun the process of joining Interserve, selling our home and leaving the medical practice—a *good* day. Exactly one year later, February 19, 1998, I was dismissed from working at the church clinic in Aden—an extremely *bad* day! Now a lovely, godly and happy function was to be held on that same date, the anniversaries of which would always ease the pain of what had transpired in Aden. This choice of the wedding day was from the Lord, cleansing and hallowing that date, which for us had been so marred.

As the weeks and months ticked by, we gradually regained our physical and spiritual strength. Adele took the opportunity to attend a six-month course of studies at the Technical and Further Education (TAFE) College at Penrith, to give her more competence in bookkeeping. She not only enjoyed the course but did well, being awarded the Certificate 2 in Accounting, with Distinction. As we prayed and reflected on our situation, the Lord began to gradually stir our spirits again with concern for the eternal welfare of Yemenis. The previous year Adele had felt that what she'd been contributing to the ministry of the Jibla hospital was not vital and was certainly not worth *dying* for. But as the days in Blaxland crept by, she realised that working at Jibla was worth *living* for—and she probably wouldn't die there anyway. Also, life for her in Australia at that time didn't seem as worthwhile as living and serving the Lord in Jibla. So, calmly and prayerfully we began to map out what we'd need to do if we decided to turn our faces towards the mission field again.

The first step was to buy a home. It was three years since we'd sold the one in Springwood; and Dell wanted a little place to call our own, and to which we could return when we came home from overseas. Before long we found one for an excellent price at Werrington, on the Sydney side of the Nepean River and we moved in on December 16, 2000.

The next step for us was to contact our friends at Jibla to see if they needed us, Dell to help again with the bookkeeping, and myself to resume work in the out-patients department. We sent off an email with our tentative enquiries, more than a year since we'd sadly notified them that we were unable to return. The staff members had been struggling with the load over those 12 months, and unbeknown to us, Bill, the hospital administrator, was almost at breaking point. In his sixties, overwhelmed and exhausted, he and his wife had almost decided to announce their retirement and return home to the USA. He especially found the financial side of the work too much for him. Our email was a godsend for him. He trusted Adele. They'd worked well together, and the fact that she now had bookkeeping qualifications only added to his relief, and to his eagerness to welcome her back as soon as possible. An email was immediately sent back in reply to ours. *Yes!* Adele's return was eagerly awaited; I would be welcomed back into the out-patient department with open arms and they had a bigger house for us this time!

My renewed contract with the medical practice only required three months' notice of my intention to resign, and it was the middle of November when I let them know. That meant we'd be free to fly out in mid-February 2001. As we prepared to set out, we found Deuteronomy 31:8 helpful.

'*The Lord himself will lead you and be with you. He will not fail you or abandon you, so do not lose courage or be afraid.*'

* * *

After almost eighteen months in Sydney, we arrived safely to a warm welcome back in Jibla on Thursday, February 22 and rapidly settled into life and work again. We were both busy, with Adele in the business office and me in the out-patients department, and very comfortable in our three-bedroom-plus-study home on the compound.

The security situation seemed stable, but things were tighter than before.

ON THE WAY

For example, to travel beyond the nearby city of Ibb, we had to have a soldier with a machine gun in the vehicle with us.

The same restrictions applied when speaking about Christian things, of course, although that didn't stop one Yemeni man starting a conversation with me one day. He was sitting beside my desk, waiting for me to complete a request for pathology tests for his sick son.

'Christians are excellent!' he said, smiling at me. Providentially the Yemeni staff member allocated to assist me was out of the room, so I had a few seconds in which to say something in reply.

'My brother,' I said. 'I am from Australia and you are from Yemen, but we are both sons of Adam (as they express it in Arabic)—brothers. If you see anything good in my life, it is because Jesus the Messiah lives in my heart.'

Immediately he responded, 'I want Jesus the Messiah to live in my heart!'

I began to say that if anyone asks Jesus to come into his or her heart, he will come in. But at that moment my Yemeni 'helper' burst into the room, apparently realising that we were talking about Christian things. He hustled the man and his son outside, so I didn't have a chance to speak to him any further.

It was frustrating, of course, to have that conversation cut short, but the Yemeni staff were under pressure from government security personnel to prevent any of us from talking about the Lord Jesus with the patients or their relatives—and to report us if we did. How encouraging it was to remember that the Lord is not restricted from working in peoples' hearts, and also to see evidence that he was drawing people to himself. Most of the patients were pleased with the care they received, and some expressed tremendous gratitude. They knew we were Christians, and many of them came considerable distances to be treated there, passing other hospitals on the way. If someone had asked us what we were achieving in Yemen, we could tell them that much of what we did was breaking down barriers. Most Muslims are taught that Christianity is synonymous with the decadent West that they see portrayed in certain magazines, as well as on TV and videos. But in Jibla they could see that we were not like that at all. By our life, speech and dress we were seeking in every way to 'make the teaching about God our Saviour attractive.' I met at least fifty Yemeni patients and their family members each day in the out-patients department and I had a lot of fun with some of the Yemeni staff with whom I became friends. They were able to watch closely how we, as Christians, lived among them. Much of our work could be likened to a farmer breaking up the hard soil, preparing it to receive the seed.

All the while a few of the other expatriate staff were having excellent opportunities. One Yemeni man said to an expatriate staff member that many Yemenis were unwilling to come to the hospital because they were afraid that they would discover that Christianity is better than Islam, and they wouldn't know what to do!

Well, some may have decided what to do, because at about that same time a news item was printed in the English-language 'Yemen Times' which greatly interested us. On a page summarising news reports from the various Arabic-language Yemeni newspapers for the previous week, the 'Al-Jamaheer' newspaper was reported as publishing the following three-sentence article.

'Quoting Islam World News issued from Mecca, this Ba'thist weekly reported that the Yemeni security authorities are carrying out investigations to verify the truth in reports which claimed that a number of Yemeni youth have converted their religion to Christianity. The investigations are to concentrate on the sides which lured the youth to Christianity as well as to hammer out the sides which carry out missionary in Yemen. The Mecca claimed that the security authorities have discovered that a number of Yemenis have converted their religion in Jibla area of Ibb Province.'

Shortly after that report, the government security tightened their control at the hospital even further. Now we had to have a soldier with a machine gun in the car even if we were only driving to Ibb for shopping. Before, for longer trips we had to fill out a travel form and hand it to the Yemeni security officer at least an hour before driving out of the hospital; now we filled out a similar form even on such short trips. We were not sure if this was to protect or to restrict us. However, the government did seem to be trying to prevent terrorism, and to restrain the fundamentalists, incorporating Islamic schools into the government education system, for instance. (After this happened, we were all confined to the compound for a few days in case there was a violent reaction.)

The restrictions, particularly on speaking to Yemenis about the Lord, were irksome, but God spoke to many people's hearts. We simply had to have more faith than might have been necessary, had we been able to share the Gospel openly—faith to see people saved, even if we were not permitted to say much. God was the only one who was able to save them anyway; and he could do it, no matter what obstacles were in the way.

However, things were about to get even more interesting. On September 11, 2001, aircraft flew into the Twin Towers in New York, an event which would shake the entire world.

We were busily occupied at Jibla when we discovered what had happened, and like most people were shocked. The next day we received an email from my younger brother Ross, Professor of Strategic Studies at the Australian National University in Canberra. He was attending an international conference of similar experts in Geneva, Switzerland, and advised everyone at Jibla to carefully take stock of our situation in the light of what had happened, and what was likely to follow.

I shared his email with the hospital leadership. 'But we're not planning to leave,' I told them.

In the aftermath, over the next few days, there were global warnings that if Afghanistan or any other Muslim country suffered retaliatory attacks, now or in the future, Americans would be hunted down worldwide and killed, and American interests destroyed. We already had cause to believe that there was a Bin Laden group in the nearby town of Ibb because, as previously mentioned, the hospital had received a truly horrible letter purporting to have been written by 'students of Bin Laden in Ibb', threatening to blow up the hospital and kill us all. Of course, Jibla Hospital was American, and the largest staff contingent were Americans, and over the next five days, several staff members from other countries were directed by their international leaders to leave Yemen as soon as possible.

On September 17, the Australian Embassy in Saudi Arabia sent us an email saying that if commercial flights were suspended to Yemen, Australians may not have alternative means of leaving the country[130]. The British Embassy in Sana'a rang us too and encouraged all Australians to leave the country as soon as possible.

Also, on September 17, the hospital administrator called a meeting of all non-Yemeni staff. 'If need be, Americans can be evacuated by a flight the embassy arranges,' he told us. 'But no other nationalities would be allowed on board.' He assured us we were all free to go if we wished to do so, and that we should make immediate plans to leave the country if we heard that airlines were beginning to suspend flights to Yemen.

The next day we heard that Lufthansa had suspended flights to and from Yemen. On that same day, a wealthy, intelligent and influential Yemeni man I had come to know well in the out-patients department made a special, brief journey to the hospital, not for his health, but for the sole reason of warning me personally as a friend to leave. 'You must get out soon, and certainly within two or three weeks,' he said in private.

On the 19th, Interserve gave us the option of choosing to fly either back to Australia, or to Jordan or Oman. The Interserve leader in Jordan said that accommodation was available, and that there were things which Adele and I could do. However, although some staff members were leaving urgently, Dell and I felt that for the sake of the hospital, we couldn't leave before the end of the month.

Over these days, Dell had been struck during her daily Bible readings by Jeremiah 50:8 and 51:6, where she read, 'Flee from Babylon! Run for your lives!' Then later we were both surprised to discover that this same instruction cropped up again on September 22, but this time in my set readings for that day in Isaiah 48:20, which seemed to confirm the decision we were feeling led to make.

On the evening of Thursday, September 20, we rang Royal Jordanian Airlines and made a tentative booking to fly to Jordan on Monday, October 1, praying that it wouldn't turn out to be too late to leave the country. That same evening, we received a further email from my brother, this time from a similar conference in London. He was now much more emphatic in advising us to leave the country, for some time at least. He wrote in a guarded manner, but we understood him to say that intelligence information predicted that almost certainly some people in situations like ours would be killed in the weeks ahead.

On September 23, two representatives of the American Southern Baptist international leadership flew to Yemen and said that any of their missionaries could leave if they wished (and most of them did), and that they would be flown out of the country. They also felt that the widespread hostility towards Americans could be adversely affecting how the local people thought of the gospel message; and that Yemeni employees, patients and their relatives could now be in danger because of a possible attack on the hospital.

Proverbs 22:3 and 27:12 also played a part in our decision to leave. 'The prudent see danger and take refuge, but the simple keep going and suffer for it.' Obviously, the Lord leads some along one path and others on different paths, but we felt that he was leading us to leave, though in an orderly manner.

The blessings we received as we moved to Jordan seemed to be confirmation that we were on the path the Lord had planned for us. We landed at dawn on October 1 and were met at the airport in Amman by Shaun, an Interserve partner. He and his family made us welcome and helped us register with the government and set up an email account quickly. Then a lovely, fully furnished apartment in a good location opened up for us on our second day there, and we moved in that same afternoon. Within a week, I had visited some clinics for refugees and had been asked to start another on the outskirts of the city for a month. Dell found some bookkeeping and work to do for a few different Christian groups.

Our time in Jordan allowed us some unique experiences. We were most interested to meet ten young Christian Arab men and women who, in a recently established school, were training to go out as missionaries to other Muslim countries, potentially risking their lives by doing so. As well, it was wonderful to be living near some Biblical sites. We were fascinated to discover that our landlord and his wife were Christian Moabites from the same village in which Ruth (King David's great-grandmother) was born and grew up. Several times we crossed the stream beside which Jacob wrestled with the angel, and we drove up Mount Nebo from where Moses viewed the Promised Land before he died. We also saw the site of Elijah's tiny home village of Tishbe, near the western edge of the plateau overlooking the Jordan Valley. Later, down in that valley, we saw where he was taken up to heaven in the whirlwind, and where Jesus was baptised at Bethany-beyond-Jordan.

Things had fallen into place well, although we missed Jibla, and our friends. That's where we felt we belonged, and where we knew we were needed. And as I wrote to a friend at the time, I had never been happier anywhere in my life than at Jibla.

* * *

Our time in Jordan ended up being just two and a half months. Grateful for the strength and encouragement the Lord gave us while we were there[131], we were keen to get back to Yemen and made plans to return to Jibla, probably after Ramadan, at the end of December.

We received a great welcome when we returned to Jibla earlier than expected, on December 17, and both quickly settled back into our work. We were grateful to receive some of our luggage sent from Jordan by airfreight just a week after we arrived, on Christmas Eve. This was so good because all the little Christmas gifts we'd bought in Jordan for our friends were in that luggage. The Lord certainly knows how to time things to perfection!

The Yemen Government seemed to be redoubling its efforts to prevent anything bad happening and because of this the US Government was now pouring aid of various kinds into Yemen. If it hadn't been for the BBC radio news which we listened to each day, we'd scarcely have known that there were any problems in the world to be concerned about. Everything seemed so calm and normal. Winter in Jibla was like spring in the Blue Mountains, and we had a magnificent view down a valley, looking through some thorn bush and eucalyptus trees, and over the rooves of the hospital which was down the slope from our house. Further away to the east, the valley ended at the base of a hamlet-dotted, north-south mountain ridge towering up behind Ibb about seven or eight kilometres away.

ON THE WAY

Occasionally Dell and I went out for breakfast to a restaurant about half-an-hour's drive away where there's another magnificent view. We hired a hospital car, drove to Ibb, and then headed west, climbing a winding road until we reached the top of a mountain pass and turned south onto a rough and narrow dirt track near the top of the ridge[132]. The almost sheer drop on our right-hand side to the valley floor far below us was dramatic, with no fence to obstruct our view, and after driving a little way, we came to a small, two-storey restaurant which stood alone at a wider part of the track.

Our soldier sat on a shaded bench watching the vehicle while we went inside and chose a table at the west-facing window. The view was a bit like that from The Conservation Hut restaurant at Wentworth Falls, looking down The Valley of the Waters. However this Yemeni valley was about three times as deep, with virtually no trees; the sides of the valley were almost entirely covered by terraces, with various crops in different stages of growth. Numerous hamlets were dotted around on the slopes, with a bigger village on the valley floor several kilometres away. The tarmac road zigzagged down to the bottom of the valley and then headed west into the distance. It was apparently possible to eventually reach the coast that way, but it would have been rough and slow. As well as the usual vehicles, flocks of animals could be seen being herded up the road—no doubt on their way to market; and here and there we could spot people working on the terraces in the early morning sunshine.

The decor and facilities of the restaurant were basic, but it was one of our favourite haunts. For about $1.50 Australian each, we enjoyed scrambled eggs, with onion and tomatoes mixed in, or a dish of something like small broad beans in an onion sauce. The food was presented on cheap plastic or enamel plates with pictures painted on them, served with flat, Lebanese-type bread, which also was used in place of utensils; you just broke off pieces of the bread and scooped the food up. Accompanying the meal was black or white tea served in small china or glass mugs.

Our breakfast outings were enjoyable and relaxing. Another encouragement around this time was a personal letter from the hospital administrator to Adele and me[133], which read as follows.

...Your continuing faithfulness is such an encouragement to us. The following chart lists patients and the amounts used to provide their medical care from your gift.

Michael it is a joy to work with you in the clinic. Your early arrival in clinic helps to start and keep the day calm.

Adele, I greatly appreciate you and your skill and dedication to the book work. Your work with the books and your follow up on the liaison work gives me great comfort, knowing the job will be done well...

Demonstrating the difference between our reception at Jibla Hospital and at Aden, this letter meant a great deal to us.

Yet another encouragement came on 31 October, with the birth of our first grandchild, Liam Charles Michael Babbage! How we praised God for his birth. It was extraordinary to realise that almost twenty-nine years before, Adele and I had been there at Jibla Hospital while our parents waited in Sydney to hear the news of our first child, Andrew's safe birth. After all the places Adele and I had lived and worked in over the intervening years, here we were, right back at Jibla Hospital again; but this time, the roles and locations were reversed. We were the ones waiting to hear the news from this same Andrew of his son's safe arrival in Sydney—our first grandchild!

The encouragements were much needed, with new uncertainties on the horizon. First, with heightened tension in the Middle East, the Yemen government increased the security at the hospital still further, often parking a large, army utility truck at the front entrance with an enormous machine gun mounted on the back; and the usual guards were joined by an extra contingent of soldiers. Second, the American Southern Baptists finally decided to withdraw their financial support from Jibla Hospital, which would mean major changes ahead.

Putting plans into motion to hand over to Yemeni administration took time, and the first four months after we heard the news were a difficult time for us. Initially Adele and I didn't want to even think about leaving Jibla, particularly because I'd hoped to continue working at the hospital for years to come, being so happy there. But after much thought, prayer and consulting with colleagues, we felt that we couldn't plan to stay on under the envisaged new management, and the changed working and living conditions. We carefully considered other possible places to work, both in Yemen and elsewhere in the Middle East; we actually applied to go and work at the American Mission Hospital in Bahrain, but then found I could not get a work visa because the following July, I would be turning sixty. So, for many different reasons, we gradually came to realise that the Lord was directing us to return to Sydney.

Even though I had a conviction about it, I was anxious and uneasy. There was no longer a vacant place for me in the medical practice where I worked for many years in the lower Blue Mountains, so I didn't know what I was going to do. While earnestly endeavouring to trust the Lord and believe that all his promises applied to us, one day in weakness and desperation, I wondered if he might give me some token to demonstrate that he would provide for us throughout the years ahead.

On the coffee table in our lounge room sat a book by Ken Duncan, entitled *Let There Be Hope*. It was full of beautiful photographs of sea and landscapes, each one accompanied by a few of the words from Matthew 6:25-33, and many times during those months I settled down on a lounge chair and gained strength and encouragement from it. I also revisited a lovely old hymn which I found meaningful.

O Holy Saviour, Friend unseen,
The faint, the weak, on Thee may lean;
Help us throughout life's varying scene
By faith to cling to Thee.
Though faith and hope are often tried,
We ask not, need not, aught beside;
So safe, so calm, so satisfied,
The souls that cling to Thee.

If only I'd applied these thoughts to our situation more diligently, I need not have been so stressed, because after those months of such uncertainty, a truly wonderful couple of things happened, and the entire outlook for our future changed.

One morning we received two emails. The first one told of the provision of a car when we returned[134]. The second email contained a job offer! A doctor with whom I did my medical training, but whom I hadn't seen for about thirty-five years[135], heard from my sister Lyndall, who was one of her patients, that we were moving back to Sydney. She worked at Baulkham Hills and had been trying for eighteen months to find a male GP to work alongside her in the practice. She offered me the job, and we worked out the details quickly. The Lord had provided more than a token; he'd provided what we needed! The way this all happened seemed to us to be his hand at work and was confirmation to us that we were on the right track, and that he was caring for us.

Our arrival date in Sydney was set for January 3, 2003. We expected a relatively peaceful leave-taking and journey home, but that was not to be. We would get back to Sydney unscathed, but the times that were coming before we got there would test us beyond anything we'd yet been through.

* * *

Monday, December 30 is the date that changed Jibla Hospital forever, and which will be forever etched in our memories.

It was going to be our last day there. Adele and I were preparing to leave the hospital that afternoon, driving to Sana'a so that we could fly back to Australia later that week. Because of this, I didn't go to the out-patients department as I would have, most other days before. Everyone else though, was doing what they usually did. At about 8.30 that morning, the administrator, Bill Koehn (pronounced 'Cain'), had just returned to his office after going home for breakfast after a chapel service, as was his usual routine. He and his wife Marty lived in the adjoining unit to Adele and me, about fifty metres up the slope from the main hospital buildings. Shortly after he entered his office, Kathy Gariety, who was in charge of the hospital medical store, and Dr Martha Myers went to talk to him.

Already, the assassin had entered the hospital grounds. Knowing that everyone entering the hospital was required to leave their weapons with the soldiers at the front entrance[136], this man carried a bundle in his arms—a pretend baby—meaning the pistol hidden under his armpit went undiscovered.

His first stop was at the outer administration office, where he spoke to the Yemeni clerk, saying that he wanted to buy a phone card.

'Please wait a moment,' the clerk asked him, but the man did not. The door into Bill Koehn's office was open, and visible from where he stood, so in he went. Mr Bill, as we all called him, was sitting at his desk, and was shot in the head. Martha was standing behind Mr Bill's chair, apparently using the phone; she was also shot in the head. Kathy was shot in one arm, presumably as she tried to protect herself, and then twice in the chest.

Next, the gunman went back out into the courtyard of the out-patients department. He pointed his pistol at the elderly Filipino radiographer, but didn't shoot him, perhaps because Daniel didn't look like an American. However, the American pharmacist Don, popped his head out, and the gunman saw him. If Don had pulled the door closed behind him, he would have been safe; the door was made of solid metal. Unfortunately, he didn't think to do so, but ducked back inside to hide. The gunman went in after him, pointing his gun at the Russian girl who worked there as a pharmacy assistant. Once again, he didn't shoot; she also didn't look American, and he may have realised that he only had two bullets left. He saw Don crawling away under a long benchtop, however, and shot at him twice from behind[137].

The gunman then went out again into the courtyard. By this time, the Yemeni soldiers had come up from the entrance but because it had all happened so quickly, they stood there for a moment, apparently undecided what to do. Sarah, a Mexican doctor, looked out of one of the out-patient doctor consulting rooms[138] and saw the gunman just throw his pistol down on the ground in front of the soldiers, and then put his hands up in the air and surrender with no attempt to escape. It seems that this is what he'd planned to do, but it's also possible that he may have lost count of how many shots he'd fired; terrorists apparently often save the last bullet, and use it to commit suicide at the completion of their mission.

Bruce, an American doctor, came out of his out-patient room; he ran with Sarah to the pharmacy where they gave first aid to Don and put him on a stretcher to go to the operating theatre. It was then they were told of the shooting in Mr Bill's office. They went in and discovered our three colleagues dying there. Mr Bill's head was thrown back as if he was asleep in his chair, Martha was in a little heap on the floor behind him, and Kathy was slumped down off her chair in a kneeling position against the front of Mr Bill's desk. All three were unconscious. They were rushed on trolleys to the recovery ward beside the operating theatres, but Martha died before she even got there. Someone rang Marty Koehn who came running down from her home to be with her beloved husband. He continued breathing and groaning quietly for several minutes after she reached his side, but then he also passed away. Kathy was taken as quickly as possible into the theatre for emergency chest surgery but couldn't be saved. So, within fifteen minutes of having been shot, all three had died.

While all this took place, Adele was in an office in another building a little way up the hill, handing over the accounts to the assistant administrator, Lee. Suddenly Bruce's wife came bursting in, screaming that there'd been some shooting in the hospital, and saying that Lee was needed down there.

'Lock your door,' he told Adele, and she began ringing the list of phone numbers on the hospital directory. 'Lock your doors and hide.' At that stage it wasn't known how many gunmen there were. It was possible that more than one could have been going from house to house, shooting anyone they found.

From her locked office, Adele tried to ring me at our house, but I didn't hear the phone. Unaware of all of this, I was outside, about thirty metres further up the slope on the next terrace, attending to the necessary routine tasks to get the hospital car we'd hired ready to drive to Sana'a that afternoon. Soon she found that she was ringing people who already knew about the shooting, and she was becoming increasingly worried that I might have been down at the hospital and amongst those shot. After every phone call she made to people on the list, she rang our house, but still I wasn't answering.

She decided to cautiously leave her office; and having locked the door, she bent down and ran, doubled over, to the next house, between the office and our home.

'I've seen Michael; he's safe,' someone told her, and Adele suddenly went weak, feeling trembly and cold. She had to borrow a blanket to put around herself. It was there that she also heard that the gunman had been acting alone and had been captured, and that Bill, Martha and Kathy had died. However, despite being in a state of shock, she had the presence of mind while in that house to make an international call to her mother in Sydney, asking her to let people at home know that we were unharmed.

While all this was happening, I was completely unaware that anything was amiss, even though I was only about a hundred metres from the scene of the horror. If I did hear any shooting, it didn't register in my mind as anything to be concerned about. There was always a fair amount of noise carried across the valley from Jibla township, especially in daylight hours. Fireworks and gunfire were commonplace and usually signified a celebration of some kind, rather than hostility.

A few of the expat hospital staff lived in the nearby town of Ibb, so Dell rang the Dutch Interserve accountant to warn him and his wife not to come to the hospital. Dell had forgotten that they'd taken their children to Aden for a short break, and it was there that he took the call on his mobile phone. He offered to ring the Dutch Interserve nurse who'd remained in Ibb. That nurse then rang our home number at the hospital, and since I'd just walked in to collect some luggage to carry up to the car, I answered the phone.

'I just heard there was a shooting at the hospital,' she said. 'Are you alright?'

'Shooting?' I replied. 'No. There hasn't been any shooting. It must be a mistake.'

After we'd finished our brief conversation, I carried some bags outside and up the steps to the next terrace. A few minutes later I came down again to the house for another load of luggage, when once more the phone rang. This time it was Katherine, the wife of the new Interserve leader in Yemen, ringing from Sana'a.

'Has there been a shooting at the hospital?' she asked. 'Are you safe?'

'That's strange,' I said. 'You're the second person to ask that. I think it's a mistake, but if you hold the line, I'll go next door and ask Marty if she knows anything about it.'

THE SAFEST PLACE OF ALL

I left the phone and went out to Marty's place. The solid back door was opened inwards, and through the fly screen door I could see her sitting in their lounge room, talking to someone[139]. I knocked and went in and was absolutely horrified when she calmly replied to my question. 'Yes,' she said. 'Bill's dead, and so are Martha and Kathy.'

'I'm so dreadfully sorry,' I said. With an explanation about the phone call, I hurried back to tell Katherine the terrible news[140].

The saying is obviously true that 'the safest place in the whole world for anyone is in the centre of God's will'. Adele and I could easily have been shot; we'd both been briefly in the administration office earlier that morning, and yet, when the shooting happened, we were unaware of it. Both of us were near at hand, but completely unharmed. Surely our spirits would be so much more tranquil if only we remembered that, being in our Heavenly Father's hands, everything which reaches us, his children, must have first passed through his fingers; and so nothing happens to us which he hasn't either planned or permitted.

After Dell had regained strength, she left the house where she'd been sheltering and managed to find me, but by now I knew about the shooting. When she went back to that house, she saw that our news was already on television via satellite from America—only an hour after it had happened!

* * *

We soon found out more details about the gunman. He was a fanatical Muslim from a village north of Sana'a. The day before the Jibla shooting, a man from the same village assassinated a socialist politician at a rally in Sana'a, presumably because the politician was not a fundamentalist Muslim. The gunman who came to Jibla said that there were other targets on their list. He chose the hospital because we were Christians, and because he hated Americans for supporting Israel against the Palestinians. He said that he would be drawn closer to God by killing people who were preaching Christianity.

We also found out about another incident that morning that demonstrated how the Lord cared for his people, and that he was in control of everything which had happened. The hospital was to be handed over the next day to the Yemeni Government, and the two men who headed up the work of the American Southern Baptists in Yemen set out together from Sana'a at about four in the morning so that they could complete the four-hour journey, and still have the whole of that final day ahead of them there in Jibla to assist with the last-minute handover details.

As they drove through the almost-deserted streets of Sana'a, they accidentally hit a roundabout and damaged one of their wheels. The man who was driving felt particularly stupid and chided himself severely for allowing such a thing to happen. With no option but to find another vehicle for their journey, they turned around and drove slowly back into town. Although they were soon on their way again, the delay set them back about an hour and a half. At about 9.30 a.m., as they were approaching Jibla, they were stopped by the police who'd closed the road. They learnt of the shooting from them, and it was only with difficulty that they managed to gain permission to pass the roadblock. With heavy hearts they drove through the hospital gates and were soon told what had taken place. It was then they realised that if they'd not been delayed in Sana'a, but had arrived at 8 a.m. as planned, both would almost certainly have been with Mr Bill in the administration office when the gunman entered. It was more than likely that they also would have been murdered.

I was encouraged by this incident. All too often, we condemn ourselves and feel guilty for accidents and other non-deliberate mishaps. And yet the Lord can overrule everything. I think he planned, or at least, permitted that accident to keep those two men out of danger. He may even have sent an angel to turn the steering mechanism of their vehicle to ensure that they *did* have that minor accident.

The bodies of our three murdered colleagues were laid out lovingly by several of the missionary nursing sisters. Adele and I decided not to go down to the hospital to see their bodies, preferring to remember them and their appearance as we'd known them.

In the early afternoon of that dreadful day, a crisis team and ambulance arrived from the American Embassy in Sana'a, together with a contingent from the FBI. Of course, Yemeni security personnel from the nearby city of Ibb had come earlier to investigate the crime. After the shooting, virtually no-one was allowed to enter or leave the compound. Although we had planned to, we didn't leave that afternoon either.

All the remaining tasks for our murdered colleagues were solemnly undertaken. Mr Bill and Dr Martha were to be buried in the little cemetery at the top of the hospital compound, but Kathy's family in the States wanted her body flown home to America, which the US Embassy arranged and paid for.

Many Yemenis were deeply affected by the tragedy. For instance, Adele watched for a few moments from a discrete distance as a little old Yemeni hospital employee dug the double grave with tears streaming down his face, grief-stricken by the murder of these beloved missionaries.

The next morning, we had a combined funeral service at the graveside, and Bernie, the new Interserve leader in Yemen, was with us now. He'd rightly and shrewdly surmised that traffic from Sana'a would be delayed by police checkpoints, so, not to be put off, he reached Jibla by driving all the way down to the coast, and then turning south, drove right through the night and got to us by taking that long route via Taiz.

The bodies of Mr Bill and Dr Martha were placed in rough, hospital-built coffins which were carried together safely up the hill, resting sideways across the back of a small utility truck. It was a brief and simple service, with a number of Yemenis looking on through the wire perimeter fence. We were all still shocked, of course. There was also some concern in case there might be further shooting, and the American Embassy staff, having organised a convoy of those being evacuated, wanted to set out for Sana'a as soon as possible.

About mid-afternoon that Tuesday, December 31, 2002, most of the expatriates were on board as the convoy of vehicles left Jibla, although a few chose to remain on the compound, including Marty Koehn[141]. Some of the residents around the hospital were fundamentalist Muslims. As we drove away, these people were amongst those lining the road, cheering and jeering, clearly glad to see us missionaries leaving. However, the majority of the crowd were sad, and some were heartbroken, weeping openly. They'd already been sorrowful, knowing that the hospital was closing temporarily, at least, and was being handed over to the Yemeni Government, with most of us expats leaving. Apart from anything else, many of their livelihoods were connected with the hospital. Those men and women didn't want us to go, and the three murders seemed to deepen their grief enormously.

But why had the Lord allowed the murders to happen—and just before the hospital was closing as a Christian entity after thirty-four years of active service? My thinking is simply that the Lord knows what he's doing. He knows how to build his church, establish his kingdom and glorify his name. I'm reminded of the saying, 'The blood of the martyrs is the seed of the church.' The early church in Jerusalem grew rapidly in numbers after Stephen was martyred. If a grain of wheat falls into the ground and dies, a stalk of wheat grows up where that seed was planted, and at harvest time it produces many more seeds. The Lord certainly didn't allow these three to be murdered for nothing. He saw it as a necessary part of his campaign to win the battle raging in the spiritual realm over Yemen[142].

Why did he select these particular ones to be honoured with a martyr's crown? Again, only the Lord knows; but of all the missionaries and expatriate staff at the hospital, these three were especially popular with the local population. Many widows, orphans, prisoners and other poor people held these three in the highest regard, grateful for the love, kindness and generosity they'd been shown. Bill, Martha and Kathy had been there for many years, and they *loved* the people. Their murders caused not just sadness, but a tremendous outpouring of grief and expressions of love from many of the local people. One of the young Yemeni men in the maintenance department said to me in English, with tears in his eyes, 'I love Mr Bill. I love Mr Bill.'

At the same time, of all the missionaries at the hospital, those three were perhaps most unsure of what they'd do after the hospital was handed over to the Yemeni Government. For various reasons, none of them sensed any leading from the Lord or inclination to move elsewhere; but at the same time they knew they couldn't continue working at Jibla as they had before. They simply had no idea what they would do. The reason of course, was that the Lord did not intend for them to serve him any longer on earth but was calling them home to heaven.

At this point, I'll recount a most extraordinary coincidence. On November 6, 1973, Dell and I arrived at Jibla Hospital for the *first* time to await the birth of our baby, but were shocked to discover that little Lydia, the daughter of RSMT colleagues, had died there earlier that day. The next morning, we attended her burial in the top corner of the hospital compound. There in Jibla, about two-and-a-half weeks later, I wrote a prayer letter in which I quoted the verse, 'Except a corn of wheat fall into the ground and die, it abideth alone: but if it die, it bringeth forth much fruit'.

Now, in a most tragic coincidence, on the *last* day that Adele and I had planned to be at Jibla, three of our colleagues died just a few hours before we were to leave. We were still present the next day as two of them were buried close to Lydia's little grave. More than twenty-nine years had passed since Lydia's death, and many Yemenis had been born into God's family during those years. They'd sprung up like new shoots where none had been before, and now we were trusting and expecting that many more souls would be saved in the years following the death of these three colleagues.

As our convoy travelled to Sana'a a police vehicle led the way, while an army truck with a huge machine gun mounted on the back brought up the rear. Because one of the vehicles had mechanical problems, we could only crawl along, which made the journey slow and exhausting. It was dark by the time we drove into the capital. The entire third floor of the Sheraton Hotel had been engaged and paid for by the American Southern Baptists, and it was there that we were all accommodated, after being brought in through a back entrance to avoid the hordes of reporters who'd gathered in the front foyer.

Wolfgang and others based in Sana'a came to express their shock and sorrow, and to say goodbye as we prepared to leave. He and a visiting friend then set out to search for a shop open at that late hour, to buy a suitcase for me because the handle on one of ours had come off. They didn't find one, but the friend brought an empty suitcase of his own which he gave me as a gift, solving our problem perfectly. Once again, we could see the Lord's hand at work in caring for our every need, and at 4.30 the next morning, on January 1, 2003, Adele and I were driven to the airport to catch our flight home as previously planned. Our time in Yemen had finally come to an end.

Epilogue

2003-2020: Age 59-76

For three months following our return to Sydney we were involved in deputation meetings for Interserve, before I returned to general medical practice for five and a half years, but this time in Baulkham Hills. I retired when I reached 65, in 2008. In 2013 we moved into an Anglican Retirement Village, and we love living here. In mid-2018 we began attending a charismatic community church, affiliated with the Crosslink Christian Network of approximately 100 churches throughout Australia. It has a strong emphasis on local and overseas missions, including Interserve, and we're glad to be part of it.

As the years tick by, and we gradually take on the role of senior citizens and members of the older generation, Adele and I realise how blessed we've been to have had prayerful parents and many godly friends and acquaintances who've faithfully brought us, our children and grandchildren before the Lord in prayer. Many of those 'saints' have already gone to their reward in heaven, but I want to acknowledge the enormous debt of gratitude I owe them for the wonderful and innumerable ways which, partly in answer to their prayers, the Lord has cared for us over the decades. I believe that they rejoiced to see him moving on our behalf. We can say, 'The Lord ... has not stopped showing his kindness to the living and the dead'.

The occasional news that trickles through to us concerning people amongst whom we've worked overseas confirms to us that the Lord is continuing to answer our prayers, and those of our faithful friends—even prayers offered up decades ago. In recent years the number of believers in

Yemen has been multiplying immensely, and the church is established, even though still largely underground[143].

Isaiah 63:9 perfectly summarises my main purpose in compiling this work; and so I quote that passage, not only with heartfelt praise and thanksgiving for all that has happened in the past, but also with trust and reverent expectancy for the future.

I will tell of the kindnesses of the Lord, the deeds for which he is to be praised, according to all the Lord has done for us—yes, the many good things he has done. ... according to his compassion and many kindnesses. He said, 'Surely they are my people', ... and so he became their Saviour. In all their distress he too was distressed, and the angel of his presence saved them. In his love and mercy he redeemed them; he lifted them up and carried them all the days of old. (Isaiah 63:7-9)

Michael and Adele outside their front door, continuing 'on the Way' (April 2019).

Acknowledgements

Firstly I'd like to thank my wife Adele for the enormous help she has been to me in writing this book, such as the filing, in chronological order, of a large number of letters and other relevant material we gathered from 1971 through to 1997, which I was then able to draw upon. Secondly, some friends in recent years have suggested that I should write this account, and then encouraged me to make a start when I was hesitating; so now I'd like to say to each one of them a truly heartfelt thank you! Thirdly, I'm extremely grateful to the many people and church congregations who've prayed for us, supported us financially, and assisted us in numerous other ways, especially during our years of missionary service. Without their backing, much of what is recorded in these pages could not have even happened.

It is important to acknowledge the contribution that Cecily Paterson has made to this book. She has done an exceptionally good job of editing and I'm truly delighted with the outcome.

Maps and Reference Books

1. The Amplified Bible, Zondervan. Grand Rapids, Michigan 49530, USA 1987
2. Analytical Concordance to the Holy Bible, Eighth edition. Robert Young, Lutterworth Press, London 1939
3. The Australian Concise Oxford Dictionary, Fourth Edition. Bruce Moore (Editor), Oxford University Press, South Melbourne, Australia, 2004
4. Christian Hymns, The Evangelical Movement of Wales, Bryntirion, Wales, 1977
5. Daily Light on the Daily Path. Morning and Evening Readings, Samuel Bagster, Great Britain, 1850 (approx)
6. Golden Bells, Scripture Union & C.S.S.M. London
7. The Hebrew-Greek Key Study Bible, King James Version. AMG Publishers. Chattanooga, TN 37422. USA, 1991
8. The Holy Bible, King James (Authorised) Version
9. The Holy Bible, New International Version, International Bible Society. Broadman & Holman Publishers, Nashville, Tennessee, 1986
10. Hudson Taylor and the China Inland Mission. The growth of a work of God, Dr and Mrs Howard Taylor, The Religious Tract Society, London, 1918
11. Hudson Taylor in early years. The growth of a soul, Dr and Mrs Howard Taylor, The Religious Tract Society, London, 1911
12. The Living Bible, Kingsway Publications, Eastbourne, BN23 6NT, United Kingdom, 1971
13. Matthew Henry's Commentary in One Volume, Rev Leslie F Church

(Editor), Zondervan Publishing House, Grand Rapids, USA, 1961
14. The New Bible Commentary, F Davidson, AM Stibbs, EF Kevan (Editors). The Inter-Varsity Fellowship, London, 1954
15. The New Bible Dictionary, JD Douglas (Organizing Editor), The Inter-Varsity Fellowship, London, 1962
16. Operation World, Seventh Edition. Jason Mandryk, Biblica Publishing. 1820 Jet Stream Drive, Colorado Springs, CO 80921, USA. 2010
17. The World Book Encyclopedia, World Book – Childcraft International, Inc, USA 1979
18. Yemen, Bernard Gerard, Editions Delroisse, Boulogne, France, 1973 (approx)
19. Yemen – A Lonely Planet Travel Survival Kit. Third Edition, Pertti Hamalainen, Lonely Planet Publications, Hawthorn, Victoria, Australia, 1996

Map of Pakistan

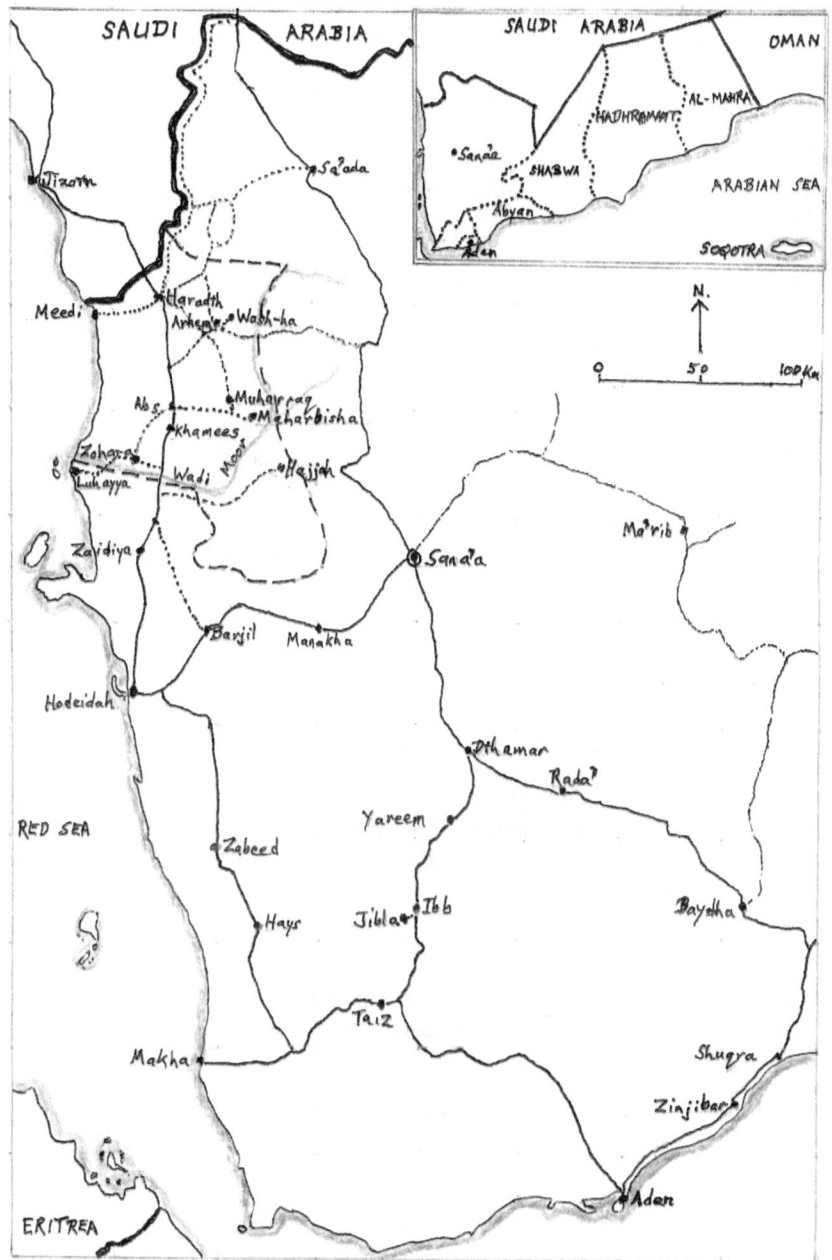

Map of Yemen

Notes

BIRTH TO NEWCASTLE, AND A SPECIAL GIFT

1   I had to repeat Second Year.

2   Acts 28:15.

3   I met Annette Bossley (later to become Mrs John Hor) through that fellowship. She was a Christian nurse working within the hospital and was to be a real blessing to Adele and me in the first few years after we left for the mission field. It was through her that I came to know the Rev David Fry, an Anglican minister who had formerly served with CMS in Northern Australia and was now a curate at Maitland. I invited David to speak at one of our monthly fellowship teas. Not long after, he was appointed to a parish in Newcastle, and he and his wife Nada proved to be an enormous help to me. We prayed about things together, and I was always encouraged by my visits to their home. We keep in touch to this day.

'YOU DON'T SPEAK ARABIC BY ANY CHANCE?'

4   By contrast with the Red Sea Mission Team, the Church Missionary Society, for instance, *does* let their financial needs be known. For years I'd contributed financially to their work, and I agreed with both principles. I once heard the Rev (later Bishop) Ken Short make a helpful point concerning this matter. He said that both methods are acceptable to God, giving the example of Elijah. God sent Elijah to hide beside the Brook Cherith (Kerith Ravine) where he would be living 'by faith', because the ravens would bring him bread and meat twice a day, and he would drink from the stream. Later, God sent him to be cared for at Zarephath where he *asked* the widow for food and drink, thus letting his needs be known. The Lord blessed both methods, but I preferred the thought of living 'by faith'.

5   Two and a half years later, after Adele and I were married, Bishop Jack Dain wrote to congratulate us, and shared that the day of our wedding, November 2, was the same date as his own wedding anniversary.

6   Something I didn't realise at the time was that the SIL team prepared a confidential report about each student at the end of the course. This provided the sending missions with invaluable information, not only about the student's language-learning ability, but how each student coped with the pressures of living and working with other people. The hot and humid climate in Brisbane simulated the situation into which many candidates would be heading when sent to the mission field. If any were found to be unsuited to such

NOTES

a life and ministry, how much better if this came to light while still in Australia rather than after arriving overseas somewhere! I never saw the report about myself, and only heard about this aspect of the screening process quite a long time later.

7   That was in 1956 and is documented in the book *Through Gates of Splendour* by Elisabeth Elliot.

8   I was still in Brisbane when I heard that I'd also been accepted by the Red Sea Mission Team. What I didn't know at the time was that Dr Gurney had written to Bob Colville about me. 'If he definitely feels led not to go to Bible College, I'll let him come to the field,' he said. However, Bob held on to Dr Gurney's reply and waited to see if I'd be accepted to SMBC, which I was. It wasn't till some months later that he showed me that letter.

9   This rule stemmed from a situation where an already-accepted candidate fell in love with someone who proved to be unsuitable for ministry with the Team, and then neither ended up on the mission field.

10 Because word had not yet come through from the Field Council with Adele's official acceptance, we'd consulted the Australian Home Council before arranging for our engagement notice to be printed in the papers. They gave us their permission, being certain that she wouldn't be rejected.

11 One of the blessings of being sent to the mission field by the RSMT was that they had a definite policy of never making appeals for money or taking collections at meetings. When we visited friends and churches, we could concentrate on sharing how the Lord had been working, and encourage prayer support for ourselves and the work, without ever having to speak about money. If finances were mentioned, perhaps in reply to a question, we did so in a guarded manner, aiming to avoid giving the impression that we were asking for money. However, in our own personal prayer times or in groups of RSMT personnel, of course we did bring our financial needs to the Lord. In this way we were constantly reminded to be prayerful, and found our faith strengthened as we saw the Lord providing. Also, as a Team and as individuals we aimed never to be in debt. This meant that if the Lord didn't provide the money for a particular need or project, then we knew that for some reason he did not wish us to proceed as we'd planned. We were to wait until he *did* provide for it, or until he showed us that he had a different plan from the one we had in mind. It was also Hudson Taylor's policy. He said that it is just as easy for the Lord to provide the necessary finance *before* a project is begun rather than afterwards. By this means we are given a most valuable and clear indication that it *is* his will to proceed, if he has provided the necessary money before any start is made. As Paul instructs us, 'Owe no man anything, but to love one another.'

TRAINING IN PAKISTAN

12 Amazingly, he knew my father's second cousin, Stuart Barton Babbage, well, and had taught him in Sunday School in New Zealand many years before. How wonderfully the Lord arranges things for his children!

13. Also, in the Land Rover were Andrew (who was about seven years old, the son of Doctors Henry and Indira Luther); old Dr Luther senior, Andrew's grandfather, who was also helping at the hospital; and an Australian nurse, Florence, from Blackheath! She was working with the Bible and Medical Missionary Fellowship (BMMF) but was now on loan to CMS following the evacuation of the Caravan Eye Hospital from near the Indian border due to the recent hostilities. Florence's friendship meant a lot to me during the next four months before Dell arrived towards the end of May. Florence later married a fellow missionary in Pakistan.

14. Adele had left Sydney towards the end of May, with Bob and Violet Colville, Miss Beryl Evennett and the Rev Doug and Dorothy Mill joining our family members to see her off at Sydney airport. She flew first to Singapore accompanied by Ewen, an Australian dentist who'd joined the RSMT, and who was also heading for Yemen. But at Singapore, due to different destinations, Ewen and Adele's ways parted. She stayed overnight in a hotel and then flew on to Karachi the next day where she stayed with the Rev David and Jean Penman (NZ CMS). I'd met David when he visited Quetta a few weeks before, and he'd agreed to care for Dell when she arrived. (A young English missionary met her at the airport and took her back again the next day to catch her flight to Quetta. Rather amazingly, that young missionary was one of Hudson Taylor's great grandsons!)

15. Actually, Ronnie said that trunk calls frequently *didn't* get through to Quetta, even in the best of times.

16. They planned to go to England at the end of June for a three-month furlough. One reason was that they both had irregular heartbeats and other health problems. I believe that they never returned to Pakistan as a couple; though after Joan died, Ronnie did visit several times to assist with eye surgery camps before he died in England about ten years later.

17. Another blessing which the Lord arranged was my meeting up with David Penman when he visited Quetta. Not only did David and Jean care for Dell in Karachi at first when she arrived all alone from Australia, but they also cared for us both when we were setting out for Yemen together. As we shall see, their help was far more necessary than we'd expected. Another key person we met during those months was the obliging and helpful Dr Henry Luther.

JOURNEY TO YEMEN AND LANGUAGE STUDY

18. In those days, the Chlorodyne in Pakistan contained a little opium, which is marvellous for pain relief, and which also dampens down cramping spasms of the bowel.

19. Yemen is a poor country, and a number of governments were offering assistance. The Chinese had recently built this important road from Hodeidah up to Sana'a, while a British/German consortium was building the road south along the mountains from Sana'a to Taiz. The Russians had completed the triangle with an equally good road which ran west from Taiz towards the Red Sea, and then north along the coastal plain to Hodeidah.

NOTES

20 Sana'a, we discovered, is 7,500 feet above sea level and pleasantly cool, though dusty. The population would have been about 40,000 people, but in a smaller space than Australian towns of equivalent size. The old mud-brick city wall, though crumbling, was still standing in many places, but much of the city had spilt out beyond it. The people are proud of their long and interesting history, and justly so. For instance, it's clear that the Queen of Sheba reigned in this land, and there are definite signs of an advanced, past civilisation not far from Sana'a, away to the east.

21 We later discovered that in older houses, upper rooms often had protruding, wooden, box-like structures with shuttered windows on the three sides, allowing women to see up and down the street without being seen themselves. Some women were only rarely permitted to leave the home at all; and if they did, they were usually hidden from head to toe by a long, black covering.

22 It turned out that the taxi driver had overcharged us, but we were just grateful that we'd arrived safely.

23 The Red Sea Mission Team had been founded in 1951 by Dr Lionel Gurney, a tall English bachelor with a military bearing, who'd nearly died of a heart attack a few weeks before we arrived. While taking a bath at Wolfgang's home, he had been overcome by leaking gas from a faulty hot water system and was unconscious when they found him. Now he seemed to have recovered, but when he showed me the electrocardiograph (ECG) tracing which had been taken soon after the incident, I made it clear to him that he had indeed suffered a significant myocardial infarction. Despite the episode, he strode along purposefully, and because the mail was irregular in Sana'a, he even offered to post a letter of mine when he travelled to Ethiopia.

24 For approximately 400 years until the end of the First World War, much of the Middle East was occupied by the Turks who chopped down most of the trees for firewood, and apparently made no effort to replace them. Where there had been forests in Israel and Yemen for example, barren wasteland was practically all that remained. Many Australian soldiers fought in the Middle East during the first World War, but it had already been realised that eucalypts would do well throughout the region. Since then, many tree-planting campaigns have been undertaken. Some have been more successful than others because the young trees need to be protected from goats, and the older ones from increasingly desperate people in search of firewood.

25 All of us, and especially the women, had to be careful how we dressed and behaved, so as to fit in with the Yemeni culture where possible, and not to detract from our presentation of Christian living, but rather in every way seek to 'make the teaching about God our Saviour attractive'.

26 Digging the well deeper fixed it—for about six months. Over the decades, the water table has continued to drop; and now the cities of Sana'a and Taiz especially are facing a serious water shortage —mainly due to the large pumps used to irrigate the crops.

27 As well as being the leader of the Anglican Diocese of Sydney at the time, Archbishop

Loane and his wife were close friends of my parents. He preached the sermon at their wedding, back in 1939, and at the service held to commemorate their 50th wedding anniversary!

28 There was never any intention to publicly preach the gospel message at our clinics, and Peter and Wolfgang made that clear to the government representatives. But the situation did seem serious for some months. We'd come into the country as volunteers ('technical aid workers') and were paying for all our accommodation and equipment ourselves. We would willingly work under the direction of the Ministry of Health, but as a Christian team we would not agree to stay in the country without the freedom to share what was on our hearts, when that was appropriate. In fact, as a Team, we placed restrictions on ourselves. When Adele and I arrived, we and the other newcomers were instructed not to speak to any Yemeni about Christian matters until we'd been individually in the country for two years! It was designed to allow us time to gain experience, and some understanding of what those with whom we spoke were thinking. Any Yemeni who seemed genuinely interested in Christian matters could be referred to more senior workers during those first two years.

29 Mrs Walker had died in Yareem a few months before, having suddenly collapsed in the entrance hall of their home. She was of Danish birth, and older than Dr Walker. He came home one morning to find that she had apparently suffered a massive heart attack. The fact that Yareem is about 8,500 feet above sea level may have contributed to her death due to the reduced oxygen content in the rarefied atmosphere at that altitude. She was the first person to be buried in the grounds of the American Southern Baptist Hospital, Jibla, after it opened in 1968. That whole section of hillside the hospital is built on, however, had originally been an ancient graveyard which the Yemeni President gave to Dr Jim Young as a plot of land on which to build.

WEDDING AND HONEYMOON

30 Our shipping agent Jacob, that good friend of the Team we had met in Hodeidah, told us that our luggage had been offloaded at Aden (which we'd hoped wouldn't happen), and was then brought up to Hodeidah on a little sailing dhow. This is considered a precarious way to send things, with the luggage having a definite tendency to end up in the sea, usually during loading or unloading. However, due to the busy military activity at the port, these small craft were the only vessels able to approach the docks with civilian cargo, and so our two drums, trunk and tea chest were loaded on to a lorry and brought up from the coast to Wolfgang's front gate.

31 From time to time, in the years ahead, we all had to manage with reduced allowances like this, but the Lord always provided what we needed at the right time. We could have been concerned about paying for our honeymoon, but he'd provided the money about four years earlier, long before we'd even met. Prior to Adele's beginning her two-year course at Bible College, she'd worked for two years as a dietitian and nutritionist with the NSW Department of Health. With a good salary, she had toyed with the idea of buying a car

but decided to save the money instead. How glad we now were that she'd been led to do so, since we would never have been able to afford such a lovely honeymoon without it.

32   We chose a Thursday for our wedding as most Yemeni weddings were held then with Friday being their 'Sabbath'. Also, the weekly Yemen Airlines flight from Sana'a to Asmara went on Friday mornings, so it all fitted together well.

33   The Embassy ceremony, conducted by the Queen's own representative, was meaningfully worded, and we noted that his authority to perform marriages had been signed by Sir Alec Douglas-Home, the British Foreign Secretary, who had been the British Prime Minister nine years before. Mr Noble had placed this authority on the desk for us to see.

34   Ian mentioned that the CBM was basically a humanitarian charity with some committed Christians on its staff.

35   As it turned out, I probably didn't need to feel so distressed about the money. Some months later I discovered that in Germany there was (and probably still is) a 'church tax', from which the government distributes funds to reputable organisations such as the CBM, which, I understand, was glad to add our Yemen work to the list of projects for which they provided finance and equipment. Nevertheless, they probably did feel that our order needed to be trimmed back somewhat. I also heard later that they sometimes even had difficulty finding enough projects to which they could allocate the enormous amounts of money they were given each year.

36   For instance, I thought we should radically reduce the number of stainless-steel instruments, while leaving the list of medications essentially the same.

37   As usual, I was overreacting; and of course, the Enemy of souls tries to cause us unnecessary grief. If I'd only been able to see the full picture, I need not have felt guilty at all. I didn't know at the time that the Team's nursing sisters who were serving in Yemen also had real misgivings about the project, foreseeing that they would be restricted from being free to visit Yemeni friends and to engage in outreach work, because of the need to care for the hospital and the eye surgery patients. But the Lord of Glory is the One who made me. He understood how shocked I'd be, and what I'd be thinking that Friday when Ian Lewis told me about the twenty thousand pounds.

YAREEM, LYNDALL'S VISIT AND ANDREW'S BIRTH

38   In those days there were few Europeans living in Yemen, so it was easy to have their house pointed out to us. This lovely family belonged to the Swedish Pentecostal Mission. The three of us went in and were shown a little of the work they were engaged in. I was especially glad to learn that they had an Arabic Bible study in their home every Sunday evening because I was then able to suggest to Yah-yah that he might like to attend. I do hope that he did. Back in Yareem, he'd already been given a gospel by Ewen. The next day, we were shown over the sewing and mechanical school that this Swedish couple had established, and where English classes for men were held four evenings each week. Dell and I were delighted to hear that they were having some wonderful opportunities for the

gospel.

39 Malcolm was working as a road supervisor on a West German/British joint venture, surfacing the Sana'a to Taiz road. He was rough as nails, but with a heart of gold.

40 Lyndall's Yemen Airlines ticket from Jeddah to Taiz had actually been confirmed, though there was no such flight. Anything could happen here. Some people called Yemen 'The Land of Wonders'.

41 It wasn't appropriate for everyone, however. We took it down before two Egyptian schoolteachers whom we'd invited came to visit us, because we sensed that they would be upset by it.

42 This province forms the far north-western corner of Yemen, bordered by Saudi Arabia to the north, and the Red Sea to the west. Hajjah, the provincial capital, is a town in the mountainous south-eastern corner.

43 We didn't choose the specific plot of land on this trip.

44 In effect, the bowel had 'swallowed' the gland, which had in turn dragged the intestinal wall to which it had been attached down the inside of the next portion. This had blocked the bowel so tightly that the blood supply to the 'swallowed' segment had been cut off, and so that segment died.

45 For years after that awful day I felt that I was at least partly responsible for her death; it has remained one of my most dreadful memories. However, I have come to realise that perhaps I don't need to feel guilty. I believe that I did my best for her; and I know that I was always pleading with the Lord for his help and overruling. As well as this, other doctors had also attended to her from time to time. Intussusception is a rare condition, especially in girls, and whenever I've managed to bring my memory of it all into perspective, I've realised of course, that it was our ever-loving Lord, the chief Physician, whom her parents and I were consulting and relying upon. He could most definitely have prevented her from dying—if that had been in keeping with his will. He could have stopped it from happening altogether; or else he could have put the diagnosis in my mind so that I might have arranged for Dr Young to see her sooner. Unfortunately, this is the view of things which I so often fail to see.

46 Italics added by me

47 As I read about Hudson Taylor's experiences, the Lord was training me to face similar situations. Armed with such accounts of the Lord's faithfulness and timing, I was much more able to launch out in faith to prove God's promises for myself than would otherwise have been the case. But I couldn't help asking why it was that he allowed Lydia to die? In pondering this question, I was reminded of three things. First, the Lord can see into the future, and knows all that will happen. Sometimes he takes his loved ones to heaven to spare them from a calamity which he knows they would otherwise suffer. In 1 Kings 14:13, the Lord allowed the godly prince to die for that reason—because he was godly. The Lord *rescued* him through death out of what was to become an appalling situation

and took him safely to heaven. Second, if through Lydia's death and God's working in the spiritual realm, any Yemenis were caused to turn to him, or were drawn closer to him, that would be a blessing. And for those of us who already knew him, Romans 8:28 assures us that 'In *all* things God works for the good of those who love him, who have been called according to his purpose'. Third, others observe the way that we as Christians conduct ourselves through calamities, including death. No matter what he allows to happen, we can be confident that 'the Lord is good, a refuge in times of trouble. He cares for those who trust in him' (Nahum 1:7). Even though it may be difficult to understand, we believe that Lydia's death related to the harvest of Yemeni souls we hoped for, and for which we'd all been praying. Jesus was speaking about his own approaching death when he said that, 'unless a kernel of wheat falls to the ground and dies, it remains only a single seed. But if it dies, it produces many seeds.' (John 12:20-33)

48   The fact that Andrew was born in Yemen created a few problems for us. If we wanted him to be registered as an Australian citizen, we had one year from his date of birth to arrange this. We wrote to the Australian High Commission in Nairobi, Kenya, and they were helpful; but mail was slow and sending passports and documents by post was risky. They therefore recommended that we communicate with them through the diplomatic bag from the British Embassy in Sana'a, and this method worked perfectly. In the end, Adele's passport was returned to us with Andrew's details added to it, and with several months to spare. However, he has since had to contend with complications which have arisen through having Yemen recorded as his country of birth. For instance, when, as an adult, he returned from a visit to the Philippines a few years ago, he was kept back at Sydney airport for half an hour or more by the immigration officials until they were able to satisfy themselves that he was not a terrorist threat. Also, he's had to explain how his birth came to be registered in Nairobi when he's never been to Kenya.

EARLY DAYS IN MUHARRAQ

49   Ewen had stayed there for a couple of weeks before Christmas to supervise everything as the work began on building the three stick huts, and on digging our well. A short access drive was cleared, up out of the dry wadi bed from where the road runs, and onto the terraced area which had been allocated for our use. While there, Ewen had gone on several long walks and had spoken to a number of men about the Good News. About fifteen months later, in the clinic, I met one of those men with whom he'd left an Arabic Gospel.

50   Mike returned to Hodeidah a day or two later to continue furniture building and other tasks. Unfortunately, he had to take the generator with him to get some spare parts, so we had to manage without electricity.

51   We had heard the call to prayer many times in other towns and cities, but those were far from sounding like the distant voice we heard here because the loudspeakers on their minarets were always apparently turned up to maximum volume.

52 The Christoffel Blinden Mission eye drugs, instruments and equipment had arrived, and were being kept in Sana'a until we had room for them at Muharraq. On the general medical side, we were well set up and were especially grateful to a friend of ours at home who had sent a small drum of useful clinic items such as kidney dishes and other equipment.

53 CSM had been developed in America for making bread and biscuits, but sadly, because the local women weren't accustomed to it, they often wouldn't feed it to their children. Another unfortunate factor was that it had the most enormous weevils in it, which were much bigger and healthier than the weevils in normal flour. In the end, the nutrition program we hoped to commence didn't work out, and we were only able to help a few malnourished children in this way.

54 The loss of appetite these children suffer can only be dealt with by getting protein into them, and hence the naso-gastric tube.

55 As a precaution, I also gave him penicillin and chloroquin to deal with possible latent bacterial or malarial infection. I thought that he might also have TB, but we would deal with that later.

56 As I've said before, a 'faith mission' was one which chose not to let their financial needs be generally known, but rather to bring each need to the Lord in prayer, and then to depend on him alone to provide all that he knew was needed in order to do his will in his way, while also depending on him to provide each thing at the exact point in time which he knew would be best to accomplish his purposes.

57 We particularly liked some by the Rev David Pawson, pastor of a Baptist church in Guildford, England, who was an excellent teacher. Among other topics, he'd given a series of sermons in which he systematically studied every book in the Bible, and then I especially enjoyed his series of sixteen sermons on the Holy Spirit.

58 Peter would most certainly, I'm sure, have spoken about the Good News to those men as he drove along, and so now there was possibly a little group in the Abs region in whose hearts the Lord had begun to work. Peter may even have been able to leave them with a gospel or two to read. How wonderful it was to be partnering with the Lord of Glory in his loving and merciful work of saving the lost. I believe the Lord brought those men to us in that way so they could be introduced to him.

59 We believed that Adele's watch, among other things, disappeared this way, (though Andrew, who crawled around happily, had begun 'posting' teaspoons down between the sticks in the wall of our hut —most of which we managed to retrieve, but often with some difficulty).

60 This entailed disconnecting the fan belt to prevent water from being thrown up onto the spark plugs and electrical cables. I covered those with grease and plastic bags as extra protection, because if they became wet it could cause the engine to stall mid-stream. If that happens, it's a calamity because unless the engine is running, water can flow up the exhaust pipe and into the engine, which then has to be completely pulled to pieces and

every part cleaned and dried before the engine can be put together again and started once more. Mike had taught me these and many other practical matters on our journeys in and out of Muharraq at the beginning of the year.

61 He had needed to borrow our spare wheel on that occasion to reach his destination and had seemed pleased to accept an Arabic Gospel of John after our earnest discussion.

62 After two nights in Sana'a, Peter and I set out to bring a team member, Anita from Hajjah where she had developed hepatitis. We saw that our doctor friend's car had been pulled out of that wadi, but we ourselves got stuck in a few other places, and had to be dragged out of one deep puddle by a tractor which 'just happened' to be in the nearby village. However, we completed the two-day round journey safe and sound, though rather wearily.

FURLOUGH, SHARON'S BIRTH AND TROPICAL MEDICINE

63 Our circular letters were now being sent out by Ken and Rosealie Badman with the help of some kind assistants, chiefly Ailsa Wareham and June Walker. All were members of St Philip's Church of England, Eastwood, our home church. From this point onwards, Adele drew cute, but informative little pictures for inclusion in these letters. Also, we were given permission to use the Red Sea Mission Team (Australian Council) letterhead, with a sketch of three camels and their riders steadfastly heading out across a desert landscape, having just passed a small oasis, above which was printed the RSMT motto, 'Islam shall hear', based on 1 Kings 8:41-42.

64 That date is a memorable one in Australia's history for two other reasons. Most importantly of course, it's Remembrance Day, when those killed in the First and Second World Wars and later conflicts are remembered. Secondly, she was born just a few hours before Mr Gough Whitlam was sacked from his prime ministership by the Governor-General.

65 Because this was Adele's second caesarean, I felt that it would be wisest if we didn't have any more children.

66 It is quite possible that, like her own mother before her, Dell was suffering from postnatal depression.

67 I did an intensive course in spoken Arabic in the Department of Semitic Studies at the University. It ran for two hours every night, five nights each week, for two or three weeks.

68 It wasn't until we were back in Yemen, and Sharon was thirteen months old, that we discovered that she had this intolerance; and once we'd changed her milk formula, she was immediately much happier and more settled.

'HOW SHALL THEY HEAR?' AND A MIRACLE!

69 It did seem as if we often drove this trip at night, but that was because of the length of it—about 12 hours to drive from Sana'a to Muharraq, with brief stops along the way. It would have been preferable to travel only in daylight of course but it took hours to complete all that had to be done before we set out, and to load the Land Rover (including

the huge roof rack) with everything we had to take. We did all that could be done the day before, but it was usually late morning before we set out.

The road from Sana'a to Hodeidah was sealed so we made good time doing 240 kms in about four hours. However, most often, about thirty minutes short of Hodeidah, and usually about mid-afternoon, we turned north at Barjil for another eight and a half hours on an unsealed 'road', travelling slowly on the rough, sandy tracks through the coastal plain. Some of the track was corrugated and other parts were rocky and with many potholes. If I was travelling alone, or we didn't have much of a load, it was possible to leave early, and so complete the journey before nightfall. With a load and other people, it was more difficult. Another factor was that I used to drive more slowly than other team members.

70 Mike's tasks had been made easier by the acquisition of the 'International' pick-up truck, which had been bought by Dr Young in 1967 for US $300 from the American Embassy in Aden for use at Jibla Hospital. When it broke down and they were no longer using it, Dr Young simply gave it to us. A great deal of work was needed before Mike could get it back into running order, but it was a wonderful answer to prayer.

71 Mike wanted to do everything to the best of his ability, and he did a marvellous job, no matter how much time it took. It was good when Werner, a young man from Germany, came specifically to help Mike, and stayed for two and a half months. Then in mid-November Wolfgang, Beryl and their four children came for a couple of weeks so that Wolfgang could also help Mike with the building. Wolfgang and his family had had quite a memorable trip to Muharraq in the pick-up truck, bringing a lot of much-needed supplies. At one point they had a flat tyre, and then later the accelerator spring broke. This necessitated using a rope to pull the accelerator pedal up each time! They then got thoroughly bogged near Abs. Fortunately Beryl and the children were given a lift to Muharraq in a passing car and arrived safely, though late at night. When we heard all they'd been through, Werner and I left early the next morning, driving our Land Rover to where Wolfgang had become stuck. He'd had to unload everything on his own, but then some Yemenis came by and helped him pull the truck out of the mud. We got there in time to help him load it up again.

72 Sharon's glands swelled following a BCG inoculation against TB which she was given at a Sydney hospital. She should only have developed a small, temporary ulcer on her arm, but I'd been horrified to see the elderly nursing sister give Sharon the injection intramuscularly instead of subcutaneously. The several weeks of anti-tuberculosis medications I'd given her in an attempt to cause the glands to subside had failed; so in the end, when Wolfgang and Beryl arrived for a visit, we wrapped her firmly in a towel, and while he held her, I lanced and drained the abscess. Fortunately, it all healed up soon after that, but left her with a permanent scar at the site.

73 Anti-malarial medication unfortunately didn't give complete protection, and we had not yet been able to have our new home screened against mosquitoes.

NOTES

74 Jibla was where the American Southern Baptist Hospital was, and where Andrew was born.

75 Interestingly, when my younger brother Ross was a baby, he had to be desensitised to cows' milk in a similar way, having initially been changed to goats' milk. For Sharon, in June 1978, eighteen months after we'd begun, we were making good progress with her milk desensitisation program, and we praised the Lord for that. She was now up to 27ml of powdered cow's milk each day in her Millac mixture, without any suggestion of abdominal pain, nausea, vomiting or diarrhoea. We'd reached the stage where we were adding an extra 1ml of cow's milk each day, whereas for months it was only an extra drop each day. Not long after this, as the four of us were sitting around the meal table one day, Sharon picked up Andrew's cup which was half-full of powdered milk, and before we realised what was happening, she'd drunk the lot! It must have been at least 120ml. All we could do was wait and see what happened, and to our delight she didn't develop any symptoms at all. Through this accident the Lord saved us from having to laboriously continue with the program we'd mapped out. What a relief and joy! However, it still took some months before she could eat cheese, chocolate or cream without developing colicky pains and diarrhoea.

76 The young girl had to stay for some months in Jibla Hospital but recovered well. Best of all, we heard later that she'd given her life to the Lord while she was there!

77 Roughly 75 north-south, by 40 east-west.

78 Muharraq is on the edge of the coastal plain, the Tihama, which means 'burning'!

79 The reason we had to contend with so many punctured tyres was that the thorn bushes (small, flat-topped trees found in Africa and the coastal plain on our side of the Red Sea) produced enormously long thorns that too often found their way onto the sandy roads.

80 Although we were not permitted to preach openly, in personal contacts like this we did have freedom. It was often easy to talk about the Lord, either introduced by some parable from the immediate situation, or else through a natural way that opened in the course of conversation. For example, if there were sheep nearby, we could mention the Good Shepherd and the lost sheep. If we were talking about houses I might say that I had two houses—one in Muharraq and one in heaven.

81 Not so long before, a young missionary doctor from Sydney, Brian Hill, had been stabbed to death by a fanatical Muslim in Ethiopia, on the other side of the Red Sea.

82 We learned that little prayer from a book we'd recently read entitled 'Heaven, Here I Come', by Jean Darnall, about whom I wrote earlier in this chapter. Her son had been seriously ill with frequent asthma attacks, but after special prayer for his healing, whenever she thought of his asthma she prayed, 'Thank you Lord, that you are healing him now.' Within a few days he was completely cured, and never had another episode.

83 We had taken a different vehicle to Jibla and our Land Rover had been driven by another person to Muharraq already.

84 Incidentally, this meant that as a family, we'd had nineteen moves in the thirteen and a half months since returning to Yemen from furlough.

THE EIGHT MOUNTAIN TREKS

85 I don't think I ever used these tablets in peoples' homes, but was glad of them occasionally on long, thirsty walks.

86 We liked the Scripture Gift Mission publications because they had no commentary at all. They were simply a carefully-chosen selection of verses from the Bible, put together in such a way as to carry clear teaching on some topic, such as the Way of Salvation.

87 For an hour every morning and every evening, these excellent broadcasts provided not only gospel messages, but also teaching for those who were seeking, or who were already believers. Even if I never saw the person again, by tuning in to the radio they could receive good, ongoing teaching and encouragement, and so be strengthened and enabled to grow as Christians. We had discovered that many Yemenis throughout the country listened to these broadcasts, and even more knew about them. For instance, our nurses, on one of their village visits, were delighted to learn that the sheikh gathered everyone into the little courtyard of his hamlet every morning to listen to that broadcast together.

88 This man had been interested in the gospel message for many years, having been given a Bible by a German oil exploration engineer fifteen years before. He had lent his copy to friends and had never got it back, so he was delighted when Peter met him in Hajjah not long before this time and gave him another one.

89 Twenty rials was equivalent to about two and a half pounds Sterling, or four US dollars.

90 I wanted to make it clear that I came independently, in case there might be ill-feeling anywhere towards the central government in Sana'a which could make things difficult for me. I also wanted to release the Ministry of Health from any possible connection with the message on my heart which I sought to share if the opportunity arose, should anyone who heard me be strongly antagonistic to the gospel.

91 This man apparently held a position of some responsibility guarding the cave in which the Red Cross had established a hospital on the royalist side during the revolution in the sixties. Len had met him a few years previous to my visit, and had given him two booklets, one probably being a Gospel, but I didn't see them.

92 Before giving out any scriptures, I had developed the habit of explaining simply how Jesus is the Son of God, but that Christians do not teach that Mary was God's wife. This was a great stumbling block to Muslims; and it was particularly important to explain if they were given a copy of Mark's Gospel where the first sentence mentions about Jesus being the Son of God. Once they read that, they might not read any further.

93 This man had sent some of his friends to Muharraq for gospels in the past. After I returned from this journey, he visited me again, and asked straight out for a big book. I gave him a big print New Testament and a copy of *Peace with God* by Billy Graham. We were also concerned about an epidemic in the region, which was killing many of their cattle, so

NOTES

he gave me an official letter to deliver to the veterinary people in Sana'a, asking them to come and help.

94 This was the second time that I was faced with this problem. The first time I faced this same dilemma was three and a half years before, in March 1974.

95 It would have been discovered later, perhaps by the women of the household who only ate what the men left.

96 His son believed that in three years' time, Yemen would retrieve all the territory it had lost to Saudi Arabia in the war about fifty years before.

97 Gart is widely grown in Yemen. It's rather like a privet bush, the tender young leaves of which give a mildly narcotic, dreamy effect when chewed.

98 Seeing the pine trees reminded me that many parts of the Middle East were covered by forests of such trees before the four hundred years or so of Turkish occupation, when enormous numbers of trees were carelessly chopped down for firewood or building, with apparently no attempt at reforestation.

99 I had a happy time with them and was particularly interested when they showed me a big sack, filled with large silver coins, Maria Theresa thalers, all dated 1780. Marie Theresa was the Austrian monarch back then, and her portrait was on each coin. They probably became Yemeni currency from 1839 when Britain occupied not only the southern port of Aden, but also the surrounding part of Yemen which was named the British Aden Protectorate. As part of the treaty, Britain paid an annual sum of 6,500 of these Austrian Maria Theresa thalers to the Imam who ruled Yemen at the time. The value of each coin was twenty Yemeni rials, and I bought one from them, for interest sake.

100 While it was distracting, I was interested to hear on their TV that work had commenced on a tarmac road from Jizan (the southern coastal city of Saudi Arabia). It was to cross the border into Yemen, and then continue south through the coastal plain to the port of Hodeidah. Another road was being built in an easterly direction, with the intention of linking Jizan to Sa'ada, in the northern mountains of Yemen, with the necessary finance being supplied by Saudi Arabia.

101 This exciting discovery was dampened a little however, when our Christian brother next visited us and said that this was news to him. Nevertheless, of course, the Lord knows those who are his.

102 Chris worked for Cable and Wireless in Sana'a, and we had stayed in their house the previous August.

103 A number of times over these treks I was shown the sites where major battles were fought.

104 The epidemic had been a type of viral pneumonia, and it had settled down completely some weeks before without any new cases appearing. In fact, it had settled two whole months ago in one of the areas although thirteen people, mostly children, had apparently died of it then. It was a shame we hadn't been notified, since many if not all could probably have been saved.

105 I felt how good it would have been to have shared the Good News with people in this village, but I later learned that there were five Egyptian primary school teachers living there, who helped to staff the little school. They could well have proved to be a dampening influence on any discussion about spiritual things or could even have caused trouble for me.

106 Besides, one of the men in this conversation told me that the snakes would eat me there; this only tended to confirm my thinking that another solution had to be found.

107 This armal used to be in Wash-ha and was moved to the government centre in this region. He came from this area and was a good friend of his. Peter had met him too.

108 It was unwise for our Yemeni brother to be seen at the clinic too often or for too long; and for this reason, I never visited his home, especially after he got into serious trouble because of his Christian activities. At this time, things had relaxed a good deal, but we still needed to be cautious, and not endanger him in any way.

109 If he was looking for evidence of our commitment to the patients' welfare, he needn't have looked any further than the small air conditioner which we'd installed and which was running in the medical storeroom, protecting the medicines from the high temperatures and humidity. This was the only air conditioner on the whole station, and it could only be run during the daytime when we had the larger of our two generators running. But it was installed in the medical storeroom, not in my bedroom!

110 The 'pharmacist' had absolutely no medical training other than having worked for three months in Hodeidah as a dresser. Ironically, he himself treated people with injections and intravenous fluids which they didn't need, without a doctor's supervision.

111 The idea of the Lord sending us to the Baluchi people helped to explain his purpose in sending us to Pakistan in the first place, back in 1972. We had not understood it until now, but with this thought developing, everything seemed to be falling into place.

FIVE YEARS IN PAKISTAN, AND BACK TO YEMEN

112 Interserve, a Christian missionary organisation which operates in many countries around the world, was formerly known as Bible and Medical Missionary Fellowship.

113 This had since been renamed Red Sea Team International, with its headquarters still in England.

114 It would be at our own expense, but worth it.

115 The Duke was leading a delegation of British consultants involved in a possible, enormous upgrading of the harbour facilities.

116 Adele and I thought that the Government may have been attempting to avoid a situation where Yemeni men could come under the influence of the gospel.

117 Not long after we arrived, Adele and I took a seven-hour trip in a shared taxi to Sana'a, the capital, where we'd been married exactly twenty-five years before, on November 2, 1972. We only had one minor road accident on the way. It was delightful to see the same

long, narrow, upstairs room in the Al Hamd Palace (The Palace of Praise) Hotel where we'd had the reception. Unfortunately, with the passing of a quarter of a century, it was in a poor state compared to what it had been then.

118 Incidentally, the word 'sapper' probably originates from Arabic!

119 When we later checked with a member of the staff who'd been interviewed by the visitor after he'd seen us that morning, we learned that he hadn't sounded out *that* person about the problems we'd told him of concerning the working environment of the clinic. And yet he said that he would do so before coming to his decision about us!

120 One of the two European nurses was an enthusiastic Christian with whom we'd enjoyed great fellowship. She was so upset by what had happened to us that (without our knowledge and without our influencing her in any way) she resigned from her position at the clinic. Sometime later, she came and worked at Jibla while we were there, and then continued working in other parts of the country.

THE SAFEST PLACE OF ALL

121 7.6 babies per woman, compared to Australia's fertility rate at the time of 1.8. A man in the clinic told me that he had two wives and twenty-two children, which wasn't an extraordinary occurrence.

122 The first two were those of Mrs Bernard Walker (1972) and little Lydia (1973), mentioned in Chapter Six of these memoirs.

123 Some Italian tourists were also killed around the same time, but they may have tried to drive through one of the many road blocks on the main roads without stopping.

124 Apparently, this man believed he was the prophet sent by God to supersede Mohammad. He had about 2000 local followers.

125 Firing weapons into the air in celebration wasn't without its risks. A young pregnant woman who'd been attending a wedding was rushed to the hospital while we were there, with an abdominal wound from one of those bullets which had fallen out of the sky. She successfully underwent urgent surgery, and we were also relieved to hear that the baby was unharmed. *The Lonely Planet* travel book said that 'Yemen is a heavily armed society. The number of firearms in the country is estimated at sixty million, or four times the population. All kinds of armaments from hand grenades to anti-aircraft Stingers can be freely purchased at special arms bazaars around the country, so it is no wonder that whenever tribal disputes develop into full-blown conflicts, the casualties are high.'

126 We learned that there were only four countries in the world which treated national believers more harshly than Yemen did.

127 It was actually a relay of five police cars, each with four policemen, taking it in turns to follow them.

128 One common cause of shooting in Yemen was if a couple ran off together. Her brother would often hunt them down to deal with the outrage and the damage to their family's

honour. But there were plenty of other reasons too.

129 In mid-July four Belgians were kidnapped north of Sana'a but were released unharmed after three days in captivity. Then two French tourists were kidnapped on August 20, east of Sana'a. We assumed that they were also released after the usual demands were agreed to by the government, e.g. to build a road to their village, etc.

130 On the 25th, the embassy sent us another email, this time recommending that Australians leave Yemen by commercial airlines as soon as possible.

131 One of these encouragements was when I was asked to preach at an evening service in a house church of committed Egyptian and Assyrian Christians. (The pastor stood beside me and translated my English into Arabic, sentence by sentence.) Although I didn't mention it at the time, I was thrilled to realise that I was seeing part of Isaiah 19:23 fulfilled before my eyes! 'The Egyptians and Assyrians will worship together.'

132 Our breakfast outings usually happened on Fridays when the out-patients department was closed for the Muslim sabbath. There was also less traffic on the roads. We still needed to drive carefully, though, with lots of foot traffic and animals on the roads, especially when passing through markets. Two noticeable features of Yemen were the unfortunate state of the roads, and the battered condition of many of the vehicles.

133 It was actually written in response to a gift of money the administrator had received from us to cover the hospital fees of some Yemeni patients who were too poor to pay their bills themselves. But we especially valued the other parts of the letter.

134 Before we returned to Yemen in February, 2001, I sold to Interserve for a dollar, one of our second-hand cars so that other missionaries on furlough could have the use of it. (Being used by Interserve, I thought it would be more satisfactory for it to be in Interserve's name.) The other car had died in December 2000, but the Magna proved to be a real blessing to a number of Interservers during those two years. Now we ourselves were due to return to Sydney in early January and would be grateful for the use of a vehicle. I wrote to the Sydney office and asked if we might book the Magna for the first three months of 2003; and could we possibly buy it back again? They agreed to both requests.

135 That doctor also reminded me that she and I had attended kindergarten together!

136 Visitors who handed in the weapons they carried got them back when they left the hospital. It's a startling fact of life in Yemen that many men carry weapons like machine guns, rifles or pistols besides the almost mandatory curved dagger in the front of their belts.

137 The bullets hit Don in both sides of his lower back but didn't cause any serious injury. One bullet was easily removed, and the other was not doing any harm, so he was soon out of danger.

138 This was just one door past the pharmacy, and where I would have been working normally, had I not been making preparations for our departure.

139 Marty was talking to the Russian girl who'd run up from the pharmacy. Having had the pistol pointed directly at her, and then having witnessed what she'd seen, the poor girl

NOTES

was weeping and in shock. And yet Marty, who'd just come home from being at her husband's side as he breathed his last, was comforting her!

140 Her phone call was a demonstration of the extraordinary speed at which information can travel in this modern age. Adele had rung Sydney and spoken to her mother, who'd rung the NSW Interserve office with the news. The staff there then rang the International Headquarters of Interserve in Cyprus, who in turn rang Katherine in Sana'a. She rang me, having thus heard of the shooting. And yet I didn't know about it, even though I was so close to where it had all taken place!

141 She later returned to the US, where her two daughters and their families lived.

142 Of course, it's Satan and his evil forces who are our real enemies, and not the men and women through whom their hostilities are expressed.

EPILOGUE

143 I gave more details at the end of Chapter Thirteen.

www.ingramcontent.com/pod-product-compliance
Lightning Source LLC
Chambersburg PA
CBHW020317010526
44107CB00054B/1879